BLUE-EYED DEVIL

A ROAD ODYSSEY THROUGH ISLAMIC AMERICA

BLUE-EYED DEVIL

A ROAD ODYSSEY THROUGH ISLAMIC AMERICA

MICHAEL MUHAMMAD KNIGHT

Soft Skull Press

Library of Congress Cataloging-in-Publication Data is available.

ISBN: 978-1-59376-240-7

Cover design by Adrian Kinloch
Interior design by Ben Meyers
Printed in the United States of America

Soft Skull Press
New York, NY

www.softskull.com

*To my lawyers, Christopher Beall and Adam Platt at
Levine Sullivan Koch & Schulz, LLP, and David Greene at the
First Amendment Project*

FBI #56 062
NAME: Wallie D. Fo...

FEDERAL BUREAU OF INVESTIGATION

THIS CASE ORIGINATED AT **CHICAGO, ILLINOIS**

DETROIT FILE NO. **100-5549**

REPORT MADE AT	DATE WHEN MADE	PERIOD FOR WHICH MADE	REPORT MADE BY
DETROIT, MICHIGAN	10/23/43	10/15,20,21/43	▮▮▮ WVB

TITLE
ALLAH TEMPLE OF ISLAM, also known as Moslems and Mooslems; W. D. FARD, with aliases

CHARACTER OF CASE
INTERNAL SECURITY – J
SEDITION; SELECTIVE SERVICE

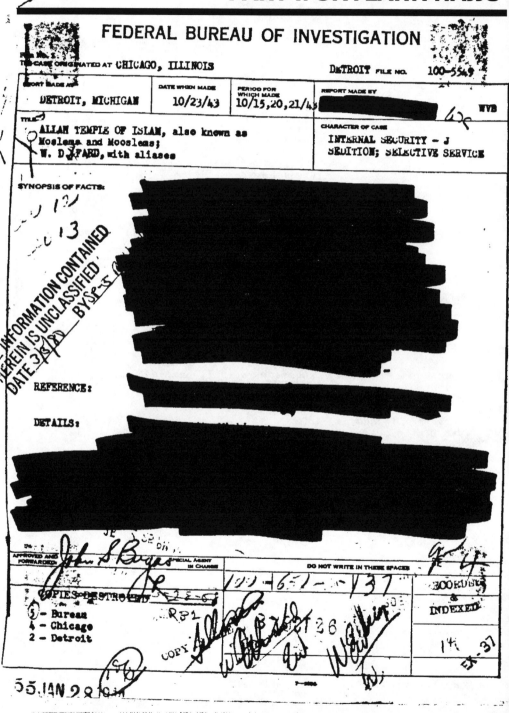

SYNOPSIS OF FACTS:

REFERENCE:

DETAILS:

APPROVED AND FORWARDED

SPECIAL AGENT IN CHARGE

DO NOT WRITE IN THESE SPACES

COPIES DESTROYED

5 - Bureau
4 - Chicago
2 - Detroit

RECORDED & INDEXED

BIOGRAPHICAL DATA

Name: Wallace Don Ford, was, Wallet Ford,
Wallie D. Ford, Wally D. Ford, W. D.
Ford, Wallace Farad, W. D. Feraud,
Fred Dodd, One Allah, W. D. Fard,
Wallace Ford, Wallie Ford, Wallace
D. Fard, Wallace Don Fard, One Fard,
A. Wallace Fard, Allah Fard, W. D.
Farad, Wallace Don Farad, W. D. Farrad,
W. D. Mohammed, Ali Mohammad,
Mohammad Ali, Wali Farrad, W. D. Feraud,
Wali Mohammad, Mohammad Wali, F.
Mohammad Ali, F. Ali Mohammad, Farrad
Mohammad, Mohammad Farrad, W. D. F.
Mohammed, W. D. Fard Mohammed, W. D.
Farrow Mohammed, W. D. Ferrad Muhammad,
Wallace Fard Muhammad, W. F. Muhammad,
W. D. Farard, W. D. Farrard, W. D.
Farrow, W. D. Ferrard, One Mahadiah,
One Mohammed, Fard Muhammad, W. D. F.
Mukmuk Mahdi*, W. F. Muck Muck*, FORD
W. F. Muhammad*, Muck Muck*, A.
Wallace Fard Mohammed*, A. Wallace
Mohammed*, W. Fard Muhammad*, W. F.
Muhammed*, W. F. Mohammed*.

Birth: 2/25/91, Portland, Ore.

Reported Birthdates
and Birthplaces: 1873
1900
2/26/77, Mecca, Saudia Arabia
1894, New Zealand

Description:

Race: White, Negro

Nationality: American, Arabian, New Zealand

Height: 5'6 3/8," 5'8"

Weight: 133 lbs., 135 lbs.

Complexion: Dark — Swarthy

Eyes: Maroon, Black

1

In 1923 William Carlos Williams wrote, "The pure products of America go crazy."

Here's a story for him:

A fifteen-year-old white kid with Dad a diagnosed schizophrenic, rapist and racial separatist and Mom fresh off her second divorce, I listened to a lot of Public Enemy and read the *Autobiography of Malcolm X* and by sixteen had a huge portrait of Ayatollah Khomeini on my bedroom wall. At seventeen I was running around Pakistan with Afghan and Somalian refugees, breaking my Ramadan fasts with Tablighs, playing cricket in Peshawar and studying Islam at the largest mosque in the world: Faisal Masjid in Islamabad, which happens to look like a spaceship.

Then I lived in Pittsburgh with a punk who'd cover himself in spikes, studs, pins and Docs while I still sported an ayatollah-sized black turban and flowing white jalab. What a scene we must have been, walking through malls together.

Years later I'd date a Pakistani-Bengali (isn't that a poem itself, child of two cultures that hate each other) whose parents called me "Johnny Walker"—*The government of Pakistan paid for his trip? He's Johnny Walker!*—as in John Walker Lindh, the infamous American Taliban.

Normal Muslim boys don't want to live in mosques overseas, they told her—just crazy American converts. And there you go.

> You claim to be a Muslim but you Irish white
> —D12, "Quitter"

You can't talk about Islam in this country without bringing race into it. There have been plenty of studies of what Islam does for the American Black Man, and African-Americans constitute nearly half of the U.S. Muslim population. The black Muslims are too established and entrenched to have any mystery, but the white Muslim (1%) remains such a culture-mutant that the sighting of one still demands an explanation. How in the wonder of Allah's creation did you happen? Had you suffered a freak laboratory accident like Dr. Octopus? Did you travel to outer space and encounter mutagenic rays like Ben Grimm? And how did your white parents feel about your new superpowers?

Back in Pittsburgh, a black kid saw me with the Qur'an and it threw his whole world into upheaval; son of a member of the Nation of Islam, he had grown up seriously believing that one of Islam's Five Pillars was the hatred of Caucasians. For him a white person reading the Qur'an was like a Jew reading *Mein Kampf.* When I assured him that I was in fact as Muslim as anyone else on the planet, he shook his head and gave me a double take.

"We have to talk," he said. A week or two later he took shahadah as a Sunni.

The only black kid in his detention home, Malcolm X described himself in those years as a mascot or a pink poodle. "I was in fact extremely popular," he writes in his *Autobiography,* "I suppose partly because I was kind of a novelty." As a white Muslim I was a pink elephant.

When I'd walk into a mosque, nobody assumed that I was Muslim; I'd greet my brothers with *as-salamu alaikum* and sometimes get a polite "hello" in reply, like *aww, isn't that cute that he tried to say salams?* There'd often be someone offering to take my coat, pour some tea or explain to me what Islam was all about. It was tempting to hide my conversion, play dumb and ask questions like "Why do Muslims wash before prayer?" or "What does Islam say about Jesus?" just because my kufr appearance made people so extra-friendly and pleasant—but when I revealed that I actually knew my shit and had taken shahadah years ago their faces would beam like I had just told them they won the lottery. In the much-hyped "war of civilizations," nothing proves the truth of Islam more than a guy that'd rather switch sides than fight. There's a White Muslim Mystique that'll get you far in the community. Communication Director at CAIR (Council of American-Islamic Relations), Ibrahim Hooper knows it. Surfer-turned-shaykh Mark Hanson/Hamza Yusuf knows it. Cat Stevens knows it, with the added value of being a mainstream celebrity. And Ingrid Mattson from ISNA (the Islamic Society of North America) knows it best, because she's the real jewel—a white *woman*.

One Pakistani brother confessed that he took delight in seeing white converts, since "black Muslims are a dime a dozen."

Often I'd try to boost my Muslim cred by wearing the right kind of hat but only ended up looking like a crazy convert with something to prove. Which I was, of course. I had taken a decent religion and made it real crazy, crazier than any of the good normal kids at my Islamic summer camp back in Rochester. All those desi teenagers would go out between lunch and Zuhr to play basketball or soccer or man-hunt and I'd sit in the office pouring through Bukhari with the imams telling me that it was okay to go outside and play, that even Prophet Muhammad enjoyed sports. I had soon read enough to teach kids my own age who had been raised with Islam around them all their lives. I remember one summer-camp afternoon when all the kids sat in a circle in the mosque and the imams asked us what we wanted to be when we grew up. I said that I wanted to be an imam or an alim and assumed that everyone else would say the same thing, but one after another it was all doctor, engineer, computer programmer. It blew me away; I thought we all wanted to live in mosques and read the Qur'an all day.

As a convert, everything I knew about Islam and Islamic culture came from books written by conservative Muslim scholars. I was led to assume that all Muslims prayed five times daily, all Muslim women wore hijab and Islam was the centerpiece of every believer's daily life. It never dawned on me that there could be half-assed Muslims like my mom's family had been half-assed Catholics, or that Islamic communities could obsess over the same concerns of materialism and social status as non-Muslims. I thought Islam did away with that and made us all brothers. I thought that if a Muslim man practiced his religion with the utmost devotion and sincerity, and just so happened to work at a gas station, any Muslim parents in the world would be proud to give him their daughter's hand. It was pretty stupid of me, I know now as I write it.

And my only socialization with Muslims came through the mosque, where everyone put on their best Super-Mumin masks and fronted like they really did wear hijab at the mall and keep to their prayers. My standard of what it meant to be Muslim became so unreachable that when I fell short, I gave up—with no idea that these good kids were boozing up, hooking up, missing prayers, even entertaining secret doubts and asking themselves horrible questions.

Funny thing about that afternoon at Islamic summer camp: when one of the older brothers in the masjid heard all the Pakistani kids saying that they wanted to be doctors, he walked over to our circle and bitched them out. You should aspire to become scholars of Islam, he said.

But that guy was a convert too, originally from Jamaica. Those crazy converts—

When asked about my religion these days I sometimes reply that I'm a Sufi following the mashrab of Hazrat Sherwood Anderson, *radi'Allahu* on him. Writing is a path itself, complete with its own inimitable sages and more sacred scriptures than any hafiz could handle. Sometimes I get more out of Walt Whitman than Prophet Muhammad and I'm sorry for that but I'll say Takbir anyway, the world came from Allah so take what He gives you—

2

So permeated is Islam with the culture of travel—from that of Ibn Khaldun's bedouin to that of the Meccan pilgrims—that Sufism falls naturally into the habit of expressing the entirety of its project in terms of wayfaring *(suluk)* in which each aspect of the Journey becomes a metaphor for an aspect of the spiritual quest.

—Peter Lamborn Wilson,
Sacred Drift: Essays on the Margins of Islam

I suppose you could say the same for America with our road novels, road movies and road songs, so maybe I could find our Star Spangled Siratul-Mustaqeem by going out there and scraping my face on the pavement. It'd be a story firmly grounded in two traditions.

In *Sacred Drift*, Wilson talks about the great saint Hujwiri who laid down some outlines for aspiring Sufi wayfarers in his classic *Kashf al-Mahjub*. Hujwiri permitted the traveler to carry only four essential items: a patched cloak to cover himself, shoes for walking, a prayer rug and staff. For the sake of the Sunna, the traveler can also carry a comb and nail scissors.

The permitted purposes of spiritual travel are as follows:

1. To see a holy site
2. To derive instruction
3. To seek knowledge
4. To visit a venerable person
5. To visit the tomb of a saint

I think if you try hard enough, insha'Allah, anything can fall into at least one of these categories; I suppose it depends on your idea of what makes a holy site or venerable person. And all real-life experience gives you knowledge of some kind, right? A lot of people have no knowledge of what it's like to go out into the world as a hobo and drift around pissing in Snapple bottles and sleeping in cars, leaving it all up to Allah. The biggest challenge could be that Hujwiri advised the seeker to avoid "sensual things," and the world was full of those.

My friend at Georgetown University did bibliographies for hot-shot scholar Yvonne Haddad and said she could put a copy of my Muslim punk rock novel, *The Taqwacores*, on Haddad's desk, so I sent one her way and said I'd stop by during one of my trips to the area. At that point I was still getting the book made at Kinko's and handing it out for free. In May 2003 I found myself in West Virginia riding a bus back to Buffalo, figured I was close enough to D.C. and hopped off at Morgantown. Morgantown's Greyhound station was right next to a homeless shelter, which worked out for me because I'd have to wait until the next day for a D.C. bus.

The guy who ran the shelter had to take down our names and raised his eyebrows at me like I must have been a troubled punk hiding from something with a fake alias. "Michael Knight's your real name? Really? For real?" (There was a television series in the early 1980s called *Knight Rider*, starring David Hasselhoff as a guy named Michael Knight who solved crimes with the help of his talking car.)

The shelter guy woke us all up at six-thirty the next morning. We folded up our blankets and then went back out to the world. I had almost ten hours to kill so I walked uphill and found the West Virginia University campus on the same street as the shelter. I checked my email at the library and waltzed through their union. Nobody was around. On a campus in the summer you can feel like the last man alive in the world. Near the school I found an emptied apartment-style dorm that had been left open for end-of-the-year cleaning so I hopped in one of their showers. Boreman Hall, I think it was called.

In the afternoon, a bus came and took me from Morgantown. We stopped to switch buses at Hagerstown, Maryland. The driver with a sweet old grandpa voice got on the PA and said, "Those of you getting off here to catch the bus to D.C… it's been a pleasure taking you this far in your journey…" and I smiled because he couldn't use a word like *trip* or *ride* but had to say *journey* with all of its sentimental and mystical connotations. He kept going: "and whatever it is you're looking for, keep looking—you'll find it." I answered that moment counting silent *insha'Allahs* on my knuckles and I believed it for each and every last one of us in this gloomy-goofy collection of Greyhound cretins. I hopped off the bus and there were more of them waiting outside, slumped everywhere with their slumped bags waiting to be picked up.

I called the Georgetown girl and told her I was on the way. She asked if I had been to D.C. before and I told her my 1997 story of riding around with the UAE's Deputy Ambassador to South Africa and hanging with his old university buddies, to which she replied, "Oh God, rich George Washington University Arabs." She explained that her half-Saudi, half-Dutch friend was all about going to club VIP rooms as GW Yemeni arm candy.

I stayed in her room at Georgetown's special Muslim housing. We kind of hooked up though it didn't amount to much, with her not sure what she wanted or didn't want and going back and forth until finally we settled on just calling it a night. As Allah wills it, so it goes; probably for the best if I was to keep in a state of holy wayfaring and all. At any rate it was fun enough to know that her roommates were all good Sunni girls who would flip out if they knew she had a boy over. I was illegal just by virtue of my lun.

The next day she took me to the MSA commencement dinner where I got to hear the headliner himself, John L. Esposito, head of Georgetown's Center for Christian-Muslim Understanding give a quick speech before leaving for another commitment. Esposito swaggered and swung through his words with authority, sure to make eye contact with a cluster of front-row hijabis at all the right points. The gist of his talk was that these graduates, as second-generation American Muslims, were poised to take their rightful place in America as previous immigrant groups had. The Italians, Irish and Eastern Europeans, Esposito explained, had all been marginalized upon arrival in this country but stuck it out and became part of the cultural fabric. The new crop of young Muslim leaders, having been born and raised in America, understands the American mentality. They participate fully in American life and speak without accents, thereby better qualified to portray Islam in the media. I can't deny his logic; the same reasoning had once made me a rising star among Rochester Muslims, groomed to lead the mosque someday. But that was a long time ago.

My friend was uncomfortable with me staying in her room again, partly for her roommates' sake and partly for our own. She apologized for being a "repressed little Muslimah" and I told her not to worry about it. I spent the night wandering Georgetown's campus through a massive rain until finding the Dahlgren Chapel open at 2:00 a.m. The altar was lit up bright, but in the pews it was dark enough to sleep. The crucifix had long skinny outstretched arms. I approached the pulpit to see where the lectionary had been left open.

"For you have said 'my kindness is established forever.'"

I liked it in Dahlgren, doing push-ups while my cell phone charged. I wondered why nobody else was in there and why nobody came to bust me. I slept with the door open and rain still falling hard outside, woke up at around eight the next morning and discovered some lonely old man walking down the aisle. I bailed before he saw me, I think.

That afternoon the Georgetown girl took me to her friend's house. She knocked to no answer but then creaked open the door, peeked in and whispered that it was okay. She crept in gingerly and I followed suit, assuming her friend was asleep but there he was on the living-room floor wide awake in sujdah—his elbows bent as he nobly palmed the floor and his bare feet arched on the end of a green rug. Georgetown went to the kitchen, grabbed something she had left there last time and then we walked out while her friend sat up with finger bobbing during the recitation of Tashahud. Turning back to look at him, I just felt bad and worse—for me that raised finger pointed to a big sign reading "MIKE KNIGHT, YOU'RE A MURTAD TURD." What happened to me, what went wrong?

At any rate, I could at least be thankful for seeing a Muslim in prayer and feeling all this rumbling in my heart over it, and I felt like my trip itself had become an act of worship.

Later that week, I was at the Smithsonian walking past a young hijabi and a little girl at a display on Moorish Spain. The little girl said to the hijabi, "You know I'm part Muslim because I'm Spanish" and the sweet hijabi replied, "Yes, but Islam is not something you're born into, it's something you believe." The girl said she knew, and they moved on together, leaving me to wonder why Allah had sent them my way. Sometimes I think He's trying to call me back, give me another chance at the deen. Staghfir'Allah. If there's no light for me, there's no light.

3

Labor Day weekend, 2003: my original plan for the Islamic Society of North America's 40th annual convention was to show up Friday with a big bag and spend three days handing out my evil novel until drawing the attention of ISNA officials and causing a massive ruckus. Then I'd issue an open challenge for anyone to meet me on top of McCormick Place, which would result in my choke-slamming an old scholar named Muzammil Siddiqi through the roof. A few Muslim friends called me suicidal or masochistic for my plans. One just closed her eyes and shook her head. Their disbelief only egged me on.

ISNA speaks for the Islam of Uplifting Hygiene: a vision of smiling professionals in cotton white hijabs, community-minded role models, politically moderate doctors, teenagers who keep their genitals clean and a perfectly sound way of life that all Americans will inevitably flock towards or at least concede an enlightened admiration. In paying my $100 registration fee online I had to click "Agree" on the term that if any member of my group caused a disturbance, my whole group would leave. I had no group. "Judgment of term 'disturbance,'" it said, "will be determined solely by ISNA officials." The convention's official website also provided a list of behaviors for Muslims to avoid and discourage while at McCormick Place: things like *fuhsh* ("indecency, obscenity, atrocity and abomination"), *fuhsha* ("shameful deeds, adultery, fornication and whoredom"), *munkar* ("ignorance, detestable behavior, reprehensible actions") and *bagha* ("rebelliousness, outrageousness and wrongdoing"). I figured that in my time at ISNA I'd have no problem hitting each at least once. My friend Sara told me that while ISNA usually had cool programs, it could often become a big hook-up place for horny young Muslims. "I guess they're not all there for speeches and stuff," she said.

The wind left my sails a week before when I learned that the Daddy of Rock n' Roll, Wesley Willis had passed away following a hard fight with leukemia in a Prospect Heights, Illinois hospice. Originally scheduled to hit Chicago for ISNA on Friday, I left early to make Wesley's memorial on Wednesday.

Wesley Willis was a 6'5", 350-pound Mercy to the Worlds.

Though the son of a Muslim, Wesley was Christian. Though not a Christian myself, I saw a lot of Christ-ness in him. Wesley came from the "least" of society: squalid Chicago projects, surrounded by poverty, crime, drugs, abuse and a hellish family life. In 1989, at twenty-six years old, he was diagnosed with chronic schizophrenia. He suffered from audio hallucinations in the form of "demons" that ridiculed him with profanity. Reacting to the voices, Wes would sometimes curse back—unintentionally disturbing or even scaring bystanders. A fellow passenger on the CTA bus, thinking that Wes had sworn at him, slashed his face with a box cutter. For the rest of his life Wesley wore a long scar across his right cheek.

Despite Wesley's pain in both his internal and external worlds, he filled everyone around him with absolute love and joy. Wes made hearts glow. He could say something as simple as "you're a good person," and you wouldn't know what to do with yourself.

In addition to the scar on his cheek, Wesley had a permanent bruise on his forehead. This came from a lifetime of "bumping heads." For Wesley the headbutt was a gesture of affection, but sometimes you'd have to ask him to go easy. There are motifs in Islamic literature of Muslims whose foreheads became calloused from repeated performances of sujdah, and traditions claim that on the Day of Judgment a believer's forehead would come up shining. With this in mind I took Wesley's bruise to be the mark of a genuine saint.

Wes loved music, and he loved rock n' roll unconditionally. One day while playing Rancid in the car (to hear Wesley's rendition of "Salvation" was priceless), I asked Wes what his favorite band was, and he replied, "Rancid." I asked him again the next day with Nirvana playing, and he replied, "Nirvana." To me it showed how much Wesley got out of every moment.

And Wesley would become a rock star himself. Tirelessly prolific, his true discography may never be known. Wesley was said to have recorded in the range of fifty albums and written two thousand songs. He counted among his fans Eddie Vedder and Billy Corgan, and once toured across the country opening for Sublime.

Wesley's music consisted of him talking and singing to a prepro-grammed keyboard beat (usually "Country Rock 8") about friends, bands, bus rides and everyday experiences. Many songs dealt with criminals; some real (Richard Speck), others imagined or replaced with imaginary characters (Mr. Magoo). He also sang a lot of what he called "bestiality songs" which were directed at his demons. Music was Wesley's therapy. Whether listening on his headphones, performing at a show or basking in love from his fans, the good sounds drowned out bad voices in Wesley's head.

For many, however, Wesley's true gift was his drawing. He loved to draw buildings and buses, and his brilliant cityscapes sold for hundreds of dollars a piece. I own a poster-sized drawing by Wes of the closed psychiatric hospital next to Buffalo State College.

As I sat at the Buffalo Greyhound station on the evening of August 25th, watching a line of buses that could just as well have been lifted from Wesley's drawings, the Earth was closer to Mars than it had been in 59,619 years. I recognized that it was an odd time.

I arrived in Chicago at around noon and then wandered with no idea where to go until finding myself on the UIC campus shuffling along concrete walkways with expressionless students. Eventually I asked for directions and was steered toward the CTA train. I rode the blue line to N. Western Avenue and lugged my big bag to John Rago and Sons Memorial Chapel. Bought a Brisk at the nearby gas station and chilled on the curb. I went to the service at four and was greeted by his former roommate, Carla Winterbottom. I looked straight ahead and there he was: in a sharp suit and tie, hands folded, eyes closed, with the big headphones he carried at all times. I knelt at the casket.

And he was thin. God, he was thin.

I met his friends Tamara Smith (whose name I had known for years from Wesley's song about her) and Dennis Cooper, who sported bright pink hair and a black shalwar kameez. Wesley's brother Ricky was there and took an interest in my Wesley Willis hoodie. "Good news is rock n' roll," it said on the back, accompanied by Wesley's face. Photocopied pages of Wesley's lyrics lined every wall. "At least I'm not a violent criminal," read one.

More of Wesley's family came in—brothers Jerry and Michael (who looked too much like Wes) and father Walter Willis Shabazz in a shalwar kameez. The room filled with friends ranging from Jim Simm, the former manager of Genesis Art Store, to Dale Meiners to Jello Biafra. I walked around reading press clippings and studying photo collages—Wesley at the beach, Wesley with a newborn baby, Wesley at various cities, Wesley all dressed up at gallery showings, Wesley with guys like Gavin Rossdale from Bush and one of the Gallagher brothers from Oasis. Several 'get well' cards were displayed, including one from Hank Williams III asking Wes to realize how appreci- ated he was. The service celebrated Wesley's boundless humor, joy and pride in himself as an artist. Songs were played, a brief film montage was shown and Jello Biafra led us all in a musical tribute. Most of us alternated evenly between laughter and tears.

Outside the funeral home, back out on the living concrete world, I slung my heavy bag back over my shoulder and walked down N. Western to Genesis, Wesley's old art store hangout. Bought a sketchbook, took a CTA back to the University of Illinois and slept outside its library.

I woke up early Thursday morning and waited for a kid to enter the Commons residence hall so I could sneak in after him and find a shared men's bathroom, hoping for a shower. No luck, so I slipped out and wandered downtown, trying to imagine all the buildings and CTA buses as Wesley would have drawn them. I found a fountain accompanying a statue of George Washington and two other guys, took my shoes and socks off and plunged my feet in. Then I unzipped my bag to discover that my shampoo bottle had busted open and damaged a mess of books. I took them all out to sun on the sidewalk. The unharmed ones I wrapped in my Wesley Willis hoodie. Poured a dime-sized circle of shampoo into my hand, threw the bottle away, mas- saged the shampoo into my hair and then rinsed it out in the fountain.

After a long and brutal walk, I stumbled upon the Jane Addams Memorial Park and its public beach. I walked in the tide with my pantlegs rolled up to the knees, and eventually just jumped in and swam. Looking out at the water with Chicago's skyline behind me, and whispering zikrs to myself, Lake Michigan felt like a new ocean that I had never thought of before.

Walking out of the water with my shirt and pants clinging like leftover skin, I felt like a new creature in evolutionary transition between species. On bare feet, blistered and tender from all my hard miles, the soft sand at once consoled and burned. I cleaned them off in the grass, put my shoes back on and began the long march to McCormick Place.

Trudged a few beautiful miles down Lake Shore Drive's bike trail with Lake Michigan forever to my left. I began walking in strange ways to assuage my hurting toes and wore my big bag of books like a backpack. Finally made it to McCormick Place, saw the sign, let the bag fall off my body and then followed it to the grass. Before long the bugs got to me and I went inside, only to find out that it was the wrong McCormick. I was in McCormick East and wanted McCormick *West*. McCormick staff directed me to the bridge that connected them.

I saw scattered brothers and sisters in kufis and hijabs setting up tables and chairs and registration counters and booths. A lady and her son whizzed by on Segway scooters. The reality of ISNA smacked me. I wondered if this was a good idea; sometimes I run so far with daydreams that I forget the flesh-and-blood people with their real sensibilities. I walked around McCormick, scavenged a volunteers' table for free pizza and Coke, found a quiet spot on level 4 and crashed onto a couch. At one point I took my bar of Dial soap into the men's room and performed a very makeshift shower. Slightly cleaner, I returned to my couch and slept. At 4:00 a.m. I woke up and found a police officer staring me in the face. He asked me what I was doing. ISNA, I said. He told me that it didn't start until tomorrow. He walked me to the elevator, put me on his little golf-cart thing and wheeled me to the main entrance. I walked out with my bag over my shoulder, feeling pretty refreshed after a good sleep. Went down to the nearby McDonald's and waited for it to open. Another officer pulled up in his car and told me that it was a bad neighborhood. I decided that it was a good day to make Fajr. I had no water to make wudhu, so I made a sort of tayammum by wiping my hands on the McDonald's window, then went out back since nobody would be needing the drive-thru at that hour and prayed by the little speaker where they take your order. Didn't know which way to face but Allah is Lord of both East and West, right?

Soon the sky became lighter and McDonald's unlocked its doors. Again, McDonald's is not my thing but I needed to rent space. I ordered hotcakes just to sit in a booth. By 8:30 I was in the Hyatt lobby. Men, women and children rolled around the lobby on Segways. It turned out that Chicago was also hosting the first national convention of Segway owners. All I had to do was stay on the lobby loveseat and allow the cartoon to unfold me before me: preppy families on $5,000 scooters, Arabic words for peace rattling off Muslim tongues, white yuppies on dumb gimmicks, bearded believers in shalwar kameezes.

A couple hours later there were Muslims everywhere. I walked around the bazaar until hearing the adhan. Then I took my shoes off, walked across a sea of cardboard, made four sunna rakats and sat for the khutbah. After a while I just got up and walked out. Most of the imam's talk consisted of melodic Arabic which just doesn't do it for me anymore, and for that I'm sorry.

The place was crawling with hijabi girls, tense and lowering their gaze. I'd have liked to talk to some girls but most of them wouldn't even make eye contact. One looked at me, I looked back and then her face tensed up. "Smile," I said. She turned toward me again from reflex, then looked away and was gone. I noticed lots of obligatory but sincere hugging; ISNA seemed an annual reunion for many people. A mother and daughter sat on the couch next to mine. I struck up a conversation. Turned out she had just finished law school. I watched the king-shit imam Siraj Wahhaj greet some fans and heard one girl gasp, "That's the THIRD time I've seen him today!" American Islam has its own celebrity culture, just as reverential and absurd as any other.

Imam Siraj Wahhaj was at one time a minister in Elijah Muhammad's Nation of Islam. After Elijah's passing he followed Warith Deen to orthodoxy but later felt that Warith had compromised Islam on issues such as polygamy and the implementation of Islamic law. Wahhaj promotes a complete over-hauling of the United States government into an Islamic caliphate. And he said that if there was ever a gay-friendly mosque, he'd burn it down himself. In 1991 Siraj Wahhaj became the first Muslim to deliver an invocation in the U.S. House of Representatives. Described by federal prosecutor Mary Jo White as a possible conspirator in the 1993 World Trade Center bombing, he testified as a character witness for Omar Abdel-Rahman. Today he sits on the CAIR advisory board and is a member of the ISNA majilis.

I sold a few books. A pair of stunning hijabis gave me ten dollars each, though I had only asked for "a couple bucks or whatever." I sold a copy to one brother but realized while we were talking afterward that it wasn't exactly his scene.

Walked around with my new friend Khalid checking out the booths. At the MPAC booth they bum-rushed us like used-car salesmen. Khalid jok-ingly told the MPAC girl that I had come to write an article about Muzammil Siddiqi. She replied with enthusiasm until I explained my plan to challenge him to a wrestling match on the McCormick roof. She didn't know what to say to that but made sure I had all her necessary MPAC pamphlets. I actually attended a Siddiqi lecture on "benevolence" and left after five minutes (without making my challenge). Went back to the bazaar and saw CAIR's booth offering a free Nike t-shirt with CAIR membership. The "Nike shirt" consisted of a swoosh with the words, "Faith in Action." Saw Siraj Wahhaj again and gave him the old stink-palm. That night I sat on a lobby couch watching young Muslims walk by until I fell asleep, later to be awakened by another cop at 8:30 a.m.

Saturday I met filmmaker Farah Nousheen, her brother Ali and friend Helena, a Polish-Mexican convert. We watched girls and pointed out the pseudo-hijabis who'd cover up at ISNA and then go out in their club gear. Met a cool girl named Samia who had come from New Orleans. "Sorry," she said. "I'm not a doctor."

"Neither am I," I replied. "I'm an engineer."

"Really?"

"No." She laughed with relief.

Ali was very cool and activist-minded. We speculated on how many Mossad agents might have been there. "There have to be some here," he mused, "at least for training." We noticed plenty of straight-postured guys with earpieces. "Are these guys feds or ISNA's secret police?" Ali wondered. "It's all the same these days."

I spent most of my time with Helena. We shared conversion stories and grievances and eventually walked far from McCormick. She took me to a coffeehouse, then the beach, then DePaul University, then her place. Sunday morning we ate in Chinatown near McCormick. Walking back to ISNA we passed a group of guys who looked to be in their early years of high school. One wore a "STOP THE OCCUPATION" shirt and they all carried ISNA bags. "Did you hear what he said?" Helena asked.

"What?"

"One of them said, 'It's ok—he's a *kufr*.'"

What did that even mean? Was it for my blue eyes? Was it for my non-*mahram* status with this girl? I threw my bag down, stretched my arms out, cocked my head back and yelled, "WHO YOU CALLING A KUFR?" They turned to look but kept on walking. "THAT'S WHAT I THOUGHT," I shouted. Then I picked up my bag and we rejoined ISNA.

At noon they screened Farah's film *Nazrah*. During it I realized a great deal not only about ISNA but Islam and my relation to it. I had been one of those guys whom Islam enters and leaves like an arrow through its game. I had abandoned the idea that there could ever be a community for me. But Farah's film, which was meant as an expression of the Muslim Woman's voice, woke me up. I heard women who dated and left the house without hijab and even a woman both Muslim and gay, and there she was on an ISNA screen. I had never imagined that there was room for these voices at a place like this. Could there be room for mine?

Helena took me to the Greyhound station. It was a long walk and my feet suffered, but it was nice going through Chicago holding hands with a brilliant young woman. It was actually depressing to get on my bus. Didn't have time for an adequate goodbye but said that I would call her and hopped aboard. With that, the Winds that Scatter took me back to Buffalo.

More than anything else, what I got out of ISNA was *people*. I missed the $150-a-plate dinner with John Esposito, but I got to stink-palm Cat Stevens as he signed autographs at the Astrolabe booth. I didn't make a disturbance and security never had to remove me, but I still considered my mission an absolute success. In the course of that three-day convention I dropped my hostilities. I never would have seen it coming, but ISNA gave me daw'ah. So I didn't challenge all the mailis to fight me on the roof, but I had a good time and met some amazing people.

I also checked off every item on ISNA's "not-to-do" list. *Fuhsh*, from my repeated acts of *istimna* in McCormick bathrooms; *fuhsha*, from my Saturday night with a beautiful convert; *munkar*, from stink-palming Siraj Wahhaj and Cat Stevens and almost fighting a group of teenagers; and *bagha*, from the dirty novel that I peddled throughout the convention.

Maybe the "old guard" still runs ISNA, and maybe the House of Saud still runs that old guard. But I saw a lot of young people there and they are claiming their spots: the med student who smoked weed, the NOFX kid, Farah the filmmaker, Rima the poet, even me, for whatever I am. Things are changing. A distinctly American Islam has already begun to take shape. Now say what you want about Islam being universal and above this kind of thing, but it's not. We don't need every Muslim in the world to think and talk and dress and act the same. There's already a Saudi Islam, a Turkish Islam, a South Asian Islam and Malaysian Islam. They are different and they should be. My own encounter with Islam has been socially South Asian and intel-lectually Black.

One of those "stunning hijabis" from the convention wrote back a few weeks later to say that after finishing my novel, she made *tauba*. Tauba! This sweet-heart who never had to repent for a thing in her life! She said my book was gross. It made her hug her Qur'an and feel good to be a "sheltered little Pakistani Muslim girl," as she put it. Everything in this dove that I would cherish had made her disgusted with me. She prayed Allah's forgiveness for having read my words.

I put on my brown wool pakul and walked down Buffalo's Elmwood Avenue, posture shrunk and gaze collapsed to the sidewalk. A sunken old guy passed me looking like a master of psychological warfare with his snaggly long hair and beard and ski cap. Elmwood Avenue had plenty of those guys. I walked behind Pano's Diner, found a dumpster and crawled in when the parking-lot attendant had his back turned. Bags of garbage cushioned me and conformed to my shape. I sank deeper in the trash. It'd be hard to get up if I wanted to.

One reader wrote calling me the "king of a new Muslim underground" but here was its glory, behind Pano's in the dumpster moaning *staghfir'Allah* to himself. My Kinko's book was a failure, or at least it had failed somebody. For Sweet Hijabi Girl all I had done was throw rotten eggs at the black velvet Kaaba-cloth. That was cool in its way, but I would have liked it to mean more.

4

For some time I had been keeping odd hours and obsessing my way through the 816 photocopied and unbound pages of the FBI file on W.D. Fard, feeling like there was something strange and wrong about me because instead of taking computer-programming classes down the street and trying to better my life I just lost myself in this secret project. If you don't know who W.D. Fard was, I hardly know where to begin, but I can say that he produced enough madness in his time to keep a lot of us going. Sometimes he was W.D. Ford, or Wallace Dodd, or Wallace Dodd Ford, or Abdul Wali Farrad Mohammed Ali or Master Fard Muhammad, and he could have been Fred Dodd.

He might have been born on February 26th, 1877 in the Holy City of Mecca, to a black man named Alphonso and a white woman named Baby Gee.

Or February 25th, 1891 in Portland, Oregon, to Zared and Beatrice Ford. Zared had been operator of Ford Bottling Works in Honolulu, Hawaii.

Or sometime in 1894, in New Zealand, to a British sailor and a Maori woman.

He has also been described as a half-Syrian/half-Jamaican, a Turkish-born Nazi agent and a London-educated Palestinian who had stirred unrest in India and South Africa.

And he could have been Arnold Josiah Ford, the black Jew from Barbados who became Marcus Garvey's choirmaster and sang at the end of every UNIA meeting. After Garvey expelled him, Arnold founded the Beth B'nai Abraham, an offshoot of the Moorish Zionist Temple. It collapsed in 1930 and Arnold was said to spend the rest of his life in Ethiopia.

Khalifa Hamaas Abdul Khaalis, the man who mentored NBA legend Kareem Abdul-Jabbar in the deen, fiercely alleged that Master Fard was a cockeyed Greek (named John Walker of all things) who had done time for raping a white girl and "stealing a carload of junk" in Gary, Indiana. By the Khaalis version, Fard died in Chicago in 1971.

From wherever he came, Wallace Dodd Ford arrived in Los Angeles around 1913 and eventually opened Walley's Restaurant at 347 South Flower Street. In 1918, he pistol-whipped a customer for refusing to put down the $2.00 deposit on a steak. A year later, he met a girl named Hazel Barton, who'd eventually move into his little apartment above the café. In 1921 or '22 she'd move out and take their baby boy with her.

On January 20th, 1926, Wallace was arrested for bootlegging and paid a fine. On February 15th he was arrested for selling morphine, heroin and cocaine out of his café and spent three years at San Quentin, where they had him working on roads and in the jute mill. In 1930, Wallace arrived in post-Depression Detroit and walked the impoverished black neighborhoods selling silks from house to house, regaling his customers with tales that he had brought his merchandise straight from the East. From there, he'd get to telling them how Africans ate, and then it'd snowball into preaching about Islam as the natural religion for black people.

Something about Wallace Dodd Ford—he looked white enough to live with a white woman in 1919, and looked black enough to preach that the white man was the devil.

His customers grew into a congregation and Wallace (now Fard) went from peddling silks to selling names. For ten dollars an initiated Muslim could drop his "slave name" in favor of an original name like Karriem, Sharrieff or Mohammed. The Master taught that black people once ruled the earth and would again soon. Fard predicted that soon the "dark races of the world" would fight "all the white races," and forbade his Muslims from registering for the United States draft.

"You are already registered in Mecca," he told them. "You are citizens in the Nation of Islam."

In 1932 or '33, a minister of Fard's named Gulam Bogans was approached by a man named Satokata Takahashi who was interested in knowing Fard's philosophy, mission and how many men belonged to the mosque. Takahashi had founded a group called the Japanese Black Dragon Society with hopes of organizing blacks to spark an American race war. He was deported and later arrested for reentering the United States. A search of his home revealed a "large quantity of subversive literature."

When Gulam Bogans was apprehended by police for failing to register for Selective Service, they found in his wallet a folded-up newspaper clipping about Takahashi's arrest. Born Elijah Poole, Gulam Bogans would go through a series of name-changes—Elijah Karriem, Mohammed Rassoull, Muck-Muck—before settling on Elijah Muhammad.

Elijah had grown up in Sandersville, Georgia and came to Detroit with his wife and two children to work at the American Wire and Brass Company for sixty cents an hour. As the Depression hit, Clara had more kids, factory jobs came and went, the family had to go on public assistance and Elijah drank hard to cope—until he came upon this door-to-door salesman who preached in crowded basements, telling black people that their ancestors didn't eat pork and didn't have last names like Smith or Jones or Poole and that the white man was only the product of a mad scientist's eugenics experiment trillions of years ago.

I tried to picture young Georgia-hayseed Elijah standing way in the back with goosebumps on his arms and a tremble in his stomach. Then he'd make his way through the post-sermon throngs to shake the man's hand and ask if he were in fact the One that had been promised in the Bible, Wallace with a smile whispering that he was but that only Elijah could know. I tried to picture them in Fard's Chevy coupe, Elijah riding shotgun and Fard behind the wheel, cruising up and down the urban squalor—Fard in his salesman suit, maybe the collar unbuttoned and the tie loosened, rambling forth all the secrets of the universe while Elijah took it in.

At that point Elijah was nowhere near being The Honorable Elijah Muhammad with his $150,000 fez. He was just an alcoholic factory-worker who had seen all of his questions answered in the most amazing way.

In 1932, following accusations of human sacrifice, Fard was apprehended, thrown in a psych ward and later ordered to leave Detroit. On May 25th, 1933 he was arrested on charges of disturbing the peace. In the interrogation room he confessed that his teachings were "strictly a racket" and was again banished from the Motor City. Fard went back to the temple, gave a farewell sermon and told his weeping faithful not to cry, that he'd come back some day and save them. Then the car took him away.

Fard continued to teach Islam in Chicago for maybe a year before disappearing for good. Some held theories of an FBI conspiracy. Others suspected that Fard's own followers had slaughtered him as a blood sacrifice, or that Elijah himself killed Fard in a power play. Elijah assumed control of the Nation, but in the Master's absence he couldn't assign original names. He instead branded new followers with the mystifying surname of "X."

As Elijah told the story, Master Fard was Allah in Person, and he had returned home to Mecca.

Not everyone bought it. Minister Osman Sharrieff, who had received instruction from Fard personally, swore that the Master would never have uttered such blasphemy and abandoned the Nation to start an orthodox group. Elijah's own brother Kallatt Muhammad opposed the new teachings and left. Tensions within the organization developed to the point that Elijah feared for his own life and moved his headquarters to Chicago.

Wherever he had gone to, Fard stayed quiet. He did, however, appear as a vision from time to time:

> … As I lay on my bed, I suddenly, with a start, became aware of a man sitting in my chair. He had on a dark suit. I remember. I could see him as plainly as I see anyone I look at. He wasn't black, and he wasn't white. He was light-brown skinned, an Asiatic cast of countenance, and he had oily black hair.
>
> I looked right into his face.
>
> I didn't get frightened. I knew I wasn't dreaming. I couldn't move, I didn't speak, and he didn't. I couldn't place him racially — other than that I knew he was a non-European. I had no idea whatsoever who he was. He just sat there. Then, suddenly as he had come, he was gone.
>
> —*The Autobiography of Malcolm X*

With Elijah as Allah's Messenger and Malcolm as Elijah's national minister, the "Black Muslims" grew to such prominence that in 1957 the FBI began a concerted effort to locate W.D. Fard. Searches of Oregon and Hawaii found no records of there ever having been a Zared or Beatrice Ford, or a Ford Bottling Works; nor could investigators determine whether Wallace had been the Fred Dodd that married Pearl Allen in Portland in 1914. At one point they suspected that Fard had died in an insane asylum under the name Abdullah Mohammed, but the lead went nowhere. They did manage to track down his Los Angeles ex, Hazel Barton (then Hazel Evelsizer) and her husband Clifford in a trailer park in Key West, Florida.

Hazel Evelsizer told agents that the last time she had seen Wallace Dodd Ford was in 1932 or '33 when he appeared in a '29 Model A Ford with California license plates and white sheets over the seats. His hair had grown long and flowing in the back. Wallace told Hazel that his "new way of life" was to eat only one meal a day. He gave her a small box of self-threading needles and said he was on his way back to New Zealand. He also left her the white sheets from his car.

She said that during his time with her, Wallace never expressed any unusual religious or political beliefs. She also said that in 1940 she arranged for her twenty-year-old son's name to be legally changed from Wallace Dodd Ford to Wallace Max Ford, and he drowned two years later while serving in the Coast Guard.

Fard's FBI file said that in July 1942, he was reported to be "Head of the Japanese Army." In 1951 a man claimed to see Allah at a Nation of Islam mosque on 115th Street in New York, and in 1953 Fard may have actually gone to Mecca. For 1955 it said, "Living; whereabouts unknown." Other than that, they had nothing. In 1963 an article appeared in the *Los Angeles Herald-Examiner* claiming that Fard, really a white man named Fred Dodd, was last seen on a boat for New Zealand. The feds had archived in their Fard file every letter from a reader asking if the article was true.

The Honorable Elijah Muhammad would insist until the very end that the Master's voice came to him like thunder in the sky.

Khalifa Hamaas Abdul Khaalis had "exposed" Fard as a cock-eyed Greek with ambitions of reforming the Nation towards the Hanafi school of Sunni Islam. For his efforts, a team of suspected NOI members slaughtered his family, putting bullets in the heads of his young children and drowning two babies in the tub and then his nine-day-old step-granddaughter in a sink.

Following Elijah's death in 1975, his son Wallace Muhammad assumed leadership of the Nation and hoped to bring its members to "real" Islam. He announced that Fard had only been a man and that just about the most un-Muslim thing you could do was associate any person or thing of this earth with Allah. He also said that he still communicated with Fard.

"I don't talk to him in any spooky way," he explained; "I go to the telephone and dial his number." After reforming its beliefs, the NOI went through a series of organizational and name changes with the goal of finally dissolving into the sea of worldwide Muslim brotherhood. To distance himself from the old ways and express his *al-Islam*, Wallace D. Muhammad became Warith Deen Mohammed.

Not everyone could accept his complete overhauling of Elijah's life's work. The traditionalists split off with Louis Farrakhan, who resurrected the old Nation of Islam and maintained that Master Fard Muhammad was in fact Allah, "Messiah of the Christians and Mahdi of the Muslims."

Over one hundred years after his birthday in Mecca, Fard (pronounced Fa-Rod) now pops up in rap lyrics:

Underground under pressure
My style is the child of a lesser God,
I Master like Fard
—Common, "Gettin' Down at the Amphitheatre"

Master Fard Muhammad comin' like a comet
when they see him, they all start to vomit
1995, Elijah is alive
—Ice Cube, "Enemy"

I'd drive back to Chicago a few months after ISNA on a search for the grave of the Honorable Elijah Muhammad. It was November 19th and there was supposed to be a meteor shower that night. I made a few turns and got on Interstate 90 westbound from Buffalo feeling like I had busted out of jail and stolen that '97 Skylark and had a lusty time lined up in the Windy City with booze and coke and girls and maybe a fistfight on the sidewalk (insha'Allah). I was twenty-six years old in real-life orbits of the *ard* around the *shams* but for all intents and purposes on that very night I wasn't a second over seventeen, and felt liable for any kind of stupid action with all the windows down in late November going seventy-two, slapping my knee, singing along to the Subhumans—ARE YOU PREPARED TO DIE FOR YOUR BELIEFS OR JUST TO DYE YOUR HAIR?

Near Cleveland (which was just another Buffalo for all I could see), 90 merged with 80 and became a goddamned toll road. I stopped for gas around Toledo. The guy working the counter read my sweatshirt and asked who Wesley Willis was.

"He's a singer from Chicago."

"What kind of stuff does he sing?"

"I don't know," I replied. "It's kind of hard to say."

"Like a blues-man?"

"Yeah, kind of. He's a blues-man." With that I got my change and walked out. The more I thought about it, the more it sounded right to call Wesley Willis a blues-man.

Near Chicago, I-90 ditched I-80 and merged with I-94. I took a random exit and found myself driving past McCormick Place, appreciating the fact that I could go straight from Buffalo to the ISNA convention on only one road. I found a place to park and walked around.

It had been warmer at the end of August and even though it had been less than a hundred days I felt like I had been three or four different people since. I sat on a bench and realized that it was a bench I tried sleeping on one of those convention nights. McCormick itself came across like a mausoleum; all the personalities that made it mean anything to me were packed up and gone. In one weekend there were thirty-thousand Muslims in and around that building, and now it was just Mike Knight. It almost seemed like McCormick's people should have had all the ISNA banners and booths and merchandise stuffed away in cardboard boxes and even the scholars and lecturers and musical acts waiting in a little room off to the side having tea until it was time to bring them back out again. Maybe my ISNA girlfriend, too.

Back at the car, I looked at a map to find Thornton.

I was deep into writing a new novel and considered sending my protagonist, a slob-drunk punk named Bombay Unger, on his own journey to Elijah's grave. It could have made a decent conclusion for the character, searching as he was for a historically rooted sense of American Islam and the journey that Islam has taken in this hemisphere. I could see this Bombay Unger character standing where Elijah's bones rest, by plan or by accident, and coming to a heightened appreciation for the drama that's taken us this far.

When constructing a setting, I'm a big fan of authenticity. If you write a story about Buffalo's Elmwood Avenue, for example, you should do it with the knowledge that someone could read that story who walks up and down Elmwood every day and knows every last store and bum that you're talking about—so get the stores right, and get the bums right. To poeticize about the outpatients in front of the Elmwood/Forest Mobil station adds myth and lyricism to something in that reader's daily life—it's real, he's there, and he sees it on the page. You've made a grimy street sacred! Reading my hometown of Geneva mentioned at the end of *Tender is the Night* awakened me to an irrational sense of holiness; my childhood haunts were real not only in this universe, but also within a meaningful imagination. You can call it shirk or kufr, but what do I care? For me to write effectively about Bombay Unger standing at the grave of Elijah Muhammad, I would have to stand there myself.

On the way there, I thought about my Bombay Unger and what he might do at the grave. I'd expect more of myself than to just have him piss on it. Driving by the Glenwood Post Office, I figured that if the stone wasn't too big and heavy I could have him steal it and ship the thing to a girl with hopes of impressing her. That'd be kind of cool, right? Here honey, I know we're broken up but I got you Elijah Muhammad's tombstone. I tried to imagine how much the stone could weigh and what it might cost to ship it somewhere like Syracuse.

Back in his campier days, Farrakhan proclaimed that Elijah had never died and you could even dig up Elijah's grave and would find no body. Taking Brother Minister up on his dare would be a story.

When I got to the place I jumped out and walked around thinking it'd be no problem to find, images dancing in my head of old sad-eyed Elijah in jewel-encrusted fez and bowtie. Turned out to be a reasonably-sized cemetery. I walked back to the office and went inside to ask the lady at the counter, middle-aged with fake blonde hair and a lot of makeup.

"I'm looking for an individual's plot," I told her. "His name was Elijah Muhammad."

"Elijah Muhammad, King of the Moozlems?"

"Yes," I replied, "King of the Moozlems."

"And what is your name, sir?"

"I'm Ibrahim Hooper."

"Mr. Hooper, I'm sorry; but we have an agreement with the Moozlems not to disclose the location of Elijah Muhammad's grave."

"I understand," I replied with a smile. "Thanks anyway." If they thought I'd go away that easy, they were sadly mistaken. I went back to my car, made a peanut butter and jelly sandwich and snuck around back to the cemetery. If I had to I'd examine every last stone in the place, odd man out and against all odds, until finding Elijah.

I had read in David Lee Roth's autobiography, *Crazy From the Heat*, that if you really want to understand a site you can't go at noon when all the tour buses are unloading idiots who have nothing to do with the place. Go at 3:00 a.m. and the spirits of the place—soldiers, kings, holy men, whatever—are there with you.

It was the middle of the day but I knew what he meant.

Most of the recent years' burials were clustered in the same areas so at least I could cancel them out along with family plots and the decorated graves of U.S. military. The ground-level stones, however, were almost all shrouded under old dead leaves that burrowed in and escaped the lawnmowers. I had to uncover each one myself, for a time sweeping the leaves away with my foot. I went through the process along one far side of the yard, making sure to check each stone. There was one with no name on it. I wondered if the Nation could have legally kept his grave unmarked. Wasn't there a law about that? I would think that a grave had to be accounted for and recognized, if there was a dead body down there. The uncarved stone had a baseball-sized oblong rock on top of it. Could that have been an arcane Fard thing? I fatwa'd to myself that if I couldn't find Elijah, that stone would have to do.

A shiny black car rolled down a distant winding lane, appearing to pause whenever I turned to face it. Must have been an employee of the cemetery, I figured, sent out to keep an eye on me. It finally went on its way and I resumed the hunt.

I walked along the side all the way to the back where a railroad track stretched itself out and disappeared into the woods on either end. A train went by quietly, but the one that followed rumbled past. I looked at some more graves, skipping one here and there and then finally passing whole packs of stones, all but surrendering. If Elijah needed his rest so damn bad, he could have it. I staggered over to sit on a stack of smooth unused stones, thought about who they might be for, imagined that one of them could be mine and whipped out my phone figuring that I was far enough removed from the actual graves for it to be no disrespect—or at least no less offensive than the trains going by.

"Yo," I said.

"Yo," my friend James said back. "What's good?"

"I'm in Thornton," I told him. "Around Chicago—I'm at the cemetery where Elijah Muhammad is buried but they won't tell me where he is, they have an agreement with the Nation of Islam to—"

And then the shiny black car was coming my way. I hung up on James, pocketed my phone and watched the driver's-side window roll down. Behind the wheel sat a ruddy-complexioned, middle-aged African-American man with scant gray facial hair and freckles.

"What are you doin' out here?" he asked.

"I'm looking for an individual's plot," I answered.

"Who you looking for?"

"Elijah Muhammad," I told him.

"What do you want to see him for?" At that moment I launched into my well-rehearsed ramble of Muslim Credibility—I was no poser, I had lived for two months at Faisal Masjid in Islamabad. I read Malcolm's autobiography at 15, took shahadah at the Islamic Center of Rochester, New York at 16, went to Pakistan at 17. I told him that I loved history, entertained a passionate interest in Islam in America and couldn't pass up the chance to see Elijah's grave while I was in the area.

The man replied that Elijah Muhammad was his grandfather, and he'd show me the grave. "Come on in," he said, nodding to the passenger seat. I ran around the front of his car and upon opening the door, felt horrible about my muddy feet—the inside was spotless. I never caught the make and model but it was some money, leather seats and all. "What's your name?" he asked.

"Michael," I replied.

"I'm Walid," he said. "Where are you from?"

"Buffalo."

"What are you doing out here?"

"Visiting friends I met at the ISNA convention," I answered, hoping the ISNA reference gave me some added weight. Walid drove us to the grave.

"There it is," he said. And there it was, with a big ground-level stone: Elijah Muhammad, though they spelled it *Mohammed*. There he was. Walid explained that much of the family was buried there too, pointing out Sister Clara, and that a great deal of the living family had stayed around Chicago.

"Where do they side on the whole Farrakhan-Warith Deen thing?" I asked. Walid answered that that was all in the past, Louis Farrakhan and W.D. Mohammed had made amends and were both Muslims doing what they could for the deen in this country. After all, he said, they were both students of Elijah twenty years ago; why fight? Farrakhan now goes to Warith Deen's events, Walid said, and Warith Deen chills with Farrakhan too.

"I mean," he added, "there was a time when, you know—" he pointed to me with an open hand. "You know, you'd be the devil." I smiled. "But we weren't reading the Qur'an back then, you know, we've moved past the white-devil stuff." He looked at his grandfather's grave. "There was some bad, and some good, but his intentions were good."

"It'd be really cool to see W.D. Fard's grave," I said, "but nobody knows what happened to him—right?"

Walid then told me the deal, alternating between calling him W.D. Fard and Fard Muhammad.

W.D. Fard/Fard Muhammad died a few years ago in or near Hayward, California, where he served as a professor and imam.

He was Pakistani and a Sunni Muslim, his real name Muhammad Abdullah.

Warith Deen Mohammed communicated with him regularly until his death.

Everyone in "the circle" knew Muhammad Abdullah, but only Warith Deen knew that the man was Fard.

"After he passed away," Walid explained, "Warith Deen just said 'that was him.'"

I tried to think about the grave in front of me like it wasn't just 1965's HONORABLE ELIJAH MUHAMMAD in there but also the regular 1930 Elijah Poole, factory grunt at American Wire and Brass Company, trying his best to feed a wife and kids... and then the 1934 Elijah Muhammad, scared that his whole world was crashing down as he drove Allah to the airport in a Model T Ford, not knowing where the Master would go or if he'd ever see him again—with Fard assuring Elijah that he didn't need him anymore and

Elijah refusing to believe him—while back at home Clara tended to their rebellious baby Wallace, and somewhere far away Malcolm Little was nine years old.

It felt like Master Fard was there in Thornton too. Fard liked to be mysterious, Walid told me; that was how he spoke and carried himself and perhaps why he disappeared the way he did. Walid speculated that Fard had some form of mental illness. "It's kind of perverted," he said, "that, you know, we all believed this man to be Allah."

Walid was there that day, he said, to find the missing headstone of his father. I wished him well with it, shook his hand and said *as-salamu alaikum.*

Wa alaikum as-salam, Walid Muhammad replied.

Even dead, Fard kept the mysteries coming. After driving 647 miles the night before, I found myself standing in an Illinois cemetery with Elijah Muhammad's grandson. Wasn't that something?

And he turned out to be a cool guy, drove me around the cemetery in his car and revealed things that blew my mind more than he probably expected. There was a positive energy when he spoke, enough to make me feel like a real bum. He also seemed to have a down-deep Islam that I had lost by my own fault long ago. What a bucket of crap I was, and Bombay Unger too.

5

I knew a girl in Chicago, a twenty-eight-year-old Pakistani psychiatrist who had emailed me a while back saying that she read *The Taqwacores* and we should have dinner if I ever found myself out that way again.

Part of me played with the idea that this Uzma girl was a set-up. Just a couple of months ago I had been in Chicago at the big mystery-god convention, handing out my nasty book and stink-palming Siraj Wahhaj the superstar imam with alleged ties to the Blind Sheikh and those nuts, and then out of the blue a girl wrote asking me to dinner—in Chicago. Wahhaj wasn't in Chi-Town, his mosque was in the Bronx but anyway I seriously wondered what I'd do in certain situations and considered buying mace or a knife but in the end said fuck it, *aoudhu billahi mina shaytani rajeem* ["I take refuge in Allah from the condemned Shaytan"] and all that. So I called her and we made plans to meet in front of the university hospital where she worked.

Uzma called me from across the street but I saw her with her phone and waved and then she hung up and we walked towards each other laughing about it.

"Hey," I said.

"Hey," she said back. We shook hands. "How was your drive out here?"

"It was great. What's the plan?"

"What would you like to do?"

"I'm in no decision-making frame of mind," I said.

"We could go to dinner."

"Okay."

"What do you like?"

"I could go for anything."

"I've downloaded the directions for a Chinese place downtown."

"That's cool," I said. "You came prepared." She laughed.

Over dinner we made introductory small talk. She asked if I had been writing anything new. I told her about an idea I had to tell the story of Imam Husain's slaughter at Karbala as an American Western—complete with cowboys and Indians and six-shooters and saloons, and Imam Husain wearing a white ten-gallon hat.

Uzma insisted on paying the whole check on the grounds that I should save my money because I was traveling. I didn't put up much of an argument.

She drove me to the hospital where she worked. The whole building was closed by then but she used her special electronic key to take us to her office on the sixth floor. I noted the clandestine coolness of being anywhere after it was closed for the day, with the lights turned off and the halls quiet and everyone gone. Didn't matter what kind of place it was.

We sat reasonably but not suspiciously close on her couch, but before long we were lying down with my arm around her. I thought about her clients lying there like clichéd Freud patients going off about their moms and traumatic toilet training. Uzma seemed a sweet person, more than likely wonderful at what she did.

"Where are you sleeping tonight?" she asked.

"My car," I told her. "I'm durable."

"Not tonight," she replied. "Please—you can stay here."

"In your office?"

"It's no problem—I have this couch, and you can check your email on my computer, and there's a bathroom right down the hall."

"It won't get you in trouble?"

"Just if you can, avoid leaving the office between six and seven. That's when the janitors come through."

"Okay. This is huge. You definitely get the Spirit Award for this one."

She pushed herself off the couch. I watched her put her shoes on. She reminded me not to leave the office between six and seven and said she'd come by around eight or so. She walked out and closed the door behind her.

I sat at her desk and kicked my feet up. By the computer sat a half-empty and flat Diet Coke, good enough for me at that hour. I finished it off, turned on her computer and checked my email. I opened Microsoft Word hoping that the night could lend itself to a work of genius but instead stared at the screen with nothing doing and couldn't get halfway through a sentence without deleting it. Felt the need to piss but knew I didn't really have to. I was weird about that sometimes. I sat up and typed the heading for an essay:

A COMPLETE HISTORY OF MY TROUBLES WITH URINATION BY MICHAEL MUHAMMAD KNIGHT

I'd have to say my hang-ups took root in January 1995, when I was a seventeen-year-old convert spending two months at the largest masjid in the world, Faisal in Islamabad. Religion had me going pretty hard on myself, and everyone around me too. Made sense, though—in the Qur'an, Allah said that every atom of good or bad we commit will be recorded and account towards our final judgment. Can you imagine an atom of good or bad? How much is that? How many atoms are in a drop of piss?

For the serious Muslims this meant that every day you could receive thousands of little blessings or commit as many microscopic sins. Inspired by the holy Tablighi supermen around me I took note of all actions, tallying every deed every day. Even now I'm a little proud that I could have maintained that kind of discipline. I didn't know any Muslims in my age group who cared for the deen like I did.

Early on in Pakistan I became obsessive-compulsive over my wudhu. It started over an unshakable fear that I'd break wind during prayer. From the time I finished wudhu at Faisal's massive facilities and hurried up the ramps to the prayer hall to the time that I greeted the angels on my shoulders I'd clench my ass up tight out of overwhelming dread that I'd fart and make it all for nothing. I imagined bubbles moving inside my body and wondered whether they escaped to the outside. I feared that the men on either side of me had heard or smelled something and suspected me of being either a munafiqun or just ignorant of my religion's dictates. It's pretty easy to convince yourself that you had failed to notice your own farting; it became a five-times-daily routine for me. I'd get up, walk back down to the wudhu faucets, wash and walk back to do it all over again.

I lost this hang-up only after reading a collection of Prophet Muhammad's sayings in which he was quoted as telling Muslims that every drop of urine a man spilled on himself would amount to a drop of hellfire—what if I had leaked and didn't know? Not only would urination break my wudhu and negate prayer, but now I had to contemplate what a single drop of Allah's incomprehensible hellfire could feel like. I began convincing myself that I felt reflexes in the end of my penis—was that a drop? Had I spilled? I'd keep going to the bathroom to check my pants. There'd almost never be anything there, though once or twice I found a wet circle almost the size of my pinkie-nail and it'd completely freak me out. I cut back on liquids and went to the bathroom a few dozen times each day, shaking and wiggling and even squeezing to remove any little drop that might have been in there. Before long it made prayer almost impossible; I no longer thought of my Creator while praying, I meditated only on my own urethra and what could push out of it each time I moved my body. More than once I left a salat feeling the urgent need to urinate, but when I got to the bathroom nothing would come out.

Finally I confided in my good friend Mukhtar, whose knowledge and experience in Islam put me in a sort of childish awe around him. He handled the matter with utmost maturity and respect, assuring me that Allah would issue no punishments for a physical problem that lay beyond my free will. I felt better about my standing with Allah but couldn't get over the feeling of having to piss all the time.

When I got home I saw a doctor, who put a finger in my ass and asked if it hurt. I told him shit yeah, it hurt. He said it wasn't supposed to hurt. I said man, you have your finger in my butt, how is that not supposed to hurt? He said I had a tender prostate and referred me to a urologist. So I went to the urologist and he pushed on my abdomen, asking if I felt the need to piss at that very moment. Yeah, I said. Well your bladder is empty, he told me. There's nothing in there. That piss is all in your head.

That's exactly what he said. He said Mike, that piss is all in your head.

I took my fingers off the keyboard and leaned back, staring at the monitor. Turned out, it was all wudhu's fault. I could have kept on going, writing through my Salafi fear of masturbating and my early explorations into the world of females and it could have ran hundreds of pages, but I was tired and my fingers hurt. I emailed it to myself and crashed on Uzma's couch.

In my half-asleep dreams I wondered how long it would take a suicide-bomber to die after his bomb went off. It had to be something unfathomably quick, like a time that would only matter to Olympic bobsled teams. A single hundredth of a second or was even that too long? A thousandth of a second? Was that long enough to feel your guts explode? Would you have time for any cognition at all? I hoped so. Because there's nobody living on this earth who has been a successful suicide-bomber, in that thousandth of a second you would be the only soul to know what you know. Too bad you couldn't write it down.

I had once flipped through a biography of Prophet Muhammad and arrived at the conclusion that it'd be perfectly *sunna* to decide to kill yourself until angel Jibril came to make you stop. This led me to contemplate two ideas:

1. Allah loves those who wage war in the name of Islam *(mujahids)* and those who martyr themselves for Islam *(shaheeds)*.

2. To some people, *The Taqwacores* had performed such a disservice to Islam that it qualified me as an enemy of the religion.

Following this logic, if I killed myself then I could be both *mujahid* and *shaheed*, fighting an enemy of Islam (myself) and giving up my life for the good of Islam. I could then disgrace the straight path all I wanted and still get my seventy-two firm-breasted *houris*.

Uzma startled me with her arrival at eight. I rolled off the couch and we went to a small diner for breakfast.

"I think we'll see each other again," she said, holding her coffee mug with both hands.

"I'll be around — I have a thing with Chicago." Then I took a sip of my chocolate milk.

"You don't drink coffee?" she asked.

"It's bad for the prostate." Our dialogue remained light but carried pregnant pauses. Gradually, without much warning, the moment came when we both knew it was that time.

She paid for us and drove to where I had parked the night before. I got in my Skylark and she drove back to the office. *Mash'Allah*, what can you do? At least she hadn't turned out to be a hired thug for Siraj Wahhaj.

29

6

Driving down the length of Indiana, I thought myself a Sufi. Maybe it wasn't Sufism that I had, or maybe it was. Maybe my sort of quasi-Sufism was only the last stop for people on their way out of Islam, or a way back in for Muslims that had failed already. The car served as a hermit's mountaintop of sorts in that I had essentially removed myself from human contact. Since I listened mainly to tapes and not the radio, there'd be no flow of information from mainstream society so long as I avoided glancing at the newspapers when paying for my gas.

Sometimes I'd trance off into space and then snap out of it so sharply that I'd hop up and down in my seat just loving the fact of being out there, the far-flung world of Indiana. I learned a lot about looking out my window while driving the state's top half where it was all flatland: the way to do it was to roll the window down and turn my head completely sideways so I couldn't even see the road in front of me—just for a second since I was driving—and look out at the never-ending dry fields. Then I'd whip my head back to the task at hand, the long I-65. And that was the proper way of looking out one's window while driving the top half of Indiana.

It was during Kentucky's share of the I-65 that I saw my first Alabama license plate, white with red numbers and starry blue field at the top with the words, "Stars Fell on Alabama."

Around nine or so I'd pull off the interstate to fuel up, empty a bottle of piss on the pavement and call Zainab (not her real name), the Pakistani-Bengali that up until then had only been an internet-and-phone girl.

"I'm an hour away," I said. She gasped and hurriedly told me which exit to take, when to turn after that and what streets I should find before coming to a park. She'd be there, she said.

The park was more parking lot than anything else but it was too dark to really matter. There was one other car there and somebody was in it. I parked fifty feet away, still unsure that it was her, and got out. The person in that other car turned its head, looked at me and jumped out. A little over five feet tall and maybe a hundred pounds. She wore a sundress over jeans. I've seen a lot of American Muslim girls do that.

We walked slowly towards each other with an energy in the air suggesting that both of us wanted to run but were too nervous. Once we were close enough to smile at each other the pace picked up and then we were close enough for me to pick her up and give her a slow spinning hug. No sooner had I set her down than she stood on her tiptoes and kissed me. Then without either of us having any control of the situation, we were walking away from the cars, holding hands.

"Wow," I said.

"Yeah," she said. We crossed a short bridge over a creek, found a bench and sat down with my arm around her and her legs flung over my lap. "I reserved you a room at the Alta Vista."

"You totally didn't have to do that, I'm a pretty rugged traveler—"

"Please take the room."

"I don't really have money for—"

"I'm giving you two hundred dollars."

"No, you're definitely not," I said as she squeezed a hand into her tight jeans pocket.

"Here."

"I can't."

"Please, you drove all this way—"

"Okay," I submitted. "Thank you."

"You're welcome." She shivered. I rubbed her hands.

"Are you cold?" I asked.

"We can go in my car."

We sat in the back seat and I was amazed to find how comfortably we fit back there. "I'm really tiny," she said.

"I guess so." We made out and I tried to put my hand in her pants but she pleaded menstruation.

"I wish I could stay all night," she said.

"Me too." She took a pen and wrote on an envelope that was lying on the floor.

"Here's how to get to the Alta Vista," she said.

"Thanks," I replied, folding the envelope and putting it in my hoodie pocket.

"Don't you want to look it over?"

"I'll be alright." We made out some more and then she crawled into the front seat. I got out and walked to my own car.

I followed her directions, took the right exit and found the hotel on top of a hill from which I could see all the lights of Birmingham. I paid for my room with her money and they gave me a key-card. Walking down the fifth-floor hallway, I approached the door with a half-suspense as though unsure of whether they'd actually give me a bed or not. Beds were gold when you lived in your car. Turns out they gave me two.

I threw all my stuff around, plopped on a firm wide mattress with tucked-in blankets and turned on the TV. I felt so good to be there it didn't even register to me what I was watching.

Zainab called me at eight in the morning and said she was coming over.

"Isn't it still Ramadan?" I asked over our free breakfast. "Are we being bad?"

"I'm on my period," she whispered.

"And I'm traveling. We're both exempt."

As we ate I daydreamed of hermits. I had read the Cynics like Diogenes and Crates and Christianity's Desert Fathers and held an interest in Hindu ascetics like Ramakrishna as well as later guys like Thoreau. I read enough to see that I had almost become a hermit myself, though I could still apparently pull gorgeous Muslim girls. My only social interaction on the road from Chicago to Birmingham had been with gas-station attendants—and they almost didn't count since it was only their role in the divine comedy to deal with these wandering patch-cloaked goofs like the faithful bringing water and food to St. Anthony in Pispir.

The sequence of thoughts led me to consider the spiritual weight of working at gas stations near long-reaching highways. I myself had once worked at a Mobil station in Geneva, New York, right by exit 42 of the I-90. Truckers used to come in ragged from the roads with heavy truck-mystique rubbing off their t-shirts and flannel shirts and jeans.

Zainab dragged me back to the real world.

"Did I ever tell you that I'm a *sayyeda?*" she asked.

"Are you serious? Who do you trace it through?"

"I'm not sure—but we actually lost the title because it's through my mom's side."

"Still, that's pretty crazy."

"So when you write nasty things about the Prophet, that's my grand-father you're talking about!"

Back in my room we flopped onto the bed and lunged at each other. Up close, her thick black hair looked like thousands of little wires. She took the moment to show me her socks, striped knee-highs in gray, black and two shades of purple. "Look," she said, "they have toes." She had to eventually go home but promised to return once her parents left the house. My face itched. I considered shaving since we were supposed to go somewhere nice later.

For dinner she drove me to a restaurant called J. Gatsby's, the whole way begging me not to go through her CD collection (especially the burned ones she made herself). I couldn't resist and batted her right hand away as she kept trying to eject her Justin Timberlake.

"What's the matter?" I asked, smiling wide.

"My taste in music isn't cool enough for you, you're all Mr. Punk Rock and I'm just a big dork."

"That's not true at all." Then I jokingly sang along to "Rock Your Body" but it only embarrassed her more.

J. Gatsby's was a nice enough place but for some reason we were the only ones there. She ordered a French onion soup, I got a chicken quesadilla. She talked about Bangladesh and how a gang of girls once held her down and cut her hair because she was fair-skinned and half-Pakistani.

"Americans are generally more diplomatic about their prejudice," she said.

"How so?"

"Americans can be as nasty and racist as anyone but they usually don't want you to know it, they're two-faced. In Bangladesh there's no concept of 'p.c.' They don't care, they'll flat-out tell you who they hate."

"Which do you think is better?"

"I don't know—hey, you can't watch me eat, I'm a messy eater." I watched her anyway; there were worse things to look at than a beautiful girl getting self-conscious with her soup. "This is my first date," she said without provocation.

"Really?"

"Yeah. Is that weird? We've already done stuff and I had never been on a date."

"I'm sorry."

"Why are you sorry?"

"I don't know—did I ruin you?" I meant it as a joke but it might have come out wrong.

"I ruined myself," she said with a smile and straightened posture. "It was my choice."

On the drive back we hit a red light every hundred feet. I didn't mind. There weren't any other cars and the streets were lined with rows of trees dressed up in white Christmas lights. Zainab had her Jeff Buckley on singing "Hallelujah" and it just seemed the right *everything* for that moment.

She came by early in the morning and we had free breakfast again. I filled up my plate with scrambled eggs and passed over the bacon. She had a danish and coffee. She asked if I drank coffee and I told her it was bad for the prostate. I looked out the window. The clouds moved to expose the sun and make me turn away.

"I have something for you," she said, going into her purse and taking out a small paperback. The front cover had a photo of the intricately detailed mihrab from a mosque somewhere far away. I knew that the patterns were words.

"The Glorious Qur'an," I read from the inside title page, "translated by Mohammed Marmaduke Pickthall."

"Now they can't say this is haram," she declared proudly, "or that I'm tempting you into hellfire. I just gave you a Qur'an!"

The window in my room gave a panoramic view of the Birmingham valley, mighty I-65 splitting through it like a river. The 65 itself was divided in halves—one side flowing toward Chicago, the other emptying out into the Gulf of Mexico down by Mobile. I didn't know whether my view came from the North or South.

"It's good that you're here," she said, wrapping her arms around me from behind.

"Promise?"

"Promise." I turned around and kissed her, inching us both towards the bed. I fell on top of her and we traded sloppy mouths. I put my arm around her and she rested her head on my chest. We talked about sex and its possibility or impossibility.

"I'm not only a virgin," she said. "I'm also just a naturally small girl, everything on me is small."

"I wonder if it can even happen—I mean, the body is made for that, right?"

"If we had sex I'd probably just close back up. I'll be a virgin forever."

"You're like a *houri*," I joked. "I could have had seventy-two of you, if I stuck to my guns." After that neither of us said anything but watched specks of dust dance in a sunbeam coming through the window. I closed my eyes to watch agitated colors on the insides of my lids. My face was warm.

We lay naked for a long time, neither of us embarrassed of anything. She said that she liked my lun better when it was short because it wasn't so scary that way. We traded stories. I told her about stupid vandalism-type things I had done in Buffalo. She told me about a poor village in Bangladesh where worms crawled through her pillow and she refused a duck that had been killed for her because the people cooked it in manure.

"I felt so bad," she said. "They had this look on their faces like they were absolutely destroyed—but I couldn't eat it, they cooked it in manure."

"I understand."

"It's like the worst thing I've ever done. But you can't put your head on a pillow with worms crawling through it, right? You can't eat a duck that was cooked in manure."

"What were you doing there?"

"It was my father's village."

"Tell me about your father," I said.

"Tell me about *your* father," she said.

"He's a rapist and a poet."

"Oh."

"He did save my mom's life, though."

"Really?"

"They were in the mountains and a rattlesnake was staring her down, poised to strike if she moved. Mom was petrified but Dad hit him with a shovel and then picked him up by the rattle and threw him."

"My dad killed a cobra when he was little. He was sent out by his brothers to do it because he was the youngest."

"How'd he kill it?"

"He killed it with fire, I think."

Her phone rang, and I watched her walk around the room talking on her cell phone in nothing but my white turtleneck sweater that swallowed up her hands and covered half her thighs. She tilted her head towards whichever side she held the phone. It was her mom on the other end so I stayed quiet.

Every time Zainab passed the mirror she'd give herself a glance. One of my dad's letters said that "the reason young girls pause at mirrors or even reflections in storefront windows, is they're waiting for the poetry they write with each step to catch up." Today my aunts have serious debates over whether Dad has a young girl tied up on his mountain.

Zainab gave her mom a *khuda hafiz* and put the phone down, then ran over to jump on me.

"I'm in trouble," she said, "but I don't care."

"You don't care?"

"Nope."

After she left I checked the sheets and found a dried red blot about the size of my fist. I then took a small pair of stainless steel scissors from my bag, snipped out a fingernail-sized square of the stain and put it in my wallet. It wasn't for any kind of chauvinistic asshole's bragging right: we hadn't had sex, I knew that it was only menstrual blood and I hadn't broken anything but this was *sayyeda* blood, Rasullullah himself spilling on an Alta Vista bed sheet from his own great-great-great-great-great-great-great-great-great-great-great-great-great-great-great-great-great-great-great-and-so-on-granddaughter, and I was sentimental enough or just creepy enough to see some beauty in that.

She called at 8:29 p.m. Her voice trembled.

Her parents had found her a doctor from Colorado. He'd be coming soon.

She said she cried when they told her.

They thought she was crying because marriage would mean her moving out of the house.

"My mother said, 'He's perfect, Zainab! He likes going to restaurants…
and *you* like going to restaurants! He likes to read… and *you* like to read!'"

The next day we went out for subs and Snapples and she drove me to
what she believed was an old pet cemetery because it had dogs on the headstones. Once I saw them I knew they were lambs.

"This isn't a pet cemetery," I told her.

"But the graves are so little!" she cried.

"They're baby graves." She gasped and buried her face in my chest. I
put my arms around her.

"Why do they have Cupids on them?"

"Cupids?" I asked. She pointed at a headstone. "That's a baby with
wings."

"Oh." She looked crushed. I hugged her tight.

It was a yard full of human beings that had come and gone in a day or
maybe a few weeks.

We walked hand-in-hand, our fingers staying interlocked even when
stubby tombstones came between us. Those lambs really did look like dogs,
she said. I asked if she would ever have a dog, what with the hadiths against
them and all. She actually did have a dog once, back in Bangladesh. They
fed it intestines and it didn't seem to enjoy its life much. Finally it got run
over, she said. And they had a rabbit for a while, but their *dhurban* ate it. In
case I didn't know, she explained that a dhurban was the gateman in front of
a house.

Then she noticed a clearing and we sat down with our subs and
Snapples.

"You want to marry this doctor?" I asked.

"No," she said. "And don't watch me eat. I'm messy."

"Who do you want to marry?"

"I want to marry you. I want two boys and a girl. You can name a boy,
I can name a boy, and then I'm naming the girl."

"I'm naming my boy David Husain," I said.

"That sounds kind of cool," she replied while staring at her own ankles.
She had rainbow-striped socks. "I want to be your Khadija."

"What's that mean?"

"The Prophet loved Khadija with all his heart. When they were together he didn't marry anyone else. And after she died and he took other wives,
they'd get jealous because he still talked about her all the time."

"That sounds alright," I told her, "except you're not dying first. I'll be
your Khadija. You can swing by my grave and have picnics."

"In Ramadan," she said.

"In Muharram," I said.

"You know, I'm wondering if I should tell my parents about you—and you know, not like 'hey I'm dating this boy' but say I want to marry you."

"So tell them."

"It's not that easy!"

"Because I'm white?"

"No, they'd love that."

"They'd have problems with the book?"

"They're actually okay with criticizing organized religion, but they still have desi morals. You write about sex a lot and that would be really hard for them to handle."

"Does it matter that I'm a writer and not a doctor?" I asked.

"Writers are cool, as long as they're successful."

"I see."

"Don't you have an agent looking at the novel?"

"Sure."

"Have they said anything?"

"There's a lot of waiting involved."

"Did you ever think of writing travel books?" she asked. "They sell."

"Can't say that I have."

"I couldn't marry you unless something big happened with your novel."

"I know."

"And you'd have to call yourself Muslim even if you quantified it with some weird Sufi thought. My parents are very contradictory about stuff like that. Like at the dinner table we can say that the Qur'an is just a pile of fables and that's cool, but if I were to marry a Sikh or something it'd destroy them."

"What would your mom do if I took your virginity?"

"Kill herself."

"Kill herself," I repeated with a smirk.

"I'm absolutely serious. She'd think she failed as a mother, that's like her whole purpose in life. I'd get slapped if she knew I was with a boy right now."

"You're twenty-three years old."

"I know," she sighed.

"If I ever saw your mom slap you, I'd slap her."

"Don't say that."

"Okay," I shrugged.

"What way are you taking home?"

"I'm thinking I'll take the I-20 to Atlanta. After that, I don't know. I might go to the beach and light fireworks for you under the Eid moon."

"Savannah's pretty. I wish I could go to Savannah with you."

"I wish I could go to Eid with you."

"No you don't."

"I've never killed a goat before," I said.

"That's the other Eid."

"Sorry, it's been a long time."

Back at the room, I got my things together and flung my bags on my back. When I closed the door we knew we wouldn't see the inside of room 531 at the Birmingham Alta Vista ever again. Made for a long sad hallway between the door and the elevator. I checked out, put my bags in my car and got into Zainab's. It took us less than two hours to reach Montgomery.

Back on the road, I asked her about the Alabama license plates.

"What do you mean?"

"Stars Fell on Alabama."

"Oh." She smiled. "In 1977 Alabama had this insane meteor shower, it was like thousands and thousands of shooting-stars all at once."

We were ninety-three miles from Birmingham, farther than Zainab had ever traveled without family. She drove us around with no agenda. I noted that Montgomery had a real civic look to it. She reminded me that it was the state capital, after all. We passed the First White House of the Confederacy, which I had seen before but was up for seeing again. We held hands while reading the sign out front stating that the house had been built by William Sayre, who was the uncle or great-uncle of Zelda Fitzgerald. My dad firmly believed that I was F. Scott Fitzgerald, though he advised me not to use the word "reincarnation."

Inside we looked at the front parlor with the chandelier-light on and it suddenly hit me that this wasn't always a historic site, it was once just a house where somebody named Jeff lived with his wife and family. We ascended the creaky stairs slowly, to politely appear as though we marveled at every detail of the walls around us. I watched as her right hand glided smoothly up the lacquered banister. She paused at the nursery to see the cribs of Davis babies while I went straight to the Relic Room full of faded battle flags and the President's personal correspondence with handwriting so beautiful that I couldn't read a word of it. Zainab soon joined me and we made out in the corner. I moved her so her back was turned to the door and reached into her jeans. Her knees buckled and she laughed. I pulled out quick. We walked a slow lap around the room, making the floor creak with each step, until hitting a display of ribbons reading "CONFEDERATE VETERAN" which amazed me because I never thought of Confederate soldiers lingering around after the war. I wondered what it would have been like to outlive the Lost Cause, how those guys carried themselves around town and how they felt about their Dixie flags rolled up and stuffed in dark attic corners. Then I wondered why I thought about things like that. Her hands were planted on my waist, reaching around to meet on the small of my back. She stood on her toes to kiss me. As I lowered my head to kiss her back she brought a hand up front to plunge down my pants. I was already hard and she jerked me with a wicked smile, stopping after maybe five reps but there was no need to finish and we both knew it, there had been enough jerking for the story to be told.

On the way out, she asked if I wanted to find the Cross Man.

"Who's the Cross Man?"

"He's this guy outside Montgomery whose whole yard is completely covered with crosses, it's really creepy. And he's got signs up that are all, YOU'RE GOING TO HELL! Everybody knows about him and there's quite a rumor mill: I've heard that he does it because his family died in a car accident, and someone even said that his family is buried in that yard; and I've heard that inside his house he's got like a million little crosses hanging from the ceiling. I'm kind of a nut but I get into people like that."

"I hear you," I said.

"It's like… the world has such *characters.*"

She thought that the Cross Man was in Prattville. We drove around, took directions from a girl at Rite-Aid, drove around more, stopped at a gas station and received a second opinion, looked for roads that turned out to be figments of someone's imagination, asked for directions from an old man sitting on his porch and those too led nowhere. We found ourselves bringing up random things just to keep the mood light.

"You ever shoot a gun?" I asked her.

"Yeah."

"Really?"

"Just a *riktiki*-rifle, but it was gun enough for me."

"A what?"

"You know how in South Asia you get all these lizards on the wall, and they're really pesky—"

"I never saw a lizard in Pakistan."

"Really? They're all over the place. In Pakistan we called them *riktikis* and in Bangladesh we called them *chipkalis*. So the riktiki-rifle was like an air gun or a BB gun or whatever to shoot them off the wall."

It wasn't too bad driving back and forth and getting lost. We held hands a lot and she told me stories. In Bangladesh the Hindus had a giant statue of Ram's ching-a-ling and put it on the qiblah side of a mosque so the Muslims would be forced to bow down to a big infidel penis. In Pakistan she knew five girls who made a pact to stab their forearms with protractors and bleed to death. "They each had their own reason," she told me. "One said her skin was too dark, and one said her mother made her do all the housework, and one said she liked a boy who didn't like her, and one got a bad grade on her test, and one—I can't remember the last one, I think she was only doing it because all her friends were." We soon gave up on Cross Man and headed back to Birmingham.

"Even if we're doomed," I said, "for a few days you made me feel like a good person."

"You *are* a good person."

"I've done bad things."

"You were sad. People do bad things when they're sad."

"I think I'll be sad again."

"We'll see what my parents say."

"Can't wait for that."

"So until further notice," she said with a finger-point, "no more greasy bacon or Canadian strippers."

"Thanks Mom," I replied.

"And no Canadian bacon," she snapped, "or greasy strippers."

My car was still back at the hotel. She pulled up next to it and got out with her car still running. I leaned up against mine and she hugged me for a long time, her hair in my face, neither of us saying anything. Then she asked if I knew how to find the 65 and of course I didn't so she said I could follow her.

"I love you," she whispered in my ear.

"I love you too."

Her arms around me, her fingers interlocked behind my neck, it took a second for us to muster up the courage to separate. Then we got in our cars.

I followed Zainab up and down the steep hills as though sitting behind her in a cheap old roller coaster until we came to route 65 of the Eisenhower Interstate System. Zainab went on the southbound ramp. I took the north.

Zainab might have been home before I switched to the I-20. For a long time I made snarling faces at other drivers though it was too dark for them to have any idea. I hated being away from her and it only made me hate Alabama too. In Georgia, the rage subsided and I turned into just a sad sack sap wishing I had kidnapped her but then missing her only led to me wanting to get as far from the South as possible. I stuck to the 20, stopping at Columbia for sleep. When I woke up it was daylight. I rubbed my eyes, rummaged around for the big road atlas, and upon brief investigation decided that I'd see the Atlantic Ocean from South Carolina.

At one point the I-20 forked into three roads—one turning into a ramp for I-95 North, another for I-95 South and the middle way just turned into route 76. I stayed in the middle and stayed with I-20 until it died. 76 went to 501 and I felt increasing excitement with all the Myrtle Beach signs and visitor centers but when I got there it was only a dead strip of tacky stores and amusements shut down for the season. I parked the Skylark, walked past the shops to the beach and stood on the sand with hands in my winter-coat pockets. The wind made my ears' outer edges alive with cold.

Every thirty or forty yards down the line moped a solitary human figure with its head down and steps slow. Like me, they were bundled up and kept their hands in their pockets; even on the beach it was two days before Thanksgiving. A congregation of bluish-black birds stood motionless like ancient stoic philosophers, every last one of them facing the same direction—a secret bird *qiblah*, I imagined. There might have been thirty birds in all. They were silent and sober, though their huddle lacked the straight lines and feet-to-feet cohesion of human salat. A gray-white seagull flew by my head without moving any part of its body. Must have been fun to be a bird and have hollow bones and just let the wind carry you like a lazy nimrod.

My right hand rested in its pocket around a paperback but I didn't even remember what it was. Took it out to find Marmaduke Pickthall's Qur'an with suras titled in English. I flipped Juz Amma pages:

THE ENSHROUDED ONE,
THE CLOAKED ONE,
THE RISING OF THE DEAD,
THOSE WHO DRAG FORTH,
THE OVERTHROWING,
THE CLEAVING,
DEFRAUDING,
THE SUNDERING,
THE MANSIONS OF THE STARS,
THE MORNING STAR,
THE MOST HIGH,
THE OVERWHELMING,
THE DAWN,
THE CITY,
THE NIGHT,

THE MORNING HOURS,
THE SOLACE,
THE FIG,
THE CLOTS,
THE EARTHQUAKE,
THE CALAMITY,
THE DECLINING DAY—

Closer to the water's edge the soft sand became hard and packed-in, dark and blotchy gray like the surface of the Moon. An older man walked across my field of vision, slumped over and only looking at his own feet. I liked that he couldn't possibly have been going anywhere, the beach didn't *go* anywhere and he couldn't have been headed for any of the obnoxious tourist-hole shops that were closed down anyway, he was just a bum of the first water plodding around the coast. The old man passed an old woman who was out there with her metal detector but neither of them said anything to acknowledge the other. I thought that it was too windy for either of them to live much longer. The sand was littered with stray seashells. I hunched over and picked up a small orange-golden one, briefly considering a drive back to Alabama just to hand it to my girl. Then I was amazed at the simple thought that I *had* a girlfriend. It felt like all the junk I had ever done or been through was only to bring me to her. I put the shell in my pocket and walked back to the car. Drove by a closed roller coaster on the way to route 17, which ran parallel to the coastline and took me to Wilmington. On the way I noted billboards for firework outlets: Nervous Charlie, Crazy D, Mr. Fireworks—maybe there were genuine characters behind those monikers, maybe Nervous Charlie really *was* nervous! I would have stopped, but I already had some fireworks in the trunk.

I drove to a strip of restaurants and souvenir shops by the ocean, parked and went in a little dive bar. Their only non-alcoholic beverage was a Coke so I ordered one and apologized to my prostate. I surveyed a wall of 4" x 5" photos of smiling Spring Break girls in Best Friends Forever pairs with spaghetti-strap tops and cute haircuts, some of those pics looking five years old or older—five years! I was so afraid of getting old, so devastated that all the cheerleaders I jerked it to in DeSales High School were now middle-class moms surrendered to the natural progress of life. Five years to me weighed more than the whole world. *Do you know what five years means?* I asked the wall. *It means from 18 to 23, or 20 to 25, or 22 to 27 or 25 to 30!* Serious transitions. All my compassion rushed to a sudden dread—where were those girls now? *We need to find them and make sure they're alright!*

Down by the water I took out a firework, acting shady about it even though the beach there was more deserted than Myrtle. SHOOTS FLAMING BALLS, read the warning tag. I cupped the fuse in the wind while flicking on my lighter. Once it sparked I sprinted like a scared boy. The firework made a neat little pop and in two seconds there wasn't even smoke to prove it ever happened.

Going through Raleigh, North Carolina I saw signs for Shaw University and sensed a chance to check my email. Parked alongside the curb and found their library in a quad. I had about a dozen spam messages and one from Zainab. She had written it the night before. "I'd choose you over anything," she wrote. "You're worth ten families and twenty communities. What does 'community' mean anyway? Just a set of expectations to keep you from doing what you want. I don't care anymore. I want to be happy."

I wrote back telling her about how sad I had been on Myrtle Beach—but don't worry, I said, it wasn't a sad-sad so much as a sweet-sad, a missing-you-sad—and I told her about the firework and the seashell and how every time I saw signs for interesting cities I wished I would have kidnapped her so we could ride those interstate strings together—the I-95 went through Richmond, Washington, Baltimore, Philadelphia, New York City, Boston and reached its final end just a little past Portland, Maine.

I wouldn't be mad if you met this doctor, I wrote. I know why you're doing it.

I can't believe I got in my car and willingly drove away from you. Right now I would kill the guy sitting next to me to be back there (no offense to him, he's just writing a paper).

Then I speed-walked out of the library to call her.

"Hello?"

"Hey!" I exclaimed as soft and cute as I could.

"Hey." She sounded like someone had died.

"What's wrong?"

"I don't think this is going to work."

"What?"

"I told my parents about you."

"Were they mad?"

"They were more sad and disappointed. My father said he wouldn't be in my life if I kept talking to you." Her voice went up and down and cracked as she spontaneously spoke and cried. "Mom said she couldn't believe that she had such a stupid daughter."

"She had no right to say that."

43

"She was like, 'How can you talk to boys on the computer? How do you know he is who he says he is?'"

"Did you tell her that we met?"

"No… that would have been too much."

"Might have helped."

"It's too late now… I'm sorry."

"What are you going to do with yourself?"

"I'm thinking about grad school."

"What does grad school have to do with anything?"

"You can't even begin to know!" she snapped, almost angry. "I live in perpetual childhood. My only chances to move out of my parents' house are a) marriage or b) go to grad school far away."

"You're twenty-three years old. You can do whatever you want."

"I know." She saw no point in further explaining herself. "This is kind of changing the subject, but I did ask Mom how we traced back to the Prophet."

"Really," I replied with flat affect.

"Yeah—it's through his grandson Husain."

"*Imam* Husain?"

"That's the one, but we're *not* Shi'a." She said it as though someone had accused her of a crime.

"Still, Muhammad's grandson through Fatima, that's cool."

"Thanks," Zainab replied. "I guess I should go."

"Yeah," I said. "Take care." She began to say something like "you too" or whatever, but I hung up.

I sat in my car about thirty seconds before starting it and heading straight to the I-40. I felt like a duck that was cooked in manure. I was sick of interstate highways, tired of spiraling off-ramps and winding on-ramps and didn't want to drive anymore. Soon enough I had to piss but couldn't bear to step out of my car again until I had moved a good distance from Raleigh so I propped my ass up to go in the gallon-jug, bumping my head on the car's ceiling. I put the lid back on and now had a jug of urine in my passenger seat as I headed for Durham and the I-85.

I had a jug of urine, and she had a doctor from Colorado.

The quick story of Michael and Zainab had a plot at the old babies' cemetery, after a life of four days. Put a lamb on the headstone.

I dwelled on bad thoughts for the whole sad crawl to the state line. Crossing into Virginia, I could feel as though some of it was behind me.

I-85 got swallowed up and merged into I-95 somewhere on the way to Richmond. The temperature was dropping and the gas prices rising as I continued north. I pulled over at a rest area, rolled down the window, leaned out and poured my jug of piss on the pavement. Steam jumped from the splashes, right back up to my face. The rest area had its own bathroom and I had to go again, so I parked the car and went inside.

Then I drove a lap around the rest area's parking lot with the heat cranked up full-blast. Before long the air in my car was thick and even the steering wheel was almost too hot to hold. That'd be good for a while, I thought. When all the heat left my car I'd wake up and return to the road. I found a place to park, put on a green Yankees ski cap and dug through the back seat before finding a second winter coat. I pushed back my seat and used the extra coat as a blanket, turning on my side and feeling old.

When I woke up it was freezing and still dark outside. I didn't feel good but car sleep wasn't meant to be healthy sleep, it just kept you alive. Without car sleep you'd drift off the road into a ditch or slowly go insane.

I remembered what I had in the trunk. I popped the trunk-lever by my seat and got out—then it was even colder—and plowed through all my garbage before finding a black bag. I hurriedly whipped it open, yanked out the rolled-up rug and kicked off my shoes, my miserable socked feet almost soothed by the frozen pavement.

The rug was soft both in texture and its shade of green, with feathery tassels on either side and flowery ornamented margins of red and yellow. At the center of the rug's design stood a mosque; could have been the Prophet's Mosque in Medina—with a single long minaret behind a bulbous dome and columns and wide-open halls for its Muslims. The sky in the rug was green. I spread it out and went to business with no wudhu or tayammum or anything and not really knowing which way to face but if the road was headed north and I was to its right then having my back to I-95 would be kind of like facing east—close enough, and at any rate Allah was Lord of both East and West so whichever direction you turned…. I touched my cold earlobes, drew a breath from deep in the bottom of my lungs and let it out with a call to prayer loud enough to be heard on the opposite end of the parking lot, including the Shi'a line about Ali just because I liked saying it.

Allahu Akbar, I touched my ears again and folded my hands just above my navel like a Sunni and recited the Qur'an's opening lines with my prettiest voice—not so pretty, but Allah forgive me I tried to sing it and all alone in the parking lot I sang it loud—*al-hamdulilahi rabbil'alameeeeeeeen, ar-rahmani raheeeeeeeeeem, maliki yawmi-deeeeeeeeeeeeeeeeeeeeeen*—

Then I went through most of the Qur'an I knew, which might have hovered somewhere below the average for American Muslim elementary-school kids. Al-Kauthar, al-Asr, al-Fil, al-Lahab, al-Ikhlas, al-Falaq. An-Nas was fun because it mentioned jinns and I was at the right time and place for mysteries. I hunched over, stood back up and brought myself to the ground, planting my forehead on the soft rug. I wasn't a Shi'a, but I had my clay turba in the car, and if I really loved the Ahlul-Bayt I was supposed to put my forehead on it when I prayed, but I couldn't worry about it. I sat up, inhaled calmly, exhaled and went back down singing loud the *Subhana Rabiyyal 'Ala* that you'd usually whisper under your breath.

After standing through a second al-Fatiha I reached deep into my archives and recited what was at least for me the big gun, the longest sura I knew: *al-Tariq.* I didn't completely remember the English but the Arabic rolled off my tongue by old habit. It began with something about a Night Visitor, I did remember that, and Allah saying that every soul had a protector, and Allah asking man to consider what he had been made from—fluid from between the loins and ribs—and after that I couldn't remember the rest but knew it ended with Allah saying that the kufrs could plan all they wanted but Allah had His own plans, so deal gently with them for awhile. Allahu Akbar, I said as I bent over again. I stood up saying *Sami Allahu liman hamidah, Rabbana lakal-hamd* and made my second set of prostrations.

Resting my forehead on the rug, my eyes getting heavy again, I said *Subhana Rabbiyal 'Ala.* Then without giving salams to the angels I turned over for no reason and lay on the pavement.

I didn't want to get up and grew to like the feeling of my cheek on cold wet ground. I cried for a minute and after the tears stopped coming so easy I tried to cry more but had nothing left. After what felt like an hour I pulled myself up, grabbed my shoes and dragged myself five feet or so to the Skylark in what could only be described as a standing crawl. Dumped my shoes in the passenger seat alongside the empty piss-jug.

The prayer rug was still a tasseled flat rectangle outside my car.

The key was still in the ignition.

I started the car and drove toward Washington, D.C. while the sun rose on a Wednesday that fell between Eid and Thanksgiving.

8

The trees just looked like big sticks as I rolled towards West Virginia. Sticks were my favorite childhood amusements since Mom wouldn't buy me toy guns. What she didn't know was that a stick could be any weapon ever made—an AK-47, M-16 or twelve-gauge shotgun, G.I. Joe Gung-Ho bazooka or even a laser to burn holes through enemy forts and then it'd just as easily make a sword if that was what I wanted. As a six-year-old *Star Wars* geek in 1983, I used sticks as canes to pretend I was a Yoda-type on his Dagobah system, an old codger Wali-Allah who had seen it all and waited patiently for a Skywalker Mahdi to come and fill the universe with equity as it was now filled with oppression.

"Welcome to Wild, Wonderful West Virginia" read the sign, which one had to respect; you don't see signs inviting you to Wild, Wonderful Rhode Island. It was still fairly early in the morning. I stopped at a gas station just to close my eyes for a minute. The background was layered, the farthest-back mountains a shade of blue just slightly darker than the sky.

My father was a confessed mass murderer, though he actually hadn't done it. After eight Dallas nursing students were found brutally murdered in 1966, my father went to the FBI headquarters in Washington, D.C., handed in his gun and confessed. I am guessing that it was after Richard Speck had been identified as the killer, because the FBI sent Dad home. But I think they kept the gun.

Dad had grown up in the hills of West Virginia, the thirteenth of twenty-one children. His parents were coal-miner evangelists who taught proper behavior through all-consuming fear of the Devil. *Wesley, finish your vegetables or the Devil will get you. Do your chores or the Devil will get you.* As a child he'd stay up all night, interpreting every creak in the hallway floor as Satan coming for him.

When he was somewhere between twelve and fifteen years old he watched his brother David get obliterated by a tractor-trailer. David was six. They literally had to scrape his body off the road with a shovel. My grandmother flipped out and attacked the trucker with a knife while my dad stood and took in the whole scene.

Somehow he blossomed in high school as a handsome, charming football player. After graduating he enlisted in the army to go out and find the world beyond West Virginia, ending up in Korea. Something happened there that I'll never know—it's not something I can ask him—but I've heard a wealth of stories about it. One aunt tells me that he signed away his consent for the government to test chemicals and drugs on him. Another says that he witnessed an ambush on refugee children. My mom thought it was an off-base jeep accident in Niagara Falls resulting in some kind of neurological impairment. For whatever the reason, Dad was discharged and to this day enjoys a veterans' disability rating of 100%.

There's a lot of sketchy history around my dad, and I'll never know which stories to believe about him. One of his sisters claims that he's a published author with a PhD in psychology. I've also heard that he did jail time, but don't know how much or what for; something to do with drugs, I think. My aunt Naomi believes he was in the Hell's Angels and tells the story of his arrival at the family home on a Harley with some terrible girl and a backpack full of books on Nazism and the occult, which prompted my grandfather to have him committed to the veterans' hospital. My aunts went to visit and found him strapped in a bed, pumped full of something.

He had been married three times before meeting my mom and had an affair with one of his mother-in-laws. Despite Dad's fondness for Nazi theory, his first wife was Puerto Rican, for which his family briefly disowned him. He once showed up in the front yard of one of his ex-wives wielding an army-surplus bazooka. Dad had two kids before me: a son named David and a daughter whose name has been forgotten. I wouldn't know where to begin looking for them. According to my father, they were killed by the Kennedys.

Dad used to write weird letters to Senator Robert Byrd about a painting of his mother's that had been stolen, and he used to shave his head and practice giving Charles Manson eyes to the mirror. And he was once an aspiring alchemist. It's all myth to me. I don't even know how he met my mom. There are two different stories—

The way Dad tells it, he was sitting on his porch one day when this girl walked by. He introduced himself, they got to talking and made plans to have dinner at her place. "And I never left," he says.

In Mom's version she was walking home with groceries when a car passed her, came to a screeching halt and then backed up. Dad rolled down the passenger-side window and told her to get in.

Dad forced two miscarriages before I was born. The first occurred because he had Mom living in a tent out in the woods, the second because he wouldn't let her eat. When Mom became pregnant with me, Dad was afraid of what he'd do; so he brought us up to her parents' house in Geneva.

It didn't help much; in the ninth month he made her sprint around the block. I'd end up coming out arm-first and my labor took over twenty-four hours. The doctor yanked me out by my soft baby skull with steel forceps, resulting in a scar on my forehead and another by my right eye. The use of forceps is now seen as a possible cause of mental retardation, traumatic brain injury and at the very least, mild behavioral disorders.

Dad then took us back south where he could do whatever he wanted, which included putting knives to my throat and threatening to kill me if Mom didn't fess up about who my real father was. Sometimes the answer he wanted to hear was the kid working at Burger King; other times it'd be Satan. Mom said and did whatever the moment called for to keep us alive. In those first two years she never let me out of her sight.

Before I could walk, I was smashing my head against the wall and covering my arms with black-and-blue teeth-marks. Mom was near comatose, zombied-out by a life that I could only compare to living in a war zone or cult compound. She resigned herself to the fact that one day he'd just kill her and that'd be the end of it—until one day when Dad pulled his usual knife-to-my-throat routine and I bit him as hard as I could on his neck, so hard that he had to put me down. Mom says that in that moment she woke up to there being something in both of us that could still be saved. She began stealing from him and hiding money in a sock. When she had enough for a taxi and plane, she waited for Dad to leave the house and we were gone. That was the last day I ever banged my head or bit myself.

Mom had been so messed up from the life we'd been living that while in the cab and even on the plane she feared that my father was watching her, ready to swoop down on us at any moment. And she was so ragged and war-torn that Nan and Gramps couldn't recognize her and walked right past us at the airport.

Back in Geneva Mom tried putting her life back together while Dad issued constant threats that he'd be hiding behind a tree waiting to snatch me away. When he came up to visit, Gramps watched over us with a shotgun. A judge informally told my father to never step foot in Geneva again, and eventually Dad faded away. Years later his sister would reveal that he had asked for her help to kidnap me.

I had stopped hurting myself but wouldn't talk until I was four and engaged in stimming activities that caused people to suspect me of autism. I'd literally run around a tree for hours if they'd let me.

I couldn't see the hidden driveway and had to turn around to find it coming back. I parked at the driveway's mouth; there was no way I'd try going up that hill with my Skylark. Only Dad's pickup would make it and in the winter he didn't drive at all, he just stockpiled months' worth of canned pork and beans and holed himself up. One year he sold the truck to one of his sisters' husbands and moved to Florida for December and January, then came home and bought the truck back.

I saw Dad's two trucks—one black, one white—at the top of the driveway, then his stashes of junk: rusty parts and long pipes, square-toothed gears and oil drums, antiquated farm equipment from Willa Cather's time, gadgets and machines whose functions I wasn't man enough to understand, and what looked like it could have been a motor. Dad also had a big shed that he had built himself. Lined up alongside the shed were about a dozen white plastic buckets filled to the brim with murky rainwater. And he had an anvil fastened onto a cut of log with long nails that had been bent over its corners.

Behind all that stood the house, with a dip in front of the door bridged by flimsy planks of board that bent when I stepped on them. I knocked and yelled, *"Hey Dad?"* His boots could be heard stomping on the other side of the door and then he swung it open, and there he was—sturdy but weathered in white t-shirt and jeans, black ski-cap on top of a head that hosted serious evil in its day—extending a glad hand. I accepted, noting Dad's big mitt that stayed smooth even with everything around him so tough and hard. I stepped into a big Unabomber-looking room with wood-burning stove, lumpy mad-man's bed and walk-in kitchen where he'd do his table-saw work (sprinkling the linoleum with fine powder sawdust) and empty his meds in the sink.

"Who are you with?" he asked, almost excited.

"Nobody."

"You came with yourself?"

"Yeah."

"You have anything on you I should know about?"

"No, Dad."

"You sit down," he said, pulling out a chair at the kitchen table. I wasn't afraid, but I knew he had a pistol on him. Dad was never without it and always asked if I was carrying too. I took my seat and glanced at the stack of yellow legal-sized notepads. Dad was prolific but illegible. Back in my old room at Mom's house I had stacks of the unknowable yellow-notepad stuff, possibly brilliant but useless either way. "I'm making coffee, you want some?"

"No thanks."

"What are you doing here? Thanksgiving?"

"No," I replied. "Actually I was on my way back up from Alabama—"

"Alabama? What's in Alabama?"

"A girl." Dad gave an isn't-that-life, I-was-young-once kind of laugh.

"Well, that's good. What's her story?"

"She's a Pakistani-Bengali girl, her name is Zainab. She's actually a *sayyeda*, she's Prophet Muhammad's granddaughter—"

"Are you still caught in the Parasitical Appendages of Islam?" Dad asked.

"I guess so, to some extent. It comes and goes but never fully goes away."

"Alright," he said, sitting down with his cup. "You want some?"

"No thanks."

"Okay." The old man poured maple syrup in his coffee. "So what is happening with this girl?"

"We were basically boyfriend-and-girlfriend for four days and then she said she couldn't handle it anymore with having this secret fling and her parents wanting her to marry a Pakistani doctor and all the pressures coming from every direction, it was just too—"

"So what have you been doing with yourself?" Dad asked. "Give me a report."

"Well, I've kind of thrown myself into the writing thing. I have a book out, it's called *The Taqwacores* and—"

"Is Bean-Bag in it?"

"Bean-Bag?"

"That's just a character I'm throwing out there. Is Bean-Bag in it?"

"No."

"Okay. What is your opinion of 9/11?" I took a second to think about it.

"I don't know," I shrugged. "What do you mean?"

"Do you accept the version of events as reported by the media, in terms of who was responsible for these attacks and the reason presented?"

"I guess I haven't seen a reason not to accept it. Have you?"

"As a matter of fact," Dad replied, "I have. And I can present this to you, with you having the full freedom to either accept or reject the hypothesis." The first time we had spoken about 9/11, Dad said that the attacks were spiritually linked to a mob hit that occurred during the World Trade Center's construction. A man had been pushed down an elevator shaft and stayed at the bottom for the next thirty years, generating bad karma that resulted in the towers' destruction. I didn't know what he'd come up with this time. "You are by no means obligated to subscribe to this line of thought," he said, "and I am by no means obligated to prove it, in order for it to be valid."

"That's fair."

"9/11 had as its root, you see, in terms of causal-and-effectual thinking, an epidemic of sex-change operations taking place in this country."

"Is that right?"

"In the procedure of sex-change operations," he explained, "which would transform the outer anatomy of a man into that of a woman, something is lost. The dreams, the ambitions, the self-identification. It's gone. And the doctors, while a sex-change patient is out cold with anesthetic, they implant his mind with suicidal impulses."

"So when he regains consciousness, he's a woman who wants to kill herself," I deducted.

"We are looking here at one person," he said, "who underwent a similar sex-change operation to go from the categorization of 'man' to the categorization of 'woman' and in doing so subjected himself to these suicidal impulses, an absolutely *shattering* crisis of personal self-identification. You understand? He is no less than *shattered* by this experience. And while in this state of crisis with new female genitalia, he finds himself seduced by what I call the Parasitical Appendages of Islam. Can you give me some skin on that?" Dad held out his hand and I slapped it. "Cool! Are you with me?"

"So far it sounds alright."

"Okay! This man who has turned himself into a woman and is now wrapped in the Parasitical Appendages of Islam—he travels to Saudi Arabia, oil-rich. He travels to Kuwait, oil-rich. He travels to Iraq, Jordan, Yemen—oil-rich." He looked at his cigarette and muttered under his breath: *oh mah God, say how it is, not how…*

I looked at the table until my old man returned to the story. "Now he's in the folds of Islam," Dad blurted, "you understand? And that is when these suicidal impulses rise to the surface."

"So 9/11 was brought on by suicidal, transsexual Muslim converts?"

"I want to talk to you about your mother now," he said, putting a cigarette in his filter. In the moment of his lighting it his whole craggy face tensed up, followed by a relief of pressure when he puffed. "Is she still alive?"

"Yeah, she's alive."

"I believe this to be valid—in her story before me and the twenty-so-odd years since her story with me, I am the only man who has ever seen every side of that woman. Am I right?"

"It makes sense."

"I have seen every side of that woman. I know what she's afraid of."

"Okay."

"I want you to tell her something; I want you to relay to your mother a message from me. Can you do that?"

"Sure."

"Tell your mother that I'm heading up to New York and I have a truck full of illegal guns, illegal drugs… and whiskey. See what she says!"

"Okay," I said.

"That'll get her. That'll really shake her up. You tell her that."

"I'm sure it will."

"What's this Pakistani girl look like? Is she pretty?"

"She's real pretty. Very petite, and—"

"Short?"

"Yeah, she's short."

"Dark hair?"

"Definitely."

"Those tiny dark-haired girls have something that is a 'GO.' You understand? They have something that I call a real *go*. Not that I prefer one to the other, but there is something particular to that experience." Mom was a tiny dark-haired girl when Dad whipped her with a belt and buried her under a pile of firewood. "Do you have complaints?"

"No," I said, "I think I'm alright."

"You drove here?"

"Yep."

"Parked down by the road?"

"You know my car wouldn't make it up here."

"And you walked up the hill?"

"Yeah."

"See any deer?"

"No," I replied. Dad said *okay* with mild disappointment.

"Whether you have complaints," he continued on the discarded subject, "should not be a question in the processes of your characters. But you need to be aware of, and prepared for, the current intellectual trap of Resolution-Solution because Resolution-Solution, in the question of your characters' complaints, is an enterprise doomed to failure."

"Right," I said.

"Your character in this novel, is he what you would qualify as an aspirant to Resolution-Solution?"

"Kind of. He has a lot of issues with sexual repression stemming from his religious experience, and he actually—"

"What I am trying to get across to you is that your character need not reach that point of Resolution-Solution toward his complaint, in order for the story to remain valid."

"Right," I said, "I get that."

"You should avoid all seductions of this Resolution-Solution paradigm that will be demanded of you by critics and intellectuals; because it is, as I stated earlier, an enterprise doomed to failure."

"Okay."

"I'm going to ask you a question, but before asking you this question I am going to tell you the answer."

"What's the answer?"

"The answer is, 'No, because I like women too much.'"

"Okay," I said. He paused a moment to gauge his son's reaction to the answer.

"The question is, 'are you a homosexual?'"

"No, because I like women too much." He laughed and shook my hand.

"If someone were to ask you for derogatory stories concerning myself, would you inform me?"

"Absolutely."

"Alright." Dad slapped the table and walked around the room. "I have somebody who falls into the category of 'S.O.B.' If he comes upon my property I will walk over to him and tell him, very seriously, that this is my property. If he does not step off my property, he will not leave on his own; they'll carry him out in a box. This is what I'm telling him, so if he comes to you at any time and asks that you provide him with derogatory stories… " He trailed off into whispers, *Oh mah god, something-something.* He put a new cigarette in his filter and lit it.

"I should probably head on out."

"Okay," said Dad. "You alright on money?"

"Yeah," I lied.

We shook hands again and stepped outside. Before letting me go Dad had to show off his recent shingle-work on the shack.

"I'd bet you've never seen shingles on a roof like that."

"No," I replied. "I don't think I have."

"I have to wait until spring to get back to it. You can't shingle in the winter." He grabbed a square of shingle off the ground and pulled on its brittle corner. "See that? It breaks off in the cold."

"Yeah."

"Good luck to you."

"Thanks."

We shook hands one more time and turned our backs to each other, the father heading inside and the son heading down the hill, quickly gathering momentum until I almost ran against my own will and had to brace myself at the hood of the car. I got in, turned it around and headed back past the sticks and state line to Winchester where I-81 took me north.

To see signs for Cumberland reminded me of William Wordsworth's "The Old Cumberland Beggar." Wordsworth was talking about a different Cumberland. There was a motel room somewhere in the Maryland one which was once my home, I just didn't know which motel and which room because I was only a baby at the time. Don't know how long I had been there; in the first two years of my life we lived in over twenty different places, ranging from that room to a big empty house with no rooms or windows. Dad thought there were people after him so we never spent more than a few weeks in the same place, and never owned anything that wouldn't fit easily in the car.

I considered a blind search for the motel but Cumberland would have meant getting off the I-81 in Hagerstown and taking I-68 quite some ways, and I didn't even have the money to get home. On the way back to Buffalo I stopped at my friend Khalida's house in Philly and she loaned me forty dollars.

9

Few have seen him… he is rumored to live in a squalid opium den in New York's Chinatown or else in a silver Gulfstream trailer somewhere in the New Jersey Pine Barrens.

—Richard Metzger, *Book of Lies:*
The Disinformation Guide to Magick and the Occult

It was January and New York State came under an arctic blast as I drove four hundred miles to meet a brilliant writer who, while not Muslim per se, goes a long way in exposing the real richness and depth of Islam.

No, it wasn't John Esposito.

Peter Lamborn Wilson has been described somewhere as an "Anarcho-Sufi." I don't know what that means but it sure as hell sounds cooler than "Progressive." In 1965 a "brilliant junky 350-pound jazz saxophonist poet" named Walid al-Taha introduced him to the Moorish Orthodox Church, after which Peter disappeared into far-flung wanderings across the Muslim world absorbing all the classical texts and tattered heretics and local scenes he could find. In Iran he applied for a two-week visa and stayed for seven years, leaving when the Revolution came. Peter has written scores of books and articles, hosted his own radio show, "Moorish Orthodox Radio Crusade," and was a founding member of the Ibn 'Arabi Society (he remains an honorary fellow), along with thought-systems like Ontological Anarchism and the Temporary Autonomous Zone (T.A.Z.). He has become something of a living myth and modern-day Hassan bin Sabbah in anarchist circles.

The Moorish Orthodox Church stemmed from the Moorish Science Temple of Noble Drew Ali, an African-American born Timothy Drew in 1886 and raised by the Cherokee Indians of North Carolina. The story goes that Ali joined the circus as a magician, found his way to Egypt, became initiated in a secret High Priesthood at the Pyramid of Cheops and journeyed on to Mecca before crossing the ocean again with a new scripture in hand: the *Circle Seven Koran*. Declaring prophethood in 1913, Ali's divine mission was to restore African-Americans to their true status as "Asiatics" and "Moors."

White beatnik poets and jazz musicians in the 1950s would obtain Moorish passports and form the Moorish Orthodox Church with a hand in everything from traditional Sufism to Timothy Leary's drug mysticism. The MOC had three informal branches to represent the three religions of Abraham: there was the Order of Jerusalem, relating to Judaism; the Order of the Paraclete, relating to Christianity; and the Fatimid Order, relating to Islam.

Wearing my Shriner jacket now punked-out with spikes and studs, I got off I-87 and stopped at a bar on the margins of the Catskill Mountains to find five or six middle-aged men and one of their wives watching the Carolina-St. Louis game on a small TV. They stared at me like tough guys but couldn't hold eye contact when I gave it back to them. I bellied up to the bar and ordered something for courtesy. On TV, the play-by-play man mentioned Carolina receiver Muhsin Muhammad, prompting the townie on my left to look up from his beer. "Muhsin Muhammad," he moaned with a tone like his dog had just pooped on the rug and he couldn't help but find it amusing.

I slept poorly in a grocer's parking lot, turning the car on every hour to blast the heat. I woke up for the last time around five or so, turned the ignition and put it in drive. As the sun came up my horizon was walled off by Catskills on every side, enclosing the land like a sanctified holy place. I felt like I was in Masshad or something if it wasn't for the blinding bright snow.

It was a decent drive passing small town cemeteries with snow-topped tombstones and old churches left half-naked by peeling paint. My eyes hurt. I called when I reached Peter's town. He asked if I could get a quart of milk on the way.

As I pulled up on his quiet side street he stood in the front door, sporting a flannel shirt and Johnny Legend beard.

"As-salamu alaikum," he said. I returned it. We shook hands and he held the door for me. I followed him up a narrow flight of stairs to his kitchen/ living room past shelves stocked with books and manuscripts. We sat on opposite sides of a cluttered table and he spun yarns reaching from North Africa to Java starring hashish-den sayyeds, scraggly-haired opium Sufis, Muharram self-mutilators and the Drooling Moron of Quetta. I opened a book on the table, something about Ahlul-Bayt Sufis, and found a personalized note on the inside cover: "To Peter Lamborn Wilson: you are the Imam of the Age." Peter made me green tea and served it in a beautifully patterned bowl.

He admired the scimitars and crescents on my Shriner jacket and said that Noble Drew Ali had drawn heavily from Shriner symbolism, influenced by a lodge of fez-wearing Black Shriners who in 1893 appeared at the Great Columbian Exhibition in Chicago. These Black Shriners may have been the first seeds of what would become the Black Muslims—especially since one of

Noble Drew Ali's early disciples and a possible challenge to his leadership, a Russo-Syrian silk salesman known as Abdul Wali Farrad Mohammed Ali, was rumored to have been none other than W.D. Fard.

There may be a weird secret to Chicago, Peter told me. In 1921 the city was headquarters to a missionary effort by Punjabi Ahmadiyyas who established a mosque at 4448 Wabash Avenue. Noble Drew Ali came to Chicago in 1925 believing that the Windy City was somehow "closer to Islam" than New Jersey. Master Fard moved operations to Chicago after his exile by the Detroit police, and Elijah would later leave Detroit for Chicago in the post-Fard power struggle.

Incidentally, ISNA holds their convention in Chicago every year. The historical root for all of this is probably lost forever but Peter said it might have something to do with a community of runaway slaves, white indentured servants and Pawnee Indians known as the Ben Ishmaels, who settled at what is now Indianapolis (incidentally again, home of ISNA's headquarters) and traveled a triangle connecting the Indiana towns of Morocco and Mecca to Mahomet, Illinois.

I told him about the three times I have been to Chicago, starting with the two-hour layover on my flight to Pakistan. Six years later I'd go back for the amazing week of Wesley Willis' memorial service and the ISNA Convention, when Earth was closer to Mars than it had been in 600 centuries. During my most recent trip I met Elijah Muhammad's grandson at a cemetery in Thornton and learned the real story of Master Fard.

So we talked about Fard, and we also talked about Malachi Z. York, founder of the Brooklyn Ansaru Allah who claimed that Fard was a Communist until the NOI allegedly told him to "get out of the Islam game—or else," after which the man fled to Georgia and built a giant pyramid in the woods. We talked about the callous on Wesley's forehead with all its holy ramifications; there was a special term for it among Sufis or Shi'as or somebody, they called it the *Gatta*. Then Peter compared the Prophet's Night Journey to Siberian Shamanism and followed with the tale of a Moorish Muslim pirate who was among the first settlers of Brooklyn, and whose descendents married into all the prominent New York families. Our dialogue went everywhere and took sharp turns on tangents—but to participate in the oral transmission of knowledge with somebody like Peter Lamborn Wilson connects you to secret chains of lineage going back to holy men in both hemispheres. He has been everywhere and knows his books but more importantly—at least to me—he knows characters, whether you're talking about an alchemist with stacks of gold bars in his closet, Prince-A-Cuba from the Five Percenters or the Moorish Governor of Baltimore, who ran a junk shop and spoke like a

"Persian poet from Alabama."

I told him my Rochester imam's old line, "there are no sects in Islam," and we shared a hearty laugh. Of course there are sects in Islam. There's a sect of Islamic Satanists in Iran! And there's a wealth of personality to be found in the fringe: Hafiz who poured wine on his prayer-rug, Ibn 'Arabi who wrote love poems to a fourteen-year old girl until they chased him out of Cairo, Rabeya who crossed out an ayat because there was "no room for hate" in her Qur'an and Haydar whose disciples spread cannabis leaves around his grave.

In Iran, Peter practiced Islam like a Shi'a; "it made no sense not to," he said. Then he told me that in Java they used to play the adhan on drums because it traveled better through forests ("the voice is for the desert"), but the Wahhabis took over and now every mosque there has loudspeakers atop its minarets just like every mosque everywhere else in the world.

According to Peter, Islam has followed the same patterns on this continent as many religions when they arrive in new societies; entering first as heresy mingled with native culture (i.e., the Nation of Islam), followed by a phase of strict orthodoxy as converts struggle to learn the proper traditions. Made sense; four of Muslim America's biggest heroes had started out in the Nation of Islam, only to later go completely Sunni: Malcolm X, Warith Deen Mohammed, three-time heavyweight champion Muhammad Ali and Imam Siraj Wahhaj.

I never thought to ask Peter what comes after the strict orthodoxy phase. On my drive home I wished I had.

10

I shall cry blood for you instead of tears.

—Imam Mahdi

The whole Muharram thing left me too tired for Shi'a/Sunni hadith-tossing contests over whether self-injurious behavior has any place in Islam. Besides, that's a religious question and Muharram wasn't completely about religion. Part of me just wanted to soak in some deliberate heartbreak, manifested through a man who happened to be Prophet Muhammad's grandson. And part of me wanted to bleed again, because it had been a long time and I almost missed it.

I used to wrestle in rings made of barbed wire. My heroes were guys like Mick Foley, Terry Funk and Sabu (billed as "the most homicidal, suicidal and genocidal man in professional wrestling"). Five years later I still have a puffy scar on my left arm that looks like a wad of bubble gum, a bumpy scar on my head from Kid Kato's botched chokeslam and a floating chip of bone in my elbow from a Thumbtack Death Match. The wrestling was performance art but the blood was real. Sometimes I'd get smashed in the head with a steel chair and would sell it by cutting myself with a hidden razor blade. The blood would trickle down my face and our audience believed it came from the chair-shot. Of course, you don't have to fake getting tossed into barbed wire; I have permanent white scratches on my arms and legs.

People asked how I could continue a match with my head split open or dozens of thumbtacks stuck in my skin when the truth was that it only pushed me harder with a sudden and euphoric adrenaline lift. Pain can be the body's natural morphine. The storm of endorphins didn't only come from the wound itself; sometimes I'd get a tingle in my spine just from watching the blood crawl out of a new cut. That's a survival instinct kicking in; you see yourself injured and your body wants to alarm you with all of its wonderful neurotransmitters. Mash'Allah.

When the rush wore off I'd usually be sitting in the shower, watching red water swirl around the drain. It's a warm slow dizzy. Like being drunk. You don't have to be Shi'a to get that. I knew a girl with cross-hatched razor scars on her arms and she had never heard about any of that Karbala stuff, she was just a regular kufr. Hazrat Iggy Pop used to cut himself on stage, but I don't know what madhab he followed.

I did have myths to uphold in Muharram, but they weren't all Muslim. I grew up Irish Catholic. When I was five Gramps would walk me to church on weekday mornings to sit down and stand up and sit down again and stand up again and kneel on the padded kneeler before a tall bloody Christ with spikes driven through his palms and a crown of thorns pressed into his head and his deep sunken eyes gazing up at the church ceiling as though at the precise second where he asks why he had been forsaken. Reliefs lining the walls depicted the Twelve Stations of the Cross and Gramps would take me around the church, reading Christ's story in stone. As a kid I didn't know what it all meant beyond that bad guys wanted to kill Jesus and he let them—but he only let them because he loved me so much. That was a hard concept to grasp, but they call these things mysteries.

At St. Francis DeSales High School they sent us on spiritual retreats with the late Father Dave. One year he gave each of us a wooden match and then passed around a tin cup. When the cup came your way you'd have to drop your match in headfirst so it made a clink sound—like a hammer striking the head of a nail. As the cup went around the room, nobody said a word. Each clink symbolized us—you, me, all sinners—driving a nail deeper into Christ's hand.

I'm no anthropologist but Blood Atonement could be the world's oldest religious idea, so old and deeply rooted that it doesn't even need religion. Tell me we don't love the fact that Malcolm X knew he'd die a violent death and just marched into it anyway. In his eulogy Ossie Davis called Malcolm "our own black shining prince... who didn't hesitate to die, because he loved us so." That's Husain-thought right there, or maybe Christ-thought. Or Dionysius-thought, or something from even farther back. And you can find it on both sides of 9/11.

Approaching Niagara Falls on the sixth of Muharram I thought of all the times I had gone to Canada for bad things, hoping a few drops of my blood could wash that out. Then Coldplay's "Yellow" came on the radio—what a sweet song but hear it while on your way to a ritual cutting party and the light-heartedness of Chris Martin singing "for you I'd bleed myself dry" is so absurd and inappropriate it's darkly funny.

When I arrived at the border I figured I'd be in for less harassment if I just said I was going to a strip club.

"Which one?" the border cop asked.

"Seductions."

"Oh yeah? Where's that?"

"Down on Lundy's Lane, right by Sundowners."

"Okay," he said, waving me on. The test passed, I drove on to Canada.

On the QEW headed towards Toronto I wondered what the hell I was doing. I wasn't even a regular Shi'a; if this Ahlul-Bayt scene was only a heresy, then I was a heresy of a heresy. Like the Mughiriyya I say Allah is a man-shaped Light. Like the Mu'ammariyya I neglect my prayers. Like the Ghaliya I say Ali is fighting his enemies above the clouds. Like the Khattabiyya I want a vocal prophet and a silent one. Like the Saba-iyya I want my Imam back. Like the Tayyariyya my soul will transmigrate into a camel, then an inferior animal, then an animal inferior to that, and so on until I am a worm thriving in feces and I keep going down until my soul inhabits clay and iron and mud and I am tormented in fire.

Like Allama Iqbal I am one who weeps for the Martyr of Karbala.

I first learned of Husain at a time when Islam was falling apart for me. My estrangement had seemed to come from all angles; when someone today asks how I became an apostate, I don't always give the same answer. I had burned out on the demands of what people call Wahhabism and was beginning to question things about Prophet Muhammad's life. I worked overnights at Hobart College as a janitor, which interfered with my daily prayers. I'd get off work at five in the morning, make Fajr and then sleep through my Zuhr and Asr. I technically kept the Ramadan fast but barely noticed because I slept all day. My intense religious life had also left me sexually crippled, praying three hundred rakats after kissing a girl and thousands of zikrs for masturbating. Just sitting next to a female would cause me to tremble uncontrollably. I hated myself. Not only had I conked out as a Muslim, but I had become a guilt-ridden mutant incapable of what I perceived as a "normal" American life.

Then I read of everything that Husain had gone through—his mother Fatima, the Prophet's own daughter being trampled to death by men who claimed to be Muslims; his father Ali brained with a poison-tipped sword; his older brother Hassan assassinated to secure power for a criminal named Yazid; the Islamic community so divided against itself that the Prophet's widow Aisha ordered arrows to be hurled at Hassan's corpse. At a time when everything for which his grandfather had fought and struggled was sullied in a civil war that killed ten thousand Muslims, Husain declared his intention to make the Hajj—not in Mecca, but Karbala—where he'd perform the pilgrims' sacrifice not with a goat but his own blood.

It may be worth noting here that Karbala can be broken into two words: *karb*, meaning grief or sorrow, and *balaa*, meaning affliction. The cursed land sits in modern-day Iraq.

Yazid, whose father had been the rival to Husain's father and whose grandmother had chewed the liver of Husain's great-uncle on the battlefield of Uhud, sent his army to Karbala. Husain had with him his wives, children and friends. Yazid's force numbered in the thousands. The army surrounded Husain's camp and cut off his access to the Euphrates River.

Cradling his six-month old son in his arms, Husain walked to his enemies unarmed and without escort. Regardless of how they felt about him, he pleaded, his baby had done nothing to harm them; could he at least have water? One of the soldiers then fired a blow dart that went through Husain's arm and pierced his son's neck, pinning them together. Husain went to wipe his baby's blood on the earth, but the earth cried that it could not bear such holy weight; he then offered the blood to the sky, but it too refused for fear that it would fall asunder. So Husain smeared the blood on his face, took the dead baby back to his camp and picked up his sword.

Yazid's army made short work of Husain's defenders; soon the Holy Imam was alone. Stuck with arrows and covered with wounds, his blood streaming down the side of his white horse, Husain sheathed his sword and made one last plea for the soldiers to remember how kindly his grandfather had treated them. He even offered to leave the Muslim world so Yazid would no longer view him as a threat to his power. Finally, he warned them of the eternal consequences that could come with taking his life. He knew that nothing he might have said would change his fate, but Husain did not mean it for the soldiers' ears; he said it for history. In giving these men one last chance to put down their weapons, he exposed the corruption of Yazid's regime for all time.

He then noticed that it was time for evening prayer and slid down from his horse, only to find himself impaled on the ground by the arrows still protruding from his body. He passed out. In a dreamlike state Husain felt the presence of heroes from earlier times: Abraham, Moses, Jesus, his grandfather Muhammad and father Ali, all grief-stricken though each of them turned away rather than watch him suffer. Then the spirit of Fatima descended upon him and cooled his forehead with her hand, vowing that her son would not be alone in his final hour.

He awakened, pulled himself up and prepared for his last salat. With no water for wudhu he performed tayammum on the burning sand. It was during Husain's prayer, his face lowered to the ground, that a soldier walked up and chopped off his head.

The details vary. This was the story as I knew it.

They rode over his body with their horses. His head was stuck onto a spear. The widows and orphans were imprisoned. Husain's horse neighed and cried and galloped off into the desert. The sky turned red with shame for what it had seen.

Husain's murder was cathartic; Islam had failed Muhammad's own blood more than it had me, and Husain hurt for it in ways that I'd never know. If someone wants to pull up history and scripture to refute these Shi'a melodramatics, have fun—but you're missing the point of mythology. I don't even need the story to be true; there are people that get like this over *Star Wars*.

I got off the QEW at Hamilton and turned onto a side street, passing a rope-chain manufacturer and gray concrete recycling plant before I came to an empty fenced-in parking lot. The mosque looked like it could have been a regular house, apart from the sign reading "ISLAMIC CENTRE" with much of its paint scratched off. It had grimy aluminum siding and was stained with rust from the bars over a window.

I parked and wondered how far I could really go with this; but how can you face Husain's mother on the Day knowing that you half-assed your *matam*?

Matam is the sanctified self-abuse in which mourners of Husain take to their own skins with knives and hooks and chains. Popular forms of matam are *zanjir-zani* (self-flagellation) and *qamma-zani* (forehead-cutting), though some Shi'as have also walked on fire—but I can't remember what kind of *zani* that is.

The parking lot was empty. I sat in my car and flipped through a booklet designed to teach children how to pray. The kid on the cover cupped his hands up by his chest instead of folding them above his navel. Everything I knew about prayer I had learned as a Sunni. The Shi'as did it their own way.

This kid on the cover might have looked as Husain did when he was a child, besides the flannel shirt and slacks. Husain's grandfather used to put him on his lap and say things like "I see you weltering in your own blood." What was it like to be so young and hear that stuff? I realized that I was getting weird and opened the car door just to reconnect with the outside world. It was put-up or shut-up time. I got out of my car and went in the mosque.

The kindly imam met me at the door and showed me where to put my shoes. Since no one was there yet he showed me the women's section, then the men's. They were basically halves of the same room, divided by a solid wall. I tried hard to impress upon him that I wasn't new to Islam but part of me felt like I was. I had never been in a mosque that had pictures of white horses on the wall, or banners with Husain's name and pictures of hands everywhere (the five fingers symbolizing Muhammad, Fatima, Ali, Hassan and Husain). I spotted a wall hanging of the Kaaba and felt relieved that at least something was familiar.

Soon enough the room filled with brothers. A visiting scholar from Pennsylvania sat before us and gave a talk in English, then said that today we would remember the martyrdom of Husain's young nephew Qasim and launched into it—out of nowhere he began screaming the story in Urdu and crying and holding his face in his hands while all the brothers up front lowered their heads. Occasionally someone yelled in Arabic and others would yell their replies. Nothing in my Sunni experience could have prepared me for this. Six teenagers entered the room carrying a little coffin on their shoulders and everyone stood up to touch the shroud that covered it. Younger boys followed with plates of fruit and cake. One had a plate of lit candles and brothers would wave their hands over the flames.

Then the men formed two columns facing each other. While a brother at the front of the room wailed in Urdu or maybe Farsi, they swayed back and forth and slapped their chests hard. Left, right, bam, bam and you could tell which guys were really getting into it because they moved their whole bodies and swung hard with full arm extension. One guy kept yelling something and everyone would yell after him; I think he was saying Ya Ali but I'm not sure. At certain spots we chanted Ya Husain, Ya Husain. I closed my eyes and zoned out on the rhythm of forty or fifty men beating their chests in unison and then I did it myself, my right hand coming down hard on my left pec. It stung but I kept going, trying to picture how pink it'd get under my Dropkick Murphys shirt. Sometimes I flexed my pectoral to brace for the hit. Sometimes I hit harder than others. If I found myself going easy I'd remember Husain's mother, curl my lip and raise my hand higher before bringing it down. Some guys were going harder than I could fathom, just straight beating the shit out of themselves. Even kids that looked to be in seventh or eighth grade were slapping hard. Men took turns reading the poems. The intensity of the hitting seemed to match whatever was going on in the recitation. At times the reading would slow down and we'd slow down our slaps, but then he'd pick up and everyone smashed their chests even harder than before. I wondered how long they'd go, and what was next—would someone whip out a dashna and smack his forehead with it? Where were the swords and chains?

When the *sineh-zani* (chest-beating) was done, the kids brought out dinner and tea. The imam sent a couple of high-schoolers over to sit with me. They asked the same questions that I'm asked in every mosque. I gave my standard answers of 1) I was raised Roman Catholic, 2) Malcolm X's autobiography inspired me to learn more about Islam and it just snowballed from there, and 3) my mom was totally cool with it—in fact she drove me to the mosque for my first shahadah. I owe my early development in Islam more to Mom than any Muslims—it wasn't Muslims that paid for my books and kufis and jalabiyyas, it wasn't Muslims that drove me forty miles to the mosque every week or sent money when I was in Pakistan.

I asked if anyone at that mosque did more of the severe stuff, like whipping and cutting and such and they said nobody did that in Canada but you could find it overseas. One of the kids told me that in Pakistan they had stories of men going so far with matam that they died, only to miraculously come back to life and even their awful scars would disappear. The kid said that I was a hero to him because while he had been born Muslim and it was all he'd ever know, I sought out the truth for myself—not only to go from Christian to Muslim, but Sunni to Shi'a—and I wanted to hurt myself again because he had no idea of how gully I had turned out. I told him that I had highs and lows and let it end there.

I left the place feeling so good that it depressed me at the border to claim I had gone to a strip club. But for the seventh of Muharram, I wanted more. Back in Buffalo I went online to find another Shi'a community, hoping that I could get into zanjir-zani or at least qamma-zani. Turned out there was a Shi'a mosque less than an hour from Buffalo, and on this side of the border—in Medina, New York.

So the next night I got off I-90 at exit 48-A and drove around Medina looking for West Avenue, just loving the fact that the town was called Medina and full of signs saying things like "MEDINA MINI-MART" or "MEDINA LIQUOR." But the mosque was dead—doors locked, lights off, no cars in the driveway. I found a flyer taped to the side-door window telling me to go back to Buffalo and hear a lecture at the University's North campus in Amherst. Pulled in at a truck stop on the way back and found a 16" x 20" framed drawing of Jesus with beads of blood rolling down his forehead and a tear on his cheek, and with the hair and beard and robe and heroic gaze he looked just like pictures of Imam Husain I had seen on the Internet. So I bought it. And if anyone asks, it's Imam Husain.

I arrived at the University, found screening room 112 and felt like a creep. Everyone seemed to sit by the aisles, so the only seat available to me without crawling over people was in the front row. The maulana was going on about how you can find no instance of Abu Talib's kufr causing any harm to Islam, or Abu Sufyan's iman helping it. For a moment I felt an incredible sense of relief, as though it somehow related to me. The scholar made some great points about the Ahlul-Bayt but remained respectful of the Sunnis; even if Sahih Bukhari slighted Ali, he told us, it was a holy book and we should all own a copy. I own a copy but haven't opened it in years.

The maulana told us of Imam Husain gathering the body parts of Qasim in his robe and carrying them to Qasim's mother. After the talk a neatly dressed man came to the podium with his forehead carved up like Bruiser Brody and wept as he recited. I could hear a man sobbing behind me. Then we all stood up and placed our hands on our hearts. I thought of the gruesome stories and the previous night's funeral procession and all the passion of men crying and slapping themselves for an event from centuries ago, realizing that what I missed in going from Catholic to Sunni could be fulfilled in the throes of Irrational Shi'a Love. It almost feels good to get sad, to cultivate a grief so thick it can coat your stomach like Pepto-Bismol. Again, I don't think it has to be a religious thing.

We did maybe five minutes of chest slapping, prayed and then everyone went home. The next night I went back to UB but the lecture went so long we had no time for matam at all, we just prayed and left. I doubted that I'd ever get to see hardcore matam. I had only until the tenth night of Muharram to find some holy cutters and this was already the seventh. Down in Jamaica, Queens they had a mosque that did zanjir-zani but I lacked the funds for another long drive.

Monday, the ninth of Muharram, I drove my friend Tundy to the liquor store on Grant so he could cash his check. In front of the store stood a life-sized statue of a white horse, flanked on either side by haggard old guys with brown-bagged bottles. While Tundy waited in line I stayed outside and sat on the curb, pretending that the horse's shade protected me from a hot Karbala sun though it was the beginning of March in Buffalo.

Slightly burned out on the sadness angle, I skipped that evening's lecture and kept to myself. Though far removed from the Shi'a scene, I considered that it was the eve of Husain's murder and made it a quiet night.

Tuesday I drove back to Medina and attended my first observance of Ashura. The alim from the UB lectures explained why Husain's martyrdom saved the entire Earth and all that it contained: Shi'as, Sunnis, Christians, Jews, Hindus and on down the line. He told the story while we all put our heads down. The youths carried out a replica coffin, draped in a white sheet that had been splattered with fake blood and followed by a parade of smaller kids carrying flags topped with hand-shaped ornaments. The coffin was placed on the floor and we rose to surround it. As someone began the recital I felt as though we were at a real funeral, and for a moment I imagined that the soft carpet was hot sand. The man had a beautifully nasal, almost feminine voice. Having entered Islam as a Sunni, it made me briefly uncomfortable to hear poetry and singing in a mosque but I got over it fast. When the tears came I tried to spread them to as much of my face as I could, hoping they were the tears that could shield my face from the Fire.

After prayer we sat on the floor for dinner. I had rice and I'm not exactly sure what else, but it was spicy and good. The brother seated next to me talked about Muharram celebrations he had seen in Africa and the different ways in which they did things. "Everyone observes it their own way," he told me. He said that some scholars issued fatwas banning matam altogether, though others allowed it as long as there was no serious or permanent injury. Then he explained that matam originated when those who had declined to join Husain at Karbala heard the news of his death and beat themselves with remorse. I had heard another story that it was started by Husain's sister. One version had her beating her head against the bar of a carriage; another said she smashed her head on the bars of a cell.

On the way home I stopped at Wegmans and purchased four packs of brass-plated thumbtacks at ninety-nine cents a pack. Through the clear plastic I could see my reflection on the heads. They made a rattling sound when I shook them.

"For home, school or office," it said on the package. Or matam.

At home I spilled my four hundred thumbtacks on the floor and gathered them closer together. Some were on their sides but most had their points straight up. From a few feet away it looked like sprinkled gold. I took off my shirt and thought of the maulana breaking down as he described Husain standing before Yazid's army. The maulana had asked us to imagine thousands of archers aiming at a single target. I tightened my body and threw myself down.

Ya Husain, Ya Husain.

Back when I wrestled in thumbtack matches I'd always do my own tack-bump rather than let the other guy toss me. I'd stand in front of the tacks, he'd give me a clothesline and I went crashing backwards of my own volition. I tried to flat-back bump but as often as not I'd lean to my left; sometimes I went completely sideways and got the bulk of them stuck in my arm. Falling on thumbtacks isn't so bad if you're already fired-up from wrestling; it's worse when the match is over and you're calming down but the things are still in you.

This time I again went sideways and most of what stuck was in my left arm. According to the package they were only five sixteenths of an inch into me but it still hurt. I figured that if I had done this alongside hundreds of other thumbtack-zanis, there might have been more of a rush; but this was a quiet kind of pain. A private little rush, maybe. Ya Husain, Ya Husain. I remembered why I used to do this all the time but was still glad I had given it up.

I pulled out a tack and my arm cried blood, sorry to have never raised a sword in Husain's defense. I watched the new hole in my skin dribble its sad red line and wondered how it would have felt if these tiny metal pricks were arrows.

11

Drove to Chicago to give a reading at Loyola. Instead of a gallon bottle of piss in my passenger seat, I had a freelance journalist named Mark Wallace. From Niagara Falls we opted to drive six hours through Canada, reuniting with the border at Detroit's Ambassador Bridge. The border cop made me pull off to the side and told us to go sit in the office. Through the window I watched them search my car.

First thing they found was a stack of Shi'a magazines that had been given to me at the mosque in Hamilton. An attractive blonde officer flipped through them while two other cops went through the trunk. I made a mental list of what they could find: the brown wool pakul hat I had bought in Pakistan; my photo album from Pakistan full of pictures of seventeen-year-old me in white jalab and kufi, with smiling Peshawar mullahs and Afghan refugees backdropped by mosques and mountains; a book about Isma'il Faruqi autographed by the author; my Egyptian Wrestling Champion belt; a road atlas marked up with markers; two Qur'ans and a Qur'an tape; a notebook listing all of my future Islamically-oriented road destinations by state; and thirty hand-bound copies of *The Taqwacores*. In the tape deck they found a cassette with one side reading "US BOMBS" in my handwriting and the other, "UK SUBS." They pulled out a stack of one-subject notebooks and I had no idea what they'd read in there, I wrote all sorts of things at strange hours of the night in greasy diners that weren't worth publishing—most of it awful either by style or content. I usually filed such work in the trunk with dirty clothes, old food wrappers, a leaking jug of engine coolant and a brick from the childhood home of Zelda Fitzgerald (9 Pleasant Avenue, Montgomery, Alabama). I was half-embarrassed at the condition of my car, but also half-amused that they'd be going through all my garbage and crusty masturbation rags.

They carried piles of my crap into a little room. I couldn't see what they were doing but the door was open and I heard one cop on the phone reading from my notebooks to somebody. God damn it, they found my untitled suicide poem.

It was one of those lousy little scribbles from a late night of driving around Buffalo feeling upset at myself in the way that everyone does at some point, when you get really melodramatic about your life and imagine that ending it all would make some impressive statement to the world. I'll admit that it's fairly adolescent. At the time of writing it I was pretty down on myself for being a loser with no career and no degree and no prospects for either at the ripe old age of 26 while still obsessed with this "capturing the American Islam" thing that may have just been a Lost Cause, at least for me, because what qualified me for such a mission? The job should have gone to someone who still prayed their Fajr, at least. So I had found a booth at Pano's on Elmwood and wrote this lousy poem, which I guess could come off as sketchy to a customs officer:

> Just a few hundred words
> is all I have left,
> and then I'm gone—
> driving to the desert
> with hard liquor

and soft religion,
to drink myself through Isha
and make pre-sunrise sujdah
on the Stars and Stripes
with a chunk
of World Trade concrete
as my turba—
I know now
that all my crying over Islam
in 1996 was premature,
the worst
was yet to come—
and I know
I don't need an ayatollah
to fatwa my ass,
I can do it myself
and cry blood for the Imam
from my right temple
so bury me
with the Egyptian belt

So he was reading it on the phone, and God knows who he was reading it to, and Allahu Alim how they would interpret it. A cop came out and called me into the little room. As six officers stood around watching he told me to empty my pockets. Out came my pens, Canadian coins and Imam Ridha turba, a small piece of clay bearing an Arabic inscription.

"What's this?" he asked.

"A turba."

"A what?"

"A turba—a religious artifact."

"Okay. Now take off your coat and hand it to the officer standing next to you." Then he told me to face the wall and extend my arms like I was flying. I reached my arms in front of me. "LIKE YOU'RE FLYING!" he repeated. How does Superman fly? With his arms in front of him, right? But he grabbed my arms and put them how he wanted, reaching out on either side like an airplane. "You have anything sharp?" he asked. "You have a knife, you have anything that's going to stick me or poke me?"

"No." I had seen this whole exchange on *Cops* more than once.

"I'm going to give you a full-body pat-down," he told me. "It's going to get personal. I'll let you know before it does, because if you jump I'm going to think that you're attacking me and I will act to defend myself. Do you understand?"

"Yes, sir."

"Spread your legs out. Wider. A little wider. There you go."

So he patted me down. Chest, back, arms, legs.

"Okay, it's about to get personal." He reached between my legs, rubbed from anus to testicles, cupped my balls in his hand and pushed around my cock for thirty seconds or so to make sure it was only me in there. On a stupid male-pride level, I wished that it wasn't so cold and that I wasn't so nervous—I could have represented my lun better. Then he sat me down and asked where I was headed.

"Chicago," I said.

"For what?"

"I'm giving a talk."

"What's your talk about?"

"I wrote a book and self-published it, so I'm talking about my experiences with that, you know, with independent publishing, and I'll be reading from the book."

"What's your book about, exactly?" asked the blonde girl.

"A house of Muslim punk-rockers in Buffalo, New York." They sent me back to the waiting room and called in Mark.

For over three hours we watched carloads of people come and go. At one point three young Arab males came in dressed for the clubs, and I thought I had made their night more difficult but they were back on the road in five minutes—must have been no Qur'ans in their trunk. The blonde officer walked around flipping through my Pakistan pictures and trying to look tough. She made eye contact with me once or twice and I glared back at her. I tried to fathom what she thought she might have been looking at. She carried herself like she expected to be wearing a medal on CNN tomorrow.

Eventually an officer showed up who looked to be a boss, and he called me back into the room where I was fondled. He seemed like a reasonable and nice enough guy, which could have been why he ran the place—the blonde would have sent me to Guantanamo Bay by now. He sat me down and said he'd try to get me out of there soon enough, he just wanted to talk. He asked me what the book was about, how I put it out myself, how much money I made from it. He asked if I had ever been anywhere besides Pakistan. Then he sent me back to the waiting room.

Mark asked the blonde for a coffee and she got it to him. Something had changed; she was smiling now. At one point she joked with another cop about some well-known and married professional football players who had tried to hit on her. Within twenty minutes they put our stuff back in the car and let us go. It was maybe five in the morning.

Somewhere in Indiana we stopped at a big fireworks barn, where I bought roughly fifty dollars' worth of rockets and smoke bombs, telling Mark that we'd shoot them off at the ISNA headquarters.

So we made it to Chicago, tracked down Tamara Smith and Dennis Cooper, who had put together the event, and got to have dinner with Amiri Baraka. I first learned of Baraka from a Beat writers' anthology with Jack Kerouac and William Burroughs on the cover. He was born LeRoi Jones in 1934, became immersed in the whole Greenwich Village scene with Allen Ginsberg and those guys, published his first book of poems in 1961, flipped out after Malcolm was killed, left his wife and the Beats and moved to Harlem, flirted with Islam in 1968 and changed his name to Imamu Amiri Baraka, only to later embrace Marxism. His status as poet laureate of New Jersey had been threatened by his 9/11 poem "Somebody Blew Up America."

Baraka asked if I was Muslim, and I never know what to say in that situation but spill my whole life-story and let someone else figure it out. Amiri ordered a Miller Lite and I couldn't help but think holy shit, I'm sitting here with Amiri Baraka watching him drink his Miller Lite and watching him watch the game on TV, watching him comment on Iverson with the same laid-back coolness that my grandfather and his war-buddies had, just regular old men who had lived long enough to finally relax and shoot off their mouths at the TV without ever giving a shit anymore. Baraka told stories of hanging out with Che Guevara and riding trains across Cuba watching farmers raise their machetes yelling "Viva Castro" while he had nothing to viva for other than Viva Thelonius Monk or Viva Charlie Parker. From the restaurant we headed straight to campus and the Galvin Auditorium for Baraka's reading.

The place was packed. I believe its maximum seating was in the 250–300 range. Tamara Smith handed out fliers for the following night's presenter—"a punk-rock Muslim writer"—and pointed to me.

I stayed at Dennis and Tamara's that night. They had an amazing apartment—the living room walls covered with old-school paintings of Jesus and every shelf crowded with two lifetimes spent accumulating stuff—thousands of books, movies, CDs and seven childhoods' worth of poseable action figures ranging from Star Trek guys to Star Wars guys to He-Man and G.I. Joe. In the hallway they had a giant marker rendering of trains by Wesley Willis. I slept on a fold-out couch that had been crashed on by the immortal Jello Biafra. There was something incredibly holy about Chicago, I had convinced myself, maybe simply because I honestly believed it—and I didn't know if it were the Ben Ishmaels who made it that way, or Noble Drew Ali or Wesley Willis but I could live like it was true.

The following night my reading was attended by maybe ten people—including Tammy, Dennis, Mark, Helena, Helena's friend and Uzma. I sold a couple of my Kinko's books. By the time Mark and I woke up the next morning, both Tammy and Dennis had gone to work. I folded up my bed and put the cushions back, took a shower and we bailed—first to the campus bookstore so I could buy my mom a Loyola shirt, then the I-65 to follow the trail of the Ben Ishmaels—

> The introduction of Mohammedan slaves into America is forbidden on account of the danger which lies in their intercourse with the Indians.
> —The Council of the Indies to the King of Spain,
> on the Dutch Slave Trade, 1687

> Many Muslim slaves fled to the Cherokees after they learned that the Cherokees shared their religion.
> —Dr. Faruq Abd al-Haqq/Robert Dickson Crane

Dr. Crane is a J.D. (Doctor of Laws) from Harvard Law School. He served as foreign policy advisor to Richard Nixon from 1963 to 1968 and in 1981 served as U.S. Ambassador to the United Arab Emirates under Ronald Reagan.

He describes Native American religion with Islamic terms like "salat" and "hajj." Cherokee pilgrims performed their *tawafs* on land belonging to his uncle Henry Bever a few miles southwest of Hillsboro, Indiana. His great-uncle, Joseph Franklin Bever, was among the last imams of the Cherokee when the federal government banned their religion in 1905. Joseph began each of his five daily prayers with "Ya Allah" and excused his adhan by saying that he was simply calling the hogs.

Crane visited the Cherokees as Nixon's official envoy, where he learned that they originally lived on an island in the Caribbean and based their religion on a book that had been brought over by ships from the East. Crane believes that the ships came from the Emir of Mali, Abu Bakr, who sent trans-Atlantic expeditions after meeting Chinese Muslims in Mecca. By that line of thought, the Qur'an makes its American debut around 1310 A.D.—though Harvard linguist Barry Fell believed in an earlier trans-Pacific voyage by Indonesian Muslims, evidenced by Death Valley petroglyphs reading "Yasua bin Maryam" in Arabic letters.

When "bad people" came attacking the Cherokees, their book was lost or destroyed; hoping to find it again, they left their island and took to the wilderness of the north.

Maybe these Muslim Cherokees were the ones who raised Noble Drew Ali.

There was no telling about any of that stuff. But I was after Pawnees, anyway.

It had been maybe two months since Peter Lamborn Wilson told me of the Ben Ishmaels, the tri-racial community that traveled nomadically between the towns of Morocco, Mahomet and Mecca and settled at what is now Indianapolis. I wanted to know why they wandered a triangle connecting towns with Muslim-sounding names and whether they were the ones who named them—they were also said to settle at what is now Cincinnati, which is near the town of Medina, Ohio—but couldn't find much information beyond what I had gotten from Wilson. One could figure that the slaves were African Muslims, and we do know that the Ben Ishmaels practiced polygamy and abstained from alcohol. Anything beyond that has been lost to history. The Eugenics movement emerged, branded the Ben Ishmaels as mongrels and deviants and chased them into exile. The tribe dispersed into cities like Chicago and Detroit, maybe providing roots for the Black Shriners or Black Muslims, and faded away with the beginning of the 20th century.

I'd suppose it was doubtful that in the century since, anyone had ever cared enough about these extinct people to travel their holy triangle; so there was no guessing what would happen to one who made the attempt. Maybe I'd be pulled with this freelance journalist into a mystical vortex and never be heard from again.

I called Peter Lamborn Wilson from the road and asked if he had any new information or at least some advice. He said that I'd be surprised at how much oral tradition survives, so if I found any really old-looking black men I should ask and see if they knew anything.

Morocco looked like a ghost town when we rolled in but we drove past some big rusty silos to find an open public library. The woman inside was extremely enthusiastic about helping us and kept going on about how she had never heard about anybody called the Ben Ishmaels. She brought out every old book on the town that they had and piled them up in front of us. Somewhere I read that the place was named Morocco because a stranger once rode into town wearing red Moroccan-leather boots.

On the way to Mahomet we drove through Crescent City and stopped at Urbana because I had the address for a mosque on the University of Illinois campus. They were about to perform Maghrib so we stuck around, Mark propping his back against the wall as I joined the prayer.

It was dark when we hit Mahomet. There wasn't much to experience besides the weirdness of signs like "Mahomet Post Office." We stopped at a Subway for dinner.

Mecca was all darkness and woods. We drove by a place called Mecca Tavern and thought about stopping for Pepsis but Mark said we'd get our asses kicked by the locals.

And that was it for Mecca. No old men who might remember, no trace of a secret Muslim past.

12

Having covered the Ben Ishmael triangle, it was time to shoot fireworks at ISNA. Coming into Plainfield I called the assistant editor I knew at ISNA's *Horizons* magazine and said maybe we'd swing by his place, but then thought better of it and went straight to the Days Inn. We woke up early and drove to ISNA's big corporate-looking headquarters. I wore my brown wool mujahideen hat and had a car full of rockets just for these bastards—but inside the hijabi ladies were so sweet and happy to help, even letting me have four free copies of the new issue, that I had no spirit to hit them with anything but smiles and salams. Another juvenile scheme foiled by warm hearts. But I'd flip through the magazine later and wish that I had started some shit—the article's editor misspelled the title of my book! *The Taquacores*, instead of *The Taqwacores*.

And my photo wasn't there, damned spiked Shriner jacket. A spiked Shriner jacket! Was that too heterodox for ISNA? The other featured writers, Mohja Kahf and Daniel Abdal-Hayy Moore had their pictures run, but the spot where I would have been was occupied by a shot of twirling Sufi boys which had nothing to do with the article other than that it was titled "Besides Rumi." Called my friend Tundy and bitched about it, and he just said that I wasn't meant to be the guy that ISNA *wouldn't* dick over.

From ISNA's headquarters it was twelve hours or so of straight driving before we hit New York City and JFK Airport where Mark had left his car four days before. He told me how to get to the bridge I needed to get to and the interstate after that, but I'm the worst at receiving directions verbally—I forgot it all and lost my way. Then the rain came down hard and my windshield wipers decided to stop working, they just froze in mid-swing and I could only see lights. I rolled the window down and stuck my head out to drive like

Ace Ventura but the water kept smashing down and it was still only March, not quite warm enough for that nonsense. I put my head back in but kept the window down, put my hazards on and drove through Brooklyn and then Manhattan at twenty miles an hour, squinting at every corner to see what street I was on. Found myself on Broadway completely by accident, knew that if I took it north I'd end up somewhere out of the city and tried to plod on, but the water was too much and one of these yellow cabs was going to kill me so I parked, rolled up the window and turned off the car. I rummaged through my clothes in the back seat for my Egyptian championship belt; if I was going to walk around in the rain like a monster I'd have to take it with me because my car doors didn't lock—actually they did, but they didn't *un*-lock. I don't know why I always imagined that someone would rather steal the Egyptian championship belt than say, my car stereo but it was a real one-of-a-kind belt custom-made by the same guy who made them for Vince McMahon. The Egyptian belt had been modeled after the old WWF belt used from 1988 to 1998 with the eagle design on the main plate, except it said "EGYPT" instead of "WORLD" and where the WWF logo would have been I had the pyramids, where the globe was on the WWF belt I had a map of Egypt and the side plates featured King Tut's sarcophagus and the Sphinx on either side. An amazing and priceless belt, even though the years have put some wear and tear on it. I swear that they'll bury me with it someday, Undefeated Egyptian Champion. I got out of the car and snapped the belt around my waist. Broadway went up through Harlem; there was a chance that if I walked far enough, I could find the Audubon Ballroom.

And there it was, 3940 Broadway between 165th and 166th Streets. Above the inside glass doors it read

KNOWLEDGE * 5.19.1925 * EL-HAJJ MALIK SHABAZZ * 2.21.1965 * COURAGE

complimented by Kufic calligraphy of squares and straight lines—I wished I knew what it said but did recognize an *Allah* here and there. Maybe it wasn't even Kufic, what the hell did I know.

Malcolm X stood at the end of a long red carpet and up four steps on his own little stage, shining under the only light left on in the place. He was lanky with straight posture, left hand in pocket and right hand driving home a point when for some reason he had frozen like that forever.

Malcolm was a Muslim and I wondered how he'd feel about being a statue now, statues being haram and all, and I wondered how he'd feel standing there in the main lobby of the Audubon Ballroom all alone every night.

75

And how would he feel about being on a U.S. postage stamp? Anyway, he was on stamps in Iran first.

Then I wondered how he'd feel about me standing out there getting slapped silly by the rain with the Egyptian championship belt under my jacket, an Imam Ridha turba still in my pocket, mourning tragedy and destruction while still somehow loving life, loving the fact that I was there at a sad place, feeling sad but thankful at the same time, if that made any sense.

The back part of the building, the part where it actually happened, had been torn down and turned into a parking lot encircled by steel bar fencing that made it look like a jail. For $8.46 an hour you could park where Malcolm X bled to death. With that I hunched over and walked back to my car.

Malcolm had me thinking that I still had a chance at being Muslim. It could have been nostalgia for the 1990s when I would watch Spike Lee's movie over and over and close my eyes during the assassination scene.

Malcolm came at a time when Islam was either a statement of racial nationalism for African-Americans or a transplanted immigrant culture with no real connection to this hemisphere. His journey brought it together, putting blacks, Arabs, South Asians and even blue-eyed devils in the same masjid, creating a common identity for all of us.

When I think of Islam's place in my life, I don't look to memories of being a little Muslim kid with Muslim Mom and Muslim Dad and Muslim Sunday school and Eid parties overflowing with cousins—as a convert, *Malcolm* was my culture. My only Islamic background was his damned movie. Even now, my grafting the motif of holy travel from both American and Islamic culture—that story had already been told for all time by Malcolm hopping on a plane for the truth...

I drove around for a long while, somehow ending up on I-87, then I-84—where it began to snow and again I had to drive twenty miles an hour— back-tracking forever through Pennsylvania until coming to the 81 at Scranton. I got off I-81 at Kirkwood, drove to the parking lot of the Penguin Books warehouse and checked out the dumpsters but came up empty. Then I rummaged around my Buick's back seat for an empty bottle to piss in and filled it about halfway. I screwed the lid on, pushed my seat back and fell asleep.

Two hours later I woke up and grabbed a firework.

It was attached to a wooden stick, which helped me submerge the rocket in urine while keeping the fuse dry. I opened my door, set the bottle outside, started the car, and sparked the lighter. I peeled out with one eye to the rear-view and watched my piss-bottle explode with a flash of green-white light.

When I was back on I-81 my friend Keith called. We had plans to meet that morning in the old Ames parking lot down the road from Binghamton University (incidentally, where Elijah's son Akbar was said to be an Associate Professor). Keith was driving to Philadelphia and I'd leave my car to come along for the ride.

13

From what I had heard, Philadelphia was a bastion of Islam where even kufr kids in the inner city would chew on siwaks and call each other *akh*. Famed soul-music producer Kenny Gamble grew up on the South Side and came back as Luqman Abdul-Haqq to rebuild his community. Celebrated poet Daniel Abdal-Hayy Moore, who Allen Ginsberg had called a "modern-day Sufi," lived here and I knew the address; maybe I could rummage through his trash and steal a discarded rough draft. Philly was also home to Temple University, where the legendary Isma'il Faruqi taught from 1968 until his brutal assassination in 1986.

On the way to Temple we passed Halal Bilal's Steak & Take on Stenton and I made Keith stop. I read their giant outside menu and realized that I'd have to experience the "Muslim Hoagie." Gave my order and $6.50 to the African-American hijabi at the first window and waited outside for ten minutes or so until an African-American hijabi at the second window called my number. The sandwich came wrapped in foil and heavy as a brick. I unwrapped it and had the thing finished within a few miles. Al-hamdulilah.

We made it to Broad Street, drove past Masjid Muhammad #12 and found long lines of red "T" banners attached to lampposts so we figured this was Temple. Keith dropped me off and went to do his thing. I looked at a map of the campus to find Anderson Hall, which turned out to be at the end of a long brick path flanked on either side by more Lenin-red flags. Though Faruqi died almost a decade before I'd ever hear of him, and there was a strong chance we wouldn't have agreed on much, I felt a tie to the man.

Isma'il Faruqi was my teacher's teacher.

A student of Faruqi's named Dr. Muhammad Shafiq, imam at the Islamic Center of Rochester, New York, witnessed my first shahadah and became kind of an Obi Wan-Kenobi figure. I remember an Egyptian brother who snarled that Dr. Shafiq was "more philosopher than imam" but that was what I loved about him. He made Islam a philosopher's religion not so much by a specific idea or theory but just the way that he carried himself with people, the way that he could welcome a Christian or Jew into the mosque and smile as he listened to them, the way he never bothered with petty gripes of bid'ah that the hardcore guys always threw at him. He was a good, gentle man.

Dr. Shafiq returned home to Pakistan in the fall of '94, just a few months before I went there. I made a special trip from Islamabad to Peshawar to see him, drinking tea in his backyard with three or four mullahs as chickens clucked around us. When someone said that we were within walking distance of Afghanistan I wanted to go check it out but then learned that the country was caught up in civil war. That was January 1995. The winners of the war would call themselves the Taliban.

Dr. Shafiq had written a book about Faruqi and reading it as a starry-eyed seventeen-year-old I imagined that whatever Shafiq meant to me, Faruqi meant to him. Dr. Shafiq had signed my copy, "to Br. Mikail with best wishes and prayers. May Allah guide you to the straight path. Work hard with patience and steadiness. May Allah bless you with success in this world and the hereafter (Amin)." That was a long time ago.

I found Anderson Hall, walked up six flights of stairs and then down a quiet narrow hall to a door marked 636. This was it. Faruqi's office. First thought in my head was that Dr. Shafiq had sat in there decades ago as a young hero-worshipper, a Faruqi groupie like I had been a Shafiq groupie in the mid-90s. Then I realized that for me, this was more about Shafiq—or at least my connection to Isma'il Raji al Faruqi through him. I didn't know much about Faruqi beyond that he and his wife were brutally stabbed in their home and that two weeks beforehand, the chief of New York's Jewish Defense League made remarks about an outspoken Palestinian-American professor being "silenced." I knew that an African-American convert known around town as Yusuf Ali had been convicted of the murders. I knew that he said he was compelled to do it by voices in his head. I knew that Faruqi was considered a pioneer of something in this country, but I wasn't sure what. I knew that Muslim students called him and his wife Papa and Mama. I knew that he had once been the governor of Galilee, before the Israeli occupation removed him and his family.

Looking at the door, I learned that his office now belonged to someone named Rebecca Alpert. I had expected a plaque or memorial of some kind—what do you do when an active professor is butchered with a hunting knife on his own kitchen floor? But there was nothing with Faruqi's name on it, and no reason for me to stay.

Walking back to the stairwell I spotted a student lounge with an unoccupied couch. I went in and sat down, groggy from living on the road the past week and especially from all my driving the night before. A nice breeze came through the windows. Directly above my head hung a plaque of al-Fatiha in black script with decorated blue and gold borders. Across the room hung a plaque of abstract mandala-looking stuff with Qur'anic calligraphy in the middle, too elaborate to actually read though I spotted Allah's Name a few times. They had been donated by the Temple MSA in 1977 and 1983, respectively—both during Faruqi's time here.

Back on Broad Street I walked towards Masjid Muhammad #12. Dr. Shafiq had told me that when he first came to the United States to study at Temple, he was turned away from a mosque because he wasn't black. It had completely stunned him, at that point having never heard of the Nation of Islam or Elijah Muhammad. I figured the mosque could very easily have been this Masjid Muhammad #12, being that it was on the same street as the university.

I walked past McDonald's and saw a haggard old African-American wearing what looked like a maroon turban, though I wasn't sure with just a passing glance. So I stopped and looked. He caught me looking and we both turned away. Then I looked back and he looked too. The scleras of his eyes were yellow. I tried coming up with something to say.

"Do you know anything about this Masjid Muhammad down the street?"

"Shit, no!" he exclaimed, gritting his teeth as he spoke. "I don't fuck around with them motherfuckers."

"Really?" I moved in closer. "Why not?"

"Man, that's a vulnerable position you get in with those guys. If I lay down and make my sa-ja, right, and I'm makin' my sa-ja, what if one of 'em wants to come by and chop off my head?" He acted it out with a hand across his neck, a cigarette resting between his index and middle fingers. In his other hand he held a small painted canvas.

"What's that?" I asked. He held it up. Looked to be something in Arabic though I couldn't make out any words besides Allah's Name and *qul*, which means "say."

"This is Solitude," he answered. "You know what solitude is? It's when you want to be alone. See that?" He pointed at some dark spots. I could tell that it was blood. "Some motherfuckers went up, behind me, you know, and—I don't even know who the fuck it was! You know what I'm saying?" Before I could reply he asked whether I went to Temple. No, I told him, I'm from Buffalo so he asked, "You have alumni up there in Buffalo?"

"Yeah, we have alumni."

"Do your alumni up there believe in playing psychological and uh, spiritual games with people? Do you think that's right? For alumni to play these psychological games and you don't even know who the fuck they is?" So I told him no, that's not right. "Man," he said, still gritting his teeth, "I was eight years old, right, walking right down here and I was going to Elijah Muhammad School at eight years old and these alumni are trying to play spiritual games with me—I was eight years old, I didn't have any spirituality!" I nodded. He asked if I got high. I said no. "What do you study?"

"Literature," I told him.

"Can you break down the three 2's?"

"The what?"

"The three 2's," he said. "You know, you got T-O, and you got T-O-O, and then you got T-W-O. Can you break that down?"

"T-O is like, 'I am going *to* the store.' T-O-O is like, I am going *too*, you know, like also. And T-W-O is the number."

"Good, good. Can you break down 'there,' you know, E-R-E and 'their,' like E-I-R?" So I broke that down for him too. Then he had me break down the difference between 'may I?' and 'can I?' Finally he asked whether I knew the difference between a baby Muslim and a grown-up Muslim.

No, I told him. What's that? "A baby Muslim," he explained, "is all 'is this okay with Imam, does Imam like this or that,' you know. A grown-up Muslim is just you and Allah, you know what I mean?"

Yeah, I said. I know what you mean.

I asked if I could take his picture. "Five dollars," he said. I was okay with that.

"Can you hold up your artwork?" I asked.

"Wait a minute!" he cried. "You want a picture of me, or a picture of my artwork? Because for me and my artwork, for five dollars, I don't know about that!"

"So what do you want?"

"Ten dollars."

"Man, come on. I can give you five, I'm on a traveler's budget."

"I don't know man, you could put that in a book and get rich and I'll come back and sue you." So I apologized and kept on walking. Thirty seconds later I turned back around and called him over.

"Okay," I told him. "Ten bucks." As I made my shots he flashed a hand-sign. "What's that?" I asked.

"That's where I'm from."

"Where you're from?"

"You know the plight of the Palestinians?"

"Yeah."

80

"Break that down for me, break down the plight of the Palestinians."

"They lost their homeland."

"Right, man. That's where I'm from, I'm Palestinian." He showed me the hand-sign again so I could get it right. "That's where I'm from."

We stood around and talked some more. I told him about my Muslim road-trip articles and how I planned to spend the whole summer on the road just stopping at mosques, meeting Muslims and slapping it all into a book. He said he wanted to come along and wrote down his number on my Halal Bilal receipt. "Call me this summer," he said. "I'm coming on your trip with you. What countries are you going to?"

"Just this one."

"Oh, okay. I'm still coming."

We exchanged salams and I headed on to Masjid Muhammad #12, looking at the phone number on my Halal Bilal receipt. The Palestinian Wali-Allah of Broad Street had also written his name: Lawrence Nixon.

The masjid was closed with a metal gate drawn over the doors so I took one more look at its giant stone star and crescent and walked to the subway. Khalida lived downtown. She was an Afghan girl who used to have pink hair and live in a house of punk boys. And she sang in a band, back in the day. She has known me longer than any Muslim that still talks to me, and she's the only person in the world to still call me by my old Muslim name, Mikail.

14

Khalida was always telling me about things that I never would have known, like the treatment of gay men in Egypt or the story of women in Pakistan who had been arrested for killing their rapists. Pakistan loved to brag about having no rapes so sexual assaults were usually prosecuted as adultery—meaning that both rapist and raped would be charged. Rather than go to jail, victims often married their assailants, committing to a lifetime of reliving the rape. One group of women, however, decided instead to kill their rapists and had been arrested for murder.

"That's my army," Khalida said.

She had recently been elected president of Al-Fatiha, the advocacy organization for gay, lesbian, bisexual and transgendered Muslims and served as one of the imams of a mosque in Philly based in an independent book-store—a female imam, giving khutbahs and leading men. I remember when she first told me about it and we both got so excited that a new kind of mosque was starting since someday these things will be all over the place and Khalida could say that she was there at the beginning. She told me that one of the most remarkable things about the new mosque, beyond female imams or being a safe space for the gay community, was that it'd have daycare.

"Churches and synagogues have always done it," she said, "but in Islam, having a place for children is somehow a revolutionary act."

Later we were joined by Khalida's friend, Scott Siraj al-Haqq Kugle. He's a tall, lanky Caucasian professor that you can find in Omid Safi's *Progressive Muslims* anthology. He wore a red and white kifaya around his neck. He wanted to see an independent film about lovers in the Israeli army but Khalida wanted to hit up Key West, a gay bar down the street. I wanted to shoot off my horde of fireworks.

I woke up the next morning to find Khalida crawling into my fold-out bed. She put her head on my chest and I had my arm around her and we just lay like that until she wondered where Keith was and looked around the place, finding a note on her table that said he had gone for a walk. I called him up and he said he'd come back. We were meeting Siraj for breakfast.

Siraj's place was too busy, so he led us to a café that he described as "a little bourgeois but acceptable." I suggested the pizza place across the street but Siraj said "eww" and we proceeded to the café. I'm not a coffee drinker, and if I was I wouldn't pay six dollars for a cup, so I took a seat.

"So you're Mikail, the author?" Siraj asked. I nodded and smiled. He explained that he couldn't get into *The Taqwacores* because his brother was once into the whole punk scene, but the bad and ugly Nazi corner of it, so to read about any kind of punks made him almost vomit.

Keith said there'd be a big protest in New York to mark the one-year anniversary of our invading Iraq, which figured to be a scene. I called Sara in Queens to see if she was going and left a message on her voicemail. After everyone finished their coffee and danishes we bounced across the street to the pizza place. Khalida ordered cheese slices for both of us. While waiting I asked Siraj if he had ever been to Halal Bilal's Steak & Take and he shuddered at the thought. This wasn't a guy that would sit with you on the curb eating Muslim Hoagies or pizza slices off greasy paper plates, and I couldn't see him dumpster-diving—but he was a nice guy and seemed to have a genuine heart, so Subhana'Allah.

We made our goodbyes to take the train back to Broad Street and Keith's car. Masjid Muhammad #12 was open so I walked up and shared salams with the clean-cut man standing in front.

"Is this a Nation of Islam mosque?" I asked.

"Yes, sir, it is."

"Oh—okay, because I had heard that Minister Farrakhan had gone Sunni, and I was thinking that maybe this was the kind of mosque that I could be welcome in now."

"What is Sunni?" the man asked. "We believe that all of Islam is the same, you know, we're following the traditions of Muhammad so why give all these different labels to it?"

"So he's not Sunni?"

"No, sir."

"So you still believe in Master Fard being Allah?"

"Yes, sir. That's the foundation of our belief. You can't have a strong house without first having a strong foundation, right?" I didn't even bother asking if he still believed that I was the grafted devil. We shook hands and I walked away like Dr. Shafiq had thirty years before. Strong house, strong foundation. It's all hustle.

I got back in Keith's car and we drove to Halal Bilal's so I could get a Philly cheese-steak with "Special Bakr Sauce." Then we headed on up to New York. On the way I thought about Halal Bilal's Steak & Take, Masjid Muhammad #12, Kenny Gamble, Lawrence Nixon and all these city kids I saw walking up the street in do-rags and ultra-baggy jeans and long white t-shirts that almost went to their knees, looking like shalwars if anything—and I realized that I can't capture the real heart of American Islam no matter how many dumb trips I go on, and I'm nowhere near it writing about Amazing Ayyub with his Confederate flag shirt. Masjid Muhammad's door stays closed to me. But Lawrence Nixon, God bless Lawrence Nixon... Lawrence Nixon is the real heart and blood of American Islam, fuck your ISNA matrimonials!

Then I imagined a voice in my head that sounded like Khalida's telling me, "It's not about being white or not white, Mikail... you're in no shape to tell the story of American Muslims because you think that only weirdoes are worth writing about, you and your Wally Fords—"

I don't know why it sounded like Khalida in my head, maybe Khalida's just my conscience but I knew that she was right—because I couldn't bum all over the country sleeping in my car or sleeping on Greyhound buses for the sake of writing on lame Progressive Muslims and I don't know that I could if I wanted to. Give me Noble Drew Ali with a Cherokee feather in his turban, selling Moorish Healing Oil for fifteen cents a bottle—and W.D. Fard in his mug shot looking like he could slit your throat without a thought—and Peter Lamborn Wilson making tea with rancid yak butter in a Chinatown opium den—and the Original Man of Pain and Light, Lawrence Nixon. These are the holy monsters that redefine Islam, not your harmless ivory-tower muez-zins. Tariq Ramadan's not reaching me with *Western Muslims and the Future of Islam* or *Islam, the West, and the Challenges of Modernity*.

But Lawrence Nixon, as of this writing I love Lawrence Nixon with all my sad heart—he could be the start of something new walking up and down Philadelphia's Broad Street like Master Fard had in Detroit's Paradise Valley, wearing his stained turban, selling the right to take his picture for ten bucks a pop like Fard sold names, blood-drops on his Solitude, knowing all kinds of terror that I don't know, a child of Elijah Muhammad School tor-tured by alumni and their psychological games, a black Palestinian with no homeland—why not? Why can't Lawrence Nixon hail from Palestine? Imam Ali himself said that the Mahdi would come as a poor stranger unknown and uncared for, not a PhD of anything, not a tenured professor of anything anywhere, and he'd start out like a tired old camel lowering its head, wagging its tail but from that point he'd build the Empire of God—

15

Armed with a check from Alternative Tentacles for one hundred and twenty dollars, a bag of Reese's peanut-butter cups, a bear-shaped bottle of honey and a copy of Peter Lamborn Wilson's *Shower of Stars: the Initiatic Dream in Sufism and Taoism* I sped out of Buffalo for Lyndhurst, New Jersey to find the grave of Mohammed Alexander Russell Webb. Webb began studying Islam while serving as Consular Representative to the Philippines under President Grover Cleveland, took shahadah, toured India and returned home to estab-lish the Oriental Publishing Company through which he released his book *Islam in America*. The first chapter was titled, "Why I Became a Muslim." He also corresponded with Mirza Ghulam Ahmad, established a mosque on Broadway in Manhattan and represented Islam at the World Parliament of Religions in Chicago in 1893, same city and year as the Great Columbian Exhibition that featured an appearance by the Black Shriners.

Webb is commonly regarded as the first white American convert to Islam, which makes me assume that he was a strange bird. All the white con-verts I've ever met were strange in some way. Just look at me, hunting down this guy's grave for no reason. He really wasn't that spectacular a figure—just a footnote in the history of American Muslims, mentioned only to prove that Caucasians take shahadah too. He died at seventy in 1916 with his life's work toward promoting Islam in this country amounting to dinky-shit and all but forgotten.

I arrived on Rutherford Avenue a little after five in the morning, parked my car at the convenience store across the street from Hillside Cemetery, took my flashlight and backpack and looked for a way in. The gates were locked so I cut my leg and almost tore my nuts off hopping a rusty fence but once I was in, I was really in—fenced off from Dirty Jersey in my own quiet yard of rolling grassy hills sprinkled with vertical stones at that weird time just before Isha slipped into Fajr. It was light enough to make out engraved pictures on tombstones but still too dark to read the words. Within ten minutes of making that observation, I had no use for a flashlight at all. The cemetery was so huge I thought I'd never find Webb but I could at least ignore the newer sections and the Jewish section too. It'd turn out that he was buried in the Freemasons section, surrounded by stones engraved with the compass.

There was nothing special to Webb's stone, nothing at all besides A.R. WEBB, 1846–1916.

Shower of Stars discussed the Sufi practice of *istikhara*, or seeking guidance in dreams. It was common for a Sufi to sleep at the grave of a saint, hoping that the saint would appear in his dreams with guidance. Webb wasn't a Sufi saint per se and I hadn't prepared myself with a month of du'as and zikrs, but there I was and there he was.

I had remembered hearing somewhere that eating honey, peanut butter or chocolate before bedtime could encourage vivid dreams so I drank from my plastic bear-shaped bottle and finished off the Reese's before slumping down on the moist grass. Closed my eyes and tried to understand the culture of Webb's American Islam in the years before Islam was a political concern—whether for racial nationalists or al-Qaeda sleeper cells. Less than a century ago, America's Islam was something we wouldn't even recognize… back when it was just the Old Orientalism of Mahomet delivered through Gibbon and Carlyle and Sahih BUCKHARDT, the ancient al-Coran mysteries, red fez-caps with tassels, sharp scimitars whose blades curved like crescents.

The real bridge from then to now would be Noble Drew Ali, who stood in Chicago's Muslim history between the Black Shriners and the Black Muslims. Ali was said to have met Webb; and someone that knew Noble Drew Ali would have to know someone who knew someone who knew someone who met someone somewhere who'd someday meet Walid al-Taha, and Peter Lamborn Wilson had known Walid al-Taha, and I knew Peter Lamborn Wilson.

While asleep I heard the passing traffic and dreamt that it was all anonymous Sufi saints in their pickup trucks, looking at me as they drove by, and maybe nodding their heads with assessments of this graveyard-crasher's progress on his path. I knew that I had more dreams but couldn't remember them—if Webb had anything to say to me, it was ignored and lost in a lonely corner in the back of my head. But that's Webb in American Islam, too.

It was light out but the cemetery hadn't opened. I hopped the fence back into Lyndhurst, crossed the street to my car and drove to Pennsylvania, passing Philadelphia for a small town called East Fallowfield, which was home to the *mazar* (tomb) of Shaykh Muhammad Raheem Bawa Muhaiyaddeen. He had been discovered in the early 1900's by holy pilgrims on a trek through the jungles of Sri Lanka and became something of a local saint, courted for guidance by soul-searchers of all religions and walks of life. He came to the United States in 1971, fed his Sufism to the hungry New-Agers and died in 1986.

Turning the corner onto Mt. Carmel Road I passed a church sign reading "REPENT, BELIEVE ON JESUS." Went down a hill, passed a farmhouse and pond and found the road marked "Fellowship Drive."

Parked my car in a gravel lot and walked up to a thinly wooded campground. There were picnic tables, a pavilion with tattered felt wall hangings of the Kaaba fluttering in the breeze, plastic chairs scattered around. On the other side, in a clearing with exceptionally green grass, stood the mazar of Shaykh Muhaiyaddeen—a little white mosque complete with dome and star-and-crescent on top. I realized how quiet this place was, the only sounds coming from a few birds.

I came to a faucet with a chair in front of it and deducted that this was for wudhu so I took my shoes and socks off and washed myself, not sure if I was doing it all in the right order but it felt alright. There was a large mailbox marked "Important Information on Lyme Disease." I opened it and found some photocopied sheets held down by a rock and box of light bulbs.

Then I took the little walkway to the mazar, carrying my shoes. I left them outside the door and stepped inside, right foot first. The long windows allowed for tons of sunlight and easy breezes. My bare feet were cool on the marble floor. In the center lay Muhaiyaddeen's coffin, cloaked in a green velvet shroud bearing crescents, stars and Allah's Name in bright colors and an almost childish design. The coffin was surrounded by soft Persian carpets, the walls decorated with wall-hangings of Islamic calligraphy, the ceiling domed high with a little skylight at the top allowing for even more sun. There were stacks of cushions along the walls and one corner looked to have shelves of Qur'ans but then I walked over to find that they were mostly books by Muhaiyaddeen. Another corner had some brochures with his face on them, so I took one thinking it'd help in dreaming about him.

Behind Bawa's mazar was a Muslim cemetery, many of the stones bearing both Arabic inscriptions and Western kufr names. I walked between the rows of graves, still in bare feet on the soft grass.

Back inside I took one of the cushions and used it for a pillow beside the coffin. I lay on my right side as Wilson said to do in *Shower of Stars*, reciting *Suratul-Kauthar* with a whisper. Before falling asleep I contemplated Shaykh Bawa's photo from the brochure. He was skinny, almost skeletal—like he didn't have enough skin for his body and it had to be stretched over his face extra-tight. His white beard looked like it had been taped on, like a fake Sri Lankan Santa Claus.

Sometimes a truth will sink in more clearly or intensely at one minute than the next. A moment came when I really, perfectly understood that I was napping next to a dead body—saint or holy man or not, an above-ground dead human body—and then the moment passed.

After all that driving, my sleep was too thick and heavy for dreams. Later I'd be pulled out of it by a male voice saying, "Sir, Sir..."

Laying on my stomach, I lifted up my head to see a middle-aged Caucasian man with a white beard looking down at me.

"Sir," he said, "you shouldn't be sleeping here."

"Sorry," I replied, still pretty much out of it. "I fell asleep." I got up and put the cushion back. "I was trying to have an initiatic dream," I explained.

"This isn't a place to be falling asleep." Then he faced Shaykh Bawa's mortal remains, got on his knees, cupped his hands and whispered a du'a while I felt like a real Muslim because the sight of a man praying to another man made me a little creeped out.

We sat outside the mazar on opposite benches and he watched me put my shoes on. "Where in New York are you from?" he asked, so I guessed that he had examined my car.

"Buffalo," I told him.

"What's your name?"

"Mike."

"I'm Muhammad Abdullah." Muhammad Abdullah! I immediately gave him the whole story of how W.D. Fard's real name was Muhammad Abdullah, thinking this guy would care but he barely seemed to know who Fard was and just nodded at me like a zombie or a burned-out cultist. I turned my head and noticed a push-mower thirty feet away. "I mow the lawns here," he said. "I should get back to it. Have a safe journey."

I walked to my car without much else that the place could give me. After meeting the mazar's landscaper I could still say with authority that every white Muslim in America was at least a little *off*. But I was glad that we had a Sufi saint's tomb on this side of the world, and glad that I found Webb where he lay in the dirt, just to holy-up the landscape a little.

16

Now I got niggaz claimin' they saw God
unfortunately he wasn't in the person of Master Fard Muhammad
—Chino XL, "Riot"

It had only been a few weeks but I drove back to Philadelphia to get Khalida before swinging up to Penn State, whose library held the entire 1975–1981 run of Warith Deen Mohammed's old newspaper *Bilalian News* on microfilm.

After *Muslim WakeUp* ran my piece on meeting Elijah Muhammad's grandson in a cemetery, a reader emailed me with advice to find the November 26, 1976 issue of *Bilalian News* for a photo of Muhammad Abdullah. *Muslim WakeUp* editor Jawad Ali then told me that he was once hanging around outside an NOI bookstore in San Francisco when none other than Louis Farrakhan walked by and an elderly member of his surrounding entourage pointed at Jawad, saying *"That* was what he looked like." Farrakhan nodded in understanding while one of his cronies even grabbed Jawad's arm for closer inspection. One of them then told Jawad that he had skin like Master Fard Muhammad though "many people think he was a black man." So even Farrakhan's camp owned up that Fard had been South Asian, kind of.

At that point I had only seen the Master's mug shots and the Nation of Islam portrait (retouched by Elijah's grandson Herbert) with Fard reading the Qur'an and his straight hair parted on the left. I wasn't even sure if they were of the same guy.

It was almost four hours from Philly to the town of State College, PA. We found the library, asked for directions to the Special Collections and ran to it. The lady there wrote down my requested reel, opened up a drawer big enough for me to sleep in, went down the rows and pulled out a fist-sized cardboard box. She reeled it up for me and demonstrated the controls. Turn right to go forward, turn left to go back, move it like this to go up and the other way to go down. Then she left me to do my thing.

I turned the knob as far right as it'd go and the print whizzed by so fast I thought I'd snap the reel. I stopped only to check the date at the top and then maybe skim a page just to see what they were doing back then. From repeatedly slanted articles I gathered that at least in 1976, Warith Deen Mohammed was cozy with Uganda's Idi Amin.

I swept through the second half of the year, finally coming to the November 19th issue and going through it slow, waiting for the date at the top to change, and then—

"ISSUE MISSING."

The screen was blank except for those words, ISSUE MISSING. I think it said something else but that was all I really saw.

Khalida's first reaction was to laugh but while my mouth hung open and I stared at the screen in shock she went to get help. I felt like Wally Ford was right there beside me, laughing his ass off.

The library staff looked in online databases to see what other college libraries might have it. Princeton archived *Bilalian News* but the lady warned that since everyone buys their microfilms from the same sources, anyone that'd have it most likely had the same reel with the same issue missing. What we'd have to do was find a place that had actual paper copies. The library's database came up with the University of Pittsburgh.

On the long ride back to Philly, Khalida said that it was pretty suspicious, that it couldn't be an accident for the only missing issue in six years of a weekly newspaper to be the one that'd have a photograph of W.D. Fard some forty years after his disappearance. She asked if I was upset or disappointed and what could I say but that it was all part of the story, that this mysterious bullshit was exactly how Fard would want it—

I dropped Khalida off at her house and then got on the I-76 to backtrack through Harrisburg and more or less cross the length of the state. I reached Pittsburgh a little after ten the next morning. The school was in a suburb of Pittsburgh called Oakland, which came as full of meaning for my state of mind at the time.

I parked the car on the corner of Fifth and something and then ran around like a backpack-wearing nut until coming across the library. At the Special Collections Room on the third floor I had to fill out a little card stating my purpose for the research. Then the man disappeared and came back with my newspaper. I sat down at a table and delicately turned pages until finding the headline.

"Professor Muhammad Abdullah leads Jumah Prayer in Oakland."

He didn't look like a madman or even a con-artist but only a normal old desi uncle in suit and tie with black-rimmed glasses, white hair and well-groomed white beard, an open Qur'an on the desk in front of him. The caption described him as a "renowned Islamic scholar."

"A historic event occurred here Friday, Sept. 17," the article began, "as Believers of Muhammad Mosque No. 77 observed their first Jumah Prayer service…"

"The Believers—many of whom had never participated in the Jumah prayer service—sensed the significance of the event." Then it dawned on me just how odd and tense a time that was for the "Black Muslims," making those first awkward reaches towards mainstream Islam. These were Muslims, but a kind that regular Muslims wanted nothing to do with—and they hadn't prayed like regular Muslims in a regular Friday congregation, ever. They most likely didn't know how one worked. I remembered my own first Friday prayer, how nervous and hopeful I was as though it were my first date with a girl, and tried to picture rows and rows of Muslim brothers, a whole mosque full of Muslim brothers going through the same thing all at once, confused, scared, not knowing if it was the right thing—barely a year had passed since the Honorable Elijah Muhammad died, how would he feel about all of this? What would he say to his son for twisting it all around?

I read on. "Professor Muhammad Abdullah, internationally known scholar, teacher and friend of Honorable Wallace D. Mohammad, Chief Minister of the Nation of Islam heightened the reverent mood established by the Adhan by opening the Qur'an and announcing his *khutbah* (sermon) from Chapter 103 entitled, 'The Time.'" Look at that: the article's author had to translate *khutbah* for these guys and referred to *suras* as "chapters!" It was kind of charming in its way.

"This chapter is often used as a portion from the Qur'an to be recited after the *fateha* (opening chapter of the Qur'an) in the *salat* (prayer)," Professor Abdullah said.

"In the khutbah, Professor Abdullah stressed the importance of the time and its proper use. He highlighted the sermon by relating incidents from the life of the Holy Prophet Muhammad (peace and blessings be upon him) and other great men of Islam... pointing slowly to his fingers, he enumerated the four principles of success given in the chapter as: 1—a belief in the unity of God; 2—the doing of good, or right living; 3—propagation of the faith, and; 4—patience under adversity."

The article gave no mention of W.D. Fard, nor did it name the university where Muhammad Abdullah served as professor. It did say that the imam had addressed the Spiritual Life Jubilee in Atlanta and the Honorable Elijah Muhammad Mosque No. 2 in Chicago, both at the invitation of "the Honorable Wallace D. Mohammad."

Comparing a clean-shaven, dark-haired man with no glasses from 1926 with a bearded, white-haired man with glasses from 1976, it could have been the same guy. Or not. Their ears were similar enough, coming out at the same angle. The man in *Bilalian News* had a fuller face than the man in the mug shot, maybe a fuller nose, and his eyes were less angry. He didn't look to be ninety-nine years old, as he would have been by Elijah's history.

After leaving the campus I had no idea how to get to I-79 which would take me up to Buffalo, so I just drove around randomly until finding myself by the silver dome of the Igloo Arena. Then I knew that I had been on these steep hills before. I turned around and drove in circles until finding Wylie Avenue, passing decayed bars, half-eaten buildings and a painted portrait of Malcolm X directly under a giant billboard for McDonalds' Fiesta Salad. Then I saw my old haunt from years ago:

"The First Mosque of Pittsburgh," read a sign above the door though you could barely read it anymore. I climbed the steps and pulled but the door was locked. Then a door off to the side opened and a black teenager came out.

"As-salamu alaikum," I said. He looked at me. I asked if the mosque was open and he pointed to the door that he had just come out of. Inside I walked up a stairwell and then all of a sudden it was 1995 again, there was my mosque! Just a big open space with stained carpets overlapping each other, old-school radiators, peeling paint, crumbling plaster, an unmanned table of oils and incense, a dingy partition to keep the women on their side, ratty couches and then the main prayer room with its windows covered by plastic wrap. I took my shoes off and went in. First thing I noticed was the brothers sleeping in a corner in their sleeping bags and I loved their being there because that was me so long ago: a young man fighting the *nafs*, conducting the inner jihad against himself and all that by sleeping in the masjid. At eighteen years old living away from home for the first time, that was how I spent my Friday nights!

I walked softly past them and offered a prayer of two rakats out of respect to the mosque. While sitting I looked at my handprints on the stained carpet. This place was like Shel Silverstein's *The Giving Tree*, where the tree gave the boy her leaves and branches and trunk and at the end could give no more, she was only a stump and the boy himself had turned into an old man who wanted nothing but a place to sit—so then he sat on the stump and the tree was happy that she had that much left for him—this mosque was so tired and used-up it looked like the roof could cave in but it kept on giving hardcore brothers a place to sleep far away from all the mischief of clubs and girls, fessing up its old crusty carpets for our foreheads, while in Pittsburgh's suburbs like Oakland you had heartless Islamic Centers for the engineers and doctors—

The teenager who had let me in asked how long I had been Muslim. I said since 1993 or 1994 and he said *al-hamdulilah*. I told him that I used to live in Pittsburgh. He said that Pittsburgh was boring and he liked to go to New York or Philly on the weekends. He added that the area was getting real bad in terms of shootings and such, and that he had seen someone die just weeks ago.

I asked about the table of oils and he said he ran it. I gave him five dollars for a bottle of Egyptian musk.

The March 2004 issue of *Monthly ILAN* (International Lahore Ahmadiyya Newsletter) pays tribute to Begum Hamida Abdullah, who had passed away on February 9th in Fremont, California at ninety-two years old. She was buried next to her husband, "legendary missionary" Master Muhammad Abdullah Sahib, at Chapel of the Chimes Cemetery in Hayward.

The newsletter says that shortly after their marriage in 1930, Muhammad accepted an invitation to teach Islam in Fiji. The first Ahmadiyya Muslim Mission in the islands was established in April 1934.

When the Abdullahs arrived in Fiji they found the school to be a bare, overcrowded hut, inspiring Muhammad to work towards the construction of a new building. The article cites Muhammad's "charismatic personality" as enabling him to raise funds from poor sugarcane farmers—as it had, I supposed, with poor factory workers in Detroit.

According to *Monthly ILAN*, Muhammad and Begum Hamida Abdullah migrated to the United States in 1959 and built a "very close relationship" with the NOI, influencing W.D. Mohammed to steer the Black Muslims toward mainstream Islam.

It'd make sense for Fard to have been an Ahmadiyya; the Qur'an that he gave to Elijah Muhammad was a translation by Ahmadiyya scholar Maulana Muhammad Ali, with a personalized inscription declaring Mirza Ghulam Ahmad of Qadian to be "the greatest religious leader of the present time." One of Fard's early names for Elijah was Gulam. The Nation of Islam's line that Fard was "Mahdi of the Muslims and Messiah of the Christians" had been lifted straight from the Ahmadiyya canon.

So I called the Ahmadiyya Anjuman in Hayward, which for some reason comes up in Sunni mosque directories as Masjid Imam Muhammad Abdullah. The imam there had only vaguely heard of a man known as "Master Abdullah" who had come from Pakistan or Fiji and was appointed imam of an NOI mosque. He said that he didn't think this Master Abdullah was Fard, and suggested that I read a biography on Elijah Muhammad entitled *The Messenger*. I already knew what it said. Using the FBI file, *The Messenger* author Karl Evanzz arrived at the conclusion that Fard was an Ahmadiyya from New Zealand—and like the FBI-propped 1963 *Los Angeles Herald-Examiner* article, had him sailing home in 1934.

Around the same time that Muhammad Abdullah left Pakistan for Fiji.

New Zealand and Fiji were in the same neighborhood of the world, only twelve hundred miles of Pacific Ocean between them. There could have been something to this.

Between the years of 1876 and 1916, the British Empire sent over sixty thousand indentured Indian laborers to Fiji to work the plantations. Today almost half of Fiji's population is of South Asian descent; Diwali and Prophet Muhammad's birthday are public holidays.

The truth came to me slow and subdued; not at all like the Master's voice coming as thunder in the sky, more like a steadily creeping sunrise...

Fard was the child of indentured laborers, basically slaves.

As a South Asian in British-ruled Fiji, he grew up much like an African in North America: a child of poverty with subhuman status, worlds away from the lost land of his ancestors, watching his parents toil their lives away to serve white wealth. So once he got the chance he left it all behind, hoping for a new life on the far side of the Pacific. But he only found more of the same.

California did have one advantage: people had no idea where he had come from. His skin was dark but not *too* dark (the FBI file describes him with words like "olive" and "swarthy") and his hair was straight. He could have been Spanish or maybe Greek and was probably taken for a Caucasian of some variety without even trying. In the face of American racism he decided to play the game, changing his name from Wali Fard to Wallace Ford and claiming to be from New Zealand so he could pass as white—to his girlfriend, police, customers at Walley's Restaurant and on his son's birth certificate.

Having encountered white supremacy everywhere he went in the world, a powder keg had exploded inside him—and then, as Warith Deen Mohammed puts it, "Dr. Fard took it upon himself to be the executor, the scourge, to punish the Caucasian for his racism, for his race supremacy. To punish him for his bad treatment of the non-Caucasian races." After the bid at San Quentin he made his way to Detroit and sold clothing door-to-door in the impoverished Paradise Valley, where he crossed paths with door-to-door Ahmadiyya preachers. At first he might have been happy to reconnect with his culture; then he may have considered what the Ahmadis were trying to do and reasoned that he could do it better.

The greatest obstacle facing Muslim missionaries was that they couldn't relate their foreign religion to the African-American experience. "They invited us to Islam," writes Warith Deen, "to Allah, and to the Holy Qur'an. They told us that Islam was a better religion, but only a few of us listened to them. Master Fard discovered the real problem, and then he designed a skillful plan to bring home the prize." Fard was a real salesman, tinkering with the product and pitch to suit a new audience.

When he visited his white ex-girlfriend and their son for the last time, he told them that he was going home. He did—to Fiji. And he spent almost three decades there.

But in 1976, more than forty years later, why was he back in California leading Black Muslims through the first real jum'aa of their lives?

I called Masjid Waritheen (formerly Muhammad Mosque #77) in Oakland and told them I was writing a story on their deceased imam, Muhammad Abdullah. They told me to call the CAIR chapter in San Jose and ask for the number of Dr. Rajabally, a dentist who had married Imam Abdullah's late daughter. After getting the number I called Dr. Ali's office in Hayward and he referred me to Muhammad's sixty-year old son Zafar Abdullah.

According to Zafar, Muhammad Abdullah was born in the Punjab in 1905 and began exchanging letters with the Honorable Elijah Muhammad while on his teaching mission in Fiji. Elijah viewed himself as Muhammad's student but refused his invitations to accept *al-Islam.*

"Elijah believed he was on a mission," said Zafar, "to reach the lowest of the low," and he did it the best he knew how. In 1956 Muhammad Abdullah visited Elijah at Elijah's Chicago mansion (now the home of Louis Farrakhan, in a neighborhood patrolled by special Nation of Islam police cars). In 1959 the Abdullahs would move to America for good, and Elijah employed Muhammad in an "advisory capacity" with the NOI. For three years he worked as personal mentor to Elijah's son Wallace.

In the early 1960s Muhammad Abdullah moved to Philadelphia and became involved with a group called the Muslim Brotherhood, teaching its members and editing the newsletter. Zafar described the organization as "non-sectarian" and while "mostly black," included Muslims of all backgrounds. Maybe it was a remnant of the same Moslem Brotherhood founded by Fard's disciple Osman Sharrieff, who left the Nation of Islam after Elijah portrayed the Master as being Allah in Person.

After Elijah passed away, Wallace became Warith and set out to dismantle his father's Nation. To kill the myth of Master Fard being a starship-pilot Allah, Warith said that he kept in touch with him by simply calling him on the phone. As part of his deracializing the community and introducing traditional Islamic teachings, he appointed a Pakistani imam—Muhammad Abdullah—to run the Oakland mosque.

After years of service, Muhammad Abdullah died of heart failure on June 18th, 1992. Shortly thereafter, Warith Deen announced that the imam had been W.D. Fard in concealment all along. The Abdullah family tried to discourage him.

"But wasn't your father Master Fard?" I asked.

"I don't *believe* he was," answered Zafar Abdullah. "Wasn't Fard a Syrian?"

> Despite the fact that this Abdullah made no claim to Fard's identity, Warith was certain of it and happily installed him as an imam in his Oakland, California temple until he died in 1992.
> —Florence Hamlish Levinsohn, *Looking for Farrakhan*

> He wanted me to know that he was Fard, but didn't want to say it with his mouth because he didn't want to be put in a situation that he would have to answer all my questions and be exposed to all my rage. I thought he was very wise to never say to me that he was Fard.
> —Warith Deen Mohammed

I faced the possibility that Warith Deen had conjured the whole thing up or was seriously mistaken. Either way could paint him as touched in his own right.

It's easy to see Imam W.D. Mohammed purely as Sunni redeemer of the NOI who had served on the ISNA board, represented Islam at the 1993 Parliament of World's Religions, had audience with the Dalai Lama, addressed one hundred thousand Catholics at the Vatican, sat at Bill Clinton's inauguration, became the first man ever to recite Qur'an in the White House and whose organization was invited to represent Islam by George W. Bush and Rudy Giuliani after 9/11—but he had also grown up with Elijah's craziness of Ezekiel Wheels and nine-foot tall Martians, the same craziness that would later spawn Farrakhan claiming to have been abducted by UFOs. All those guys seemed to like issuing jaw-dropper statements.

But even if W.D. Fard's reappearance in California was just another myth for the pile, I'd bet that Warith Deen's intentions were good. For a community that had believed the silk salesman to be Supreme Ruler of the Universe, Muhammad Abdullah provided a flesh-and-blood man who not only worshipped the One True Allah, but came complete with documented death and physical grave. It may have been the only way to finally put the Master to rest.

Zafar Abdullah put me in email correspondence with his brother Akbar, who taught Warith Deen's son for three years just as Muhammad had taught Warith Deen. Akbar, 73, asked me for the names of books or articles that referenced Warith Deen's claim of his father being Fard but never answered my question as to whether it was true.

Fard or not, Muhammad Abdullah did his part. Despite the persecution that Ahmadis take from their brothers all over the world, and *takfir* declarations that they aren't even Muslim at all, an Ahmadiyya professor did more for what you'd call "true" or "mainstream" Islam in America than any of these Wahhabi or Salafi jerks, more than Siraj Wahhaj or any of 'em, yeah that's what I said.

17

I'm swellin' devils' melons for my man Fard Muhammad.
— Gravediggaz, "Graveyard Chamber"

My rhyme torments MCs with the fear of God
you'll be cursed like Fard, and struck by the iron rod.
— RZA (as Bobby Digital), "Mantis"

Louis Farrakhan seduced a crowded mosque in Russia by telling the congregation that Master Fard's own mother had come from their land; according to Nation of Islam history, her name was Baby Gee and she was a white Muslim from Chechnya. I could sit in a mosque alone at night and rock back and forth with my eyes closed, just letting the idea take me to strange places: since the black man was God and the white man was Satan, a mulatto Master Fard would have been the divine union of opposites, the Perfect Man (*al-insan al-kamil*), a walking yin-yang symbol.

You dwell on strange ideas long enough, they might as well become true. I almost self-identified as a devil. There was certainly no reason not to when I looked at history and the current state of the world and my Nazi Dad and even my own story in Islam of starting out alright but crudding up later.

Once you accept that you're wicked by nature, what does that mean? Is it a lost cause? Do you just slit your wrists and save the world from your evil?

I was reading an old Nation of Islam document called *The Supreme Wisdom Lessons*, a series of exams given by W.D. Fard to Elijah Muhammad that served as NOI catechism, and came across the following:

9. Why does Muhammad make the Devil study from thirty-five to fifty years before he can call himself a Muslim son? And wear the greatest and only Flag of the Universe? And he must add a sword on

the upper part of the Holy and Greatest Universal Flag of Islam?

Answer: So that he can clean himself up. A Muslim does not love the Devil regardless to how long he studies. After he has devoted thirty-five or fifty years trying to learn and do like the original man, he could come and do trading among us and we would not kill him as quick as we would the other Devils—that is, who have not gone under this study. After he goes through with this Labor from thirty-five to fifty years, we permit him to wear our Holy Flag, which is the Sun, Moon and Star. He must add the sword to the upper part. The sword is the emblem of Justice and it was used by the original man in Muhammad's time. Thus, it was placed on the upper part of the Flag so that the Devil can always see it, so he will keep in mind that any time he reveals the Secrets, his head would be taken off by the sword. We give him this chance so that he could clean himself up and come among us. The Holy Flag of Islam is the greatest and only Flag known.

Could there be a devil with true knowledge of self? If my Irish-white Muslim ass was Satan, could it at least be in a poetic Javad Nurbakhsh way—an apotheosis of self-afflicting love?

I wrote a hopeful email to the Supreme Minister John Muhammad, T.H.E.M.'s youngest brother who maintained his own Black Muslim faction in Detroit. Born Herbert Poole in 1910, John came to Detroit in 1923 with the Poole family and joined the Nation of Islam in 1932. His website showed him in full navy-blue Fruit of Islam uniform with blue bowtie and crescent on his hat, holding up that red Nation of Islam flag with all his brittle strength like he's the last old veteran of a war long over, standing alone on the battlefield. Ninety-four years young, he would die in bed believing with all his heart that Allah was really Wallace D. Fard and the Japanese were going to someday descend upon America with their super-ships to slaughter the white man.

Makes me realize that they're *all* old: Warith Deen and Farrakhan are both grandfathers with maybe twenty years left between them. (*Allahu Alim.*) Forgotten in his little corner, Silas Muhammad is old. Even that crackpot kid-diddler Malachi Z. York who founded the Brooklyn Ansar Allah, he's old. At a pivotal time for getting the story down, John Muhammad's value couldn't have been taken for granted: in addition to being Elijah's blood, he might have been the last of his class, the only Muslim in the world who could say that he had studied under the Master.

And to learn from him personally would have put me in a direct *silsila* with Fard, but he never replied to my email. I then turned to the Fardiyya, who renamed Harlem Mecca and Brooklyn Medina—

18

14. Who is the 85%?

ANS. The uncivilized people; poison animal eaters; slaves from mental death and power, people who do not know the Living God or their origin in this world, and they worship that they know not what—who are easily led in the wrong direction, but hard to lead into the right direction.

15. Who is the 10%?

ANS. The rich; the slave-makers of the poor; who teach the poor lies—to believe that the Almighty, True and Living God is a spook and cannot be seen by the physical eye. Other wise known as: The Blood-Suckers Of The Poor.

16. Who is the 5% in the Poor Part of the Earth?

ANS. They are the poor, righteous Teachers, who do not believe in the teachings of the 10%, and are all-wise; and know who the Living God is; and Teach that the Living God is the Son of man, the supreme being, the black man of Asia; and Teach Freedom, Justice and Equality to all the human family of the planet Earth.
—*The Supreme Wisdom Lessons of Master W.D. Fard*

The Nation of Gods and Earths (Five Percenters) was founded in 1964 by Clarence 13X, who rejected the NOI's worship of W.D. Fard and declared himself Allah. I dug Clarence because he was only giving that same power to those that followed him; Five Percenter men today use Allah as their surname.

I began corresponding with Intelligent Tarref Allah at Eastern Correctional Facility in Napanoch, NY. "Intell," as family and friends called him, joined the Five Percenters in 1994 while at Rikers Island and was the plaintiff in a historic court decision *(Marria v. Broaddus)* awarding incarcerated Gods the rights of a recognized religion. Up until that point, correctional facilities regarded them as a violent gang.

We had been going back and forth for a while. Intell told me that he maintained a vegan diet and was enrolled in a *Writer's Digest* correspondence course. He planned on writing his memoirs, tentatively titled *The Autobiography of God.*

I asked him about his concept of the devil.

"We teach that white people are devils," he replied, "and that includes you." So in my next letter, I asked Intell if this could offer anything to one of Yacub's People. He replied that some devils have already accepted the truth of their nature. There was Ida Hakim, a white woman who studied with Silas Muhammad's offshoot of the NOI, and Dorothy Fardan, author of *Message to the White Man and White Woman in America: Yacub and the Origins of White Supremacy.*

But the real kicker: back in the beginning of the Five Percenters, Allah (Clarence 13X) had a white student. He named him Azreal, after the angel of death, and said that he was in charge of the "inhabitants of Hell," meaning Caucasians. From what Intelligent Tarref Allah had heard, Azreal maintained a circle of four or five whites, referred to as "Muslim Sons," to whom he taught the Supreme Alphabets and Supreme Mathematics.

I arrived in Harlem on Friday, just in time for jum'aa prayers at Masjid Malcolm Shabazz with the bulbous green dome. This mosque had once been the Nation of Islam's Temple No. 7 but was now run by Warith Deen's community. I checked my bag at the door and walked up a flight of stairs to the prayer hall. A brother gave me a plastic grocery bag for my shoes. I walked in right-foot-first to find security guards in suits and ties positioned throughout the mosque. One pointed to an open space in the back row so I went and did my sunna. When I sat down he came over and had me sit closer to the brother on my side. I looked around and found myself the only white guy but felt alright since we were all Sunni there, this was the Islam of Malik Shabazz. The imam's khutbah was long and went all over the place, quoting not only from the Qur'an but also the New Testament and even Elijah Muhammad, but most of the time he read directly from a Warith Deen speech. Doctrine-wise it was Sunni but he used old terms from the Nation of Islam like "trick-ster" and "grafted minds" without their racial connotations.

Muslims are usually discouraged from saying anything during a khut-bah but the women in back kept yelling things like "Tell it, brother imam!" and "Allahu Akbar!" like it was a Baptist Muslim Church while donation buckets were passed around with "SACRIFICE" written on them… the imam kept going on and for a moment I zoned out in contemplation of the green curtains and white walls, the sounds of traffic and a lonely saxophone on the street corner below, and the monumental history of this place: Malcolm X was imam here in the 50s and 60s, Louis Farrakhan was imam here in the 60s and 70s, and this was where Clarence 13X gave karate classes to the Fruit of Islam. That big green dome was like Harlem's Dome of the Rock, holy to three traditions: Warith Deen Sunnism, the Nation of Islam, and Five Percenters. Playing the role of Abraham, the common father of them all, would be none other than W.D. Fard—who had wanted to build a temple in NYC because "very wise men" would someday arise there.

We stood up and prayed, after which we did an additional funeral prayer for the recently deceased Miami imam who brought Cassius Clay to the deen, introduced him to Malcolm X and always hosted Sister Clara when she came to town.

As I drove up to the Allah School my mix tape just happened to hit NOFX's "Kill all the White Man." I steered with my right hand, and in my left I clutched my turba made from clay off the grave of Imam Ridha, Imam Riza, Imam RZA…

Maybe half a dozen Gods stood in front of the Allah School, building in a circle. "Building" in Five Percenter talk meant anything positive, usually a conversation, where you built on your knowledge. I ducked in past them and said peace to the God inside.

"Hands out of your pockets," he said. I complied and told him that I was looking for Azreal so he led me back out and into the yard on the side, and there was a middle-aged Caucasian digging in the dirt. "Azreal!" the God shouted. "He's here to see you, do you know him?"

"Yeah," said Azreal. And the God left us to build.

"Peace," I told Azreal. "My name is Michael, and I was building by mail with Intelligent Tarref Allah, and he said that Father Allah had a white student named Azreal so I came down here hoping I could find you—"

"My middle name is Michael." He asked how I came to knowledge of the Nation and I started on a whole big spiel about Fard when he interrupted me to say, "There's already a *new* W.D. Fard, and he's got blonde hair and brown eyes." So I just looked at him to explain some more but he only added, "and he's four years old."

"And he's the new W.D. Fard?"

"Hey," he said like we were about to cut a deal. We were. "Ten bucks'll get me some equality, you know what equality is? Ten bucks'll get me some earth. So you help me with some earth and I'm yours for the rest of the day." So I gave him ten bucks and we walked up the street towards Malcolm X Boulevard. "You turn right at the corner and wait for me," said Azreal. "These are West Indians, some of them are First Borns. I don't want them thinking I'm a cop." So I turned right, Azreal turned left and after a while he came out with his equality.

We sat on a bench outside the St. Nicholas projects and I whipped out my notepad to jot down all of Azreal's magnetic ("magnetic is what you get when you build with Supreme Truth") but he told me, "Right now, instead of writing I need you to be my eyes," so I looked out for cops while he rolled the equality and licked the paper. "Father Allah's the one who taught me to smoke," he said with a philosopher's puff. "And he taught me how to bring out the sun when it rains. One time there was a blizzard and he blamed me for it."

Now that he had his equality, the first thing I wanted to know was how Azreal ever found himself mixed up with the Five Percenters. He started off telling me about spending his youth in psych wards, fighting guards, getting "two hundred Jack Nicholson specials," staging daring escapes ("I drove away in the cook's car"), and on through to all the atrocities that would follow, right up to a few nights ago when some teenage boys sicced their pitbull on him. He showed me a long scar going all the way down his right calf and said that it was from kicking through a chicken-wire glass window—and he sprained that same foot jumping off a fence, and then lost a toe for some other reason. It all started because his real name was John Kennedy and when the chickens came home to roost in 1963 he just lost it. The guards at Matteawan State Hospital for the Criminally Insane were all KKK or American Nazi Party and they didn't like John Kennedy's name so they beat the shit out of him and then sent inmates into his cell, two at a time. After two weeks of that they gave him a Thorazine coma.

When he woke up, fellow inmate Clarence Smith came to him and said, "You are a righteous man."

"He told me who he was," said Azreal, "and after that I'd turn down parole. I didn't want to be outside, I knew I was getting the truth right there." Azreal then told me about when the Father was killed, how he knew he'd "go home" and "he had nothing left to give us but his life."

"Who killed Father Allah?" I asked.

"Nixon. Nixon put a hit on him."

"Where is he buried?"

"He was cremated. His ashes were scattered at Mount Morris Park. I got my mom's ashes—Mam in a Can, you know—and when I die, my ashes and her ashes are going out there too."

"Do you know what happened to Master Fard?"

"It's a mystery. It'll always be a mystery. But do you know who his first student was, even before Elijah?"

"Who?"

"J. Edgar Hoover."

"No shit?"

"I heard that from a First Born out in Medina." I mentioned Malachi Z. York's claim that Fard was an FBI agent, and Azreal replied that York was at Matteawan at the same time as himself and Allah. "But York kept to himself," he said, "and tried to steal the Father's teachings, make 'em his own."

Azreal pointed to his head and said he had all the stories in there. He had once written his three-part autobiography but burned the only copy because he was afraid of it falling into the wrong hands. "If you have it in here," he said with another point at his head, "you don't need it on paper." He showed me the number 13 tattooed on his arm. "The Father went home on Friday the 13th, June 1969, and his name was Clarence 13X, and one plus three equals Culture or Freedom. Everything leads back to the Father."

"Is the white man the devil?" I had to ask.

"The Father said that the worst devil is the black devil, because the Gods don't see him coming." He smoked and almost choked on it. "But you know, I can say that I'm Allah because I wasn't taught by a man or prophet or anything. I'm First Born; the Father was right there in front of me. We can all be angels, you know, but I believe we can be more."

"Intell told me that there are other white Five Percenters—"

"Sure. There was Ariel, he had lots of money. He was into coke, he'd go to the Caribbean and party with all the Wu-Tang... but then he got in a car accident, and he was only Wisdom Culture. He was Knowledge Born when he began building, and Wisdom Culture when he went home." He paused to smoke. "And there's a white rapper in Florida." He paused again, this time in consideration of something. "You know," he said, "somebody in the Five Percenter paper wrote that 'Eminem is the Azreal of rap.' That really offended me, you know? I was really insulted. I'd never say those kinds of things about my mother that he does."

Then of course there was the new four-year-old W.D. Fard, whose father was a "light-skinned man of understanding" and whose mother was Polish. "So they named him W.D. Fard," said Azreal. "He's a little kid, about this high. He's got blonde hair and brown eyes. His sister's the same way." Azreal told me that he bought the new W.D. Fard a blue t-shirt bearing the likeness of Allah, but it was so big that the kid could only wear it as a nightshirt.

Then Azreal told me that he was going to be John Kerry's running mate. "Kerry needs a shot in the arm," he said, "and I'm the man to do it—and I can get a lot more votes in the minority community than he ever could."

"Have you been in contact with him?"

"Not yet. It's not my time yet. But just our names alone would be a shot in the arm: Kerry-Kennedy. You see?"

I watched him build and smoke and sometimes cough, and he showed me all his scars and I knew that Azreal was meant to be Azreal and that's all I can really say about him, death-angel with the keys to Heaven and Hell, the only one who can come and go as he pleases, the Devil who met God in a mental institution... being Azreal takes a lot more guts than being any of these Career Muslims like Ingrid Mattson or a Career Enlightened Kufr like John L. Esposito. I even concocted an amazing daydream of Azreal hanging around outside the CAIR office waiting to stick Hooper with a crowbar for his Prince Talal riyals, just so he could give it all to the Nation—

Eventually I took my leave of Azreal, drove downtown and crossed the bridge into Medina (Brooklyn) to find the Ansar Allah mosque. The Ansar Allah community no longer existed since Malachi Z. York made his *hijra*, migrating to Georgia to build his pyramids in the woods, but I figured at least the masjid that he built would still be there. Maybe it was purchased by another group and continued to function as a mosque of some kind. But when I got to 719 Bushwick, the domes and minarets were all gone and it didn't look anything like the pictures I had seen. I went to the All Eyes on Egypt bookstore next door and the woman told me they were remodeling. I asked a gentleman if it was true that Farrakhan's men scared York away and he said, "If anything, it was the Sunnis."

Malachi Z. York claimed that there were actually *three* W.D. Fards. The first, whose real name was said to be Abdul Ali Mohammed, was born on February 26th, 1891 in Palestine, of Turkish-Saudi descent. He arrived in New Jersey as "Professor Fahd," attempted to sabotage Noble Drew Ali's Canaanite Temple and later joined the Ahmadiyyas. While serving time at San Quentin he was murdered and replaced by an imposter named Wallace Douglas Ford, a white Mormon who had been born in Oregon. Upon his release this W.D. Ford/Fard, an implant of Germany and Japan, headed straight for Detroit and founded the Nation of Islam. According to York, the imposter was also doing double-duty as an agent of the United States government. At one point the FBI pulled Wallace into their Detroit office and told him that he was losing control of his followers, that he was never intended to preach self-deification and violent hatred of whites. Also facing harassment from local authorities, Wallace Ford disappeared in 1934.

The third W.D. Fard surfaced in 1958 as Imam Muhammad Abdullah, who had been born in the Punjab in 1905.

19

I slept at a rest stop off I-87 and woke up around ten on Saturday morning. That afternoon I went to Napanoch.

Driving through the mountains on my way to a state prison called for Johnny Cash with all his outlaw songs and prison songs, but even that led me to contemplate Master Fard—Johnny Cash recorded an album live at San Quentin, but Fard knew what it was like behind the bars.

At the visitors' center they made me empty my pockets and take off my shoes before going through the metal detector. You can't bring any of this, said the guard. Phone, camera, keys, pens, wallet—put it in the lockers outside. I had an Ibn 'Arabi book for Intell but the guard said it was too late in the day to give an inmate anything so I locked that up too. Then I had to fill out all the paperwork for a first-time visitor.

I read the signs on the wall. Physical contact was limited to an embrace and/or kiss at the beginning and end of the visit. Hands must be visible at all times. The guards opened a door. Once I stepped through that and it closed behind me, they opened the next door. And then I was in a room of families and kids and men in green pants. I handed my sheet to the man at the desk and sat at a table. Intell came through wearing a yellow kufi skullcap.

We talked about Fard and all the theories. He told me that some inmates had been circulating the Muhummad Abdullah story, but it's hard to have a real conversation in that situation; your time is limited, so you talk extremely fast. You say everything you need to say on a topic and then let the other person say everything he or she needs to say, and then you reply in the same manner and on it goes until the clock runs out. When visiting hours were over Intell wished me a safe drive and I huddled through the door with all the wives and kids and then waited for the next door to open. I unlocked my stuff and walked out past a whole mess of women, one of them standing against a railing with tears streaming down her face, her eyes looking somewhere far away.

As I drove off it occurred to me to get a picture of the building so I pulled over and stood on top of my car with my cheap disposable camera. Then some guards drove by and told me to get down. They pulled over and had me stand by my car while they made some calls.

One guard, who seemed a nice enough guy, told me that it was against the law to photograph a state prison.

"The rationale," he said, "is that you may be trying to provide information about the facility to someone on the inside who could try to escape."

"We're going to detain you," he said. "It's a maximum security prison, whole different ballgame." So we stood around making small talk about the weather until another guard came by, examined my camera and then said I could go.

Back in my car, I turned the ignition and Johnny Cash's "San Quentin" came on blaring loud enough for the guards to hear. *San Quentin, I hate every inch of you...*

When I drove away I felt something different in my face, like the muscles I'd use in smiling couldn't work if I had wanted them to. It was a weird sobering sense that I've only felt after funerals. Soon I was back in the mountains with gusts of air blasting in from all four of my car windows, watching the sunlight peek through thick walls of trees, feeling things inside but not feeling them with any kind of gusto or spunk as all of that had been drained out of me.

I stopped at New Paltz to get some food. New Paltz is a college town with streets filled with hippies and some pop-punks standing around like they're posing for album covers. I went to the SUNY campus to go online and find out if I was anywhere near Matteawan.

Turns out, it was maybe half an hour away.

The New York State Lunatic Asylum for Insane Convicts originally opened in 1855, in Auburn. It was moved to Matteawan in 1892, renamed Matteawan State Hospital for the Criminally Insane and phased out in the 1970s to become Fishkill, a medium-security general confinement facility.

To get there I had to drive past Downstate Correctional and that was some serious evil with tall fences and coils of razor wire placed everywhere possible. At Fishkill I drove up a hill and saw a pond and some geese and learned that I couldn't get close enough to actually see the building, it was all off-limits. I wondered if those geese knew where they were.

20

Saturday night I took a break from the Gods to hang with filmmaker Cihan Kaan at a party in somebody's house. Cihan had spent all day running auditions for the lead in his next project and it was time to unwind. He was like a real-life taqwacore—a Turkish Sufi kid in his Crass t-shirt walking around this Brooklyn backyard, talking to girls and beer-pong players and watching a game of drunken fast-pitch wiffleball. He'd point at someone and be like,

"Have you ever heard of such-and-such band?" and when I'd say no he'd just go ahead and say "Well, that guy right there is the bass player." Then I met the hacker who shut down Yahoo! for a day and he didn't seem too comfortable with me knowing about it. I sat in a lawn chair and just watched the whole scene since my weekend was too bizarre for me to really connect or relate to any of these kids. I listened to two guys talk about a pills-for-porn trade and complain that the party was a sausage-fest, nearly every girl was with someone and the handful that weren't all moved together in a pack. There was this cool guy in a black derby hat and wifebeater shirt, knowing the role he was meant to play. I went inside the house where it was desolate and sank into a leather couch, going into my bag for the Ibn 'Arabi book that I wanted to give Intelligent Tarref Allah. I kicked my feet up on a glass table covered with sprinklings of leftover equality and trendy-shit magazines whose covers promised articles on "THE NEXT WAVE OF CELEBRITY DESIGNERS." Two girls came in and sat on the couch across the room. Then Cihan found his way in and sat next to me to ponder the possibilities of anything happening with them.

"There's something going on here," he said, with a quick glance in their direction.

"Is there?"

"I think there is. They're over there and we're over here, you know?"

"I'm in no frame of mind for it," I told him. "I've been living in my car and haven't changed my clothes in seventy-two hours, what am I going to say to these fuckin' girls with their Gucci bags?"

"It doesn't even matter," he said. "Confidence is like eighty-five percent of it." So from there I said that eighty-five percent of it was deaf, dumb and blind, and we started building on some Sufi shit relating to the Bektashis or Naqshbandis or Jerrahis, I don't even remember which, but Cihan had seen some amazing things in his time. He told an involved story from when he went to the Southwest with a girl and all sorts of crazy things went down revolving around a black dog with blue eyes that kept popping up at random places and the Navajo tales of a creature called the skin-walker that could assume animal forms and kill you. I looked at him with all the authority I could muster and said the dog was the devil and I could back it up with hadiths. His story was legitimately awesome and it made sense that something like that would happen to him, since he was diving deep into Sufi thought beforehand. Sometimes when you project enough energy out there, the world just reacts to it and gives you something back. At least I've found it to be like that, from time to time. Maybe it was the magnetic from building with Supreme Truth but who am I to say? Then two guys with more ambition than us came over to the girls and sat on either side of them, cracking jokes and making playful contact. So that was the end of that. We made our way out and ended up eating at a Pakistani restaurant at three in the morning, talking over kebabs about the great Muslim Punk Scene and how someday it'd become real.

In the subway station I had begun building a little on the Mathematics, trying to do something with my little baby-knowledge—being twenty-six years old, my physical degree was Wisdom Equality but two plus six equals eight and the attribute of Build or Destroy, meaning that everything you did either built or destroyed. That about summed up my whole past year.

21

Sunday morning I drove back to Harlem with Ghostface Killah in the tape deck, parked my car on 129th and walked to the Allah School to find Azreal mopping the floor. I told him that I tried going to Matteawan and he reminded me that they were all KKK and American Nazi Party there. I told him that I was almost arrested at Napanoch and he said that "once you start really building with the Gods, you'll find yourself getting 'almost arrested' all the time." We went into the yard and built. Azreal put on a suit over his yellow Gods shirt and green shorts. I gave him a pair of clean socks from my bag. Then another of Yacub's People showed up, he said he was from Sweden and doing his grad research on Afro-American religion. He went with us to get Azreal some equality at the same place as the day before. On the way back we passed the Nation of Islam's Masjid Muhammad #7 and shook hands with bow-tied brothers on the front steps. From the sidewalk I could hear a taped Farrakhan speech playing inside—that Farrakhan, he could really drive a point home when he wanted. Azreal asked a brother if we could go in. The brother said that it was too crowded but if we had asked earlier, it would have been okay.

"I don't like using who I am to get into places," Azreal told me, "but I like opening the door for others." Back at the Allah School we sat in front and shared greetings of peace with all the Gods and Earths who walked by— Azreal, the Swedish kid and me, three Caucasians occupying space in front of the Allah School of the Five Percenters, Azreal teaching me the Supreme Alphabets, nobody having a problem with us.

"We don't teach pro-black or anti-white," said an older God. "We teach pro-righteousness and anti-devilishment." Intell had said the same thing when we were building by mail.

Then a Five Percenter tour group walked by and stopped in front of the Allah School, the guide explaining how this place came to be. Azreal told me that the tour stopped at all the historic places—the elevator where the Father was shot ("It's a new elevator now... you used to be able to see the bullet-holes"), the Hotel Theresa, Mount Morris Park which was home to the first Universal Parliament when thousands of Gods greeted the Father on his return from Matteawan, and also the place where his ashes were scattered. The tour group consisted of pilgrims from all over the country, here to see their Arafat and Mina, their Cave of Hira, their Mountain of Light, their Badr. Harlem really was a Mecca. Azreal got up, grabbed a broom and swept the sidewalk in front of the Allah School.

In Harlem you can see a belief system at its beginning. Today, June 13th, 2004, was only the thirty-fifth anniversary of the Father's going home and you could still find Gods from the First Born walking around telling it as it was—parallels to the Sahabas, companions to the Prophet. There's even an Ahlul-Bayt of the Father's living grandchildren. I tried to imagine some fourteen hundred years ago or whatever it was when Islam was that young and Muslims were the Poor Righteous Teachers, a lowly five percent on the fringe of society.

Azreal, the Swede and I went back to the St. Nicholas projects so Azreal could elevate. We found a bench full of Gods and Azreal built with them. Azreal could talk and talk and talk, fueled by a genuine love for the Nation, and these Gods half his age sat and listened respectfully. He showed us this spin-move that Allah taught for when someone had a gun on him and told the story about a time when he stood in front of Allah School with Allah and Old Man Justice and asked, "If you're the Father, and Justice is the Son, then what am I... the Holy Ghost?" to which Allah and Old Man Justice laughed so hard that it brought all the young Gods outside wanting to know what was up.

The Show and Prove was just across the street at Harriet Tubman Learning Center. Inside it was almost like a smaller ISNA convention and too crowded to really get around so I bought a couple shirts and went back out to watch Gods build on the sidewalk. I met a God from Pittsburgh who offered to help me achieve knowledge, but he warned that it'd be a serious journey. Then I met Saladin, a God from Niagara Falls! So I told him I was from Buffalo and we exchanged numbers. I had to know whether Buffalo had been renamed, since Gods gave the map a flavor of mythopoeia by renaming all the boroughs and cities: Aside from Mecca and Medina, Queens was the Desert and the Bronx was Pelan, New York itself was Mecca or Now Why, New Rochelle was Now Rule, Poughkeepsie was Power Kingdom and it spread across the land… New Haven, Connecticut was New Heaven, Philadelphia was Power Hill, Pittsburgh was Power Born, Detroit was D-Mecca, Chicago was C-Medina, Milwaukee was Cream City, Atlanta was Allah's Garden, Dallas was the Sudan, Seattle was Morocco, Los Angeles was Love Allah, San Francisco was West Asia… Saladin told me that he heard one God give Buffalo the name of Bethlehem, and he called Niagara Falls Atlantis.

As I stood around in front of the Show and Prove taking it all in, they gave me nothing but love and warmth. There wasn't so much as one dirty look. Gods and Earths greeted me with "peace" and I'd give it back.

I don't understand how the Five Percenters came to be so demonized as a "hate group." If someone wants to quote a teaching or rap lyric to prove that the Gods and Earths teach hate, build on this: a blue-eyed devil can walk in the front door of the Allah School in Harlem easier than some Muslim women can enter the front doors of their mosques.

A few Gods asked my name and whether I had done my 120 lessons. I'd say that I had just started building with Azreal and had been corresponding with Intelligent Tarref Allah, trying to learn about the Five Percenters so I could build on Master Fard. I'd get into my whole obsession with Fard and how I considered myself almost a Fardiyya Sufi and they all replied with "that's peace." One God took the time to explain that Fard's father was named Alphonso Allah and he had been selected by "twenty-three wise scientists" in Mecca to have a son who would go to the West and find the Lost Tribe of Shabazz.

"And Master Fard Muhammad met with Franklin D. Roosevelt face-to-face," he told me, "and Franklin D. Roosevelt even said to him, 'trying to save your people is like putting a pair of pants on an elephant.'" When the God asked my name I said Mikail, the Arabic for Michael though I pronounced it Urdu-style, which was only my old Sunni name anyway.

Sarah from the Daughters of Hajar was interested in checking out the scene so she came through and we stayed outside just talking to random Gods. Every now and then Azreal would pop up wanting a dollar for another beer. By the time we left to find a place for Azreal to elevate again, he wasn't walking too well but he could sing and dance and tell stories about elevating behind the Apollo with Sam Cook and Patti LaBelle, and he'd point to me and call me his "Caucasian angel," which I guess I was since Mikail was one of only four angels mentioned by name in the Qur'an—and if the devil's just a fallen angel, maybe there's a chance he can go back. Azreal/John Kennedy reminded me that his middle name was Michael, and he knew how to stop the rain.

We walked back to the Show and Prove and Azreal quickly disappeared in the mass of Gods and Earths. It was hard to keep track of him because he quite literally knew everyone there and made the rounds from circle to circle, building all over the place.

Last time I saw Azreal I told him I'd write a book about him someday. He said we could all play ourselves in the movie, we didn't need to be actors since his name broke down into "As Real" and he was as real as it got.

Intelligent Tarref Allah wrote to say that my *Muslim WakeUp* article on the NGE actually earned an alright review in *The Five Percenter*, but I heard from more than one God that it brought Azreal into question. I was asked in emails if he had really said the things that I quoted him as saying, that he claimed to be Allah himself and such. I tried calling him but his math was disconnected. It worried me to remember the long scars on his legs, his lithium and thorazine-comas and institutionalizations and the long line of people that had offered him violence through the years. Azreal reminded me of a few old friends in that if you went long enough without talking to him, you just assumed that he was dead. It comes with the territory of the roles that these guys give themselves. Azreal could have been taken off the map by some Jive-Pretenders… or it could have been cops that did him for no reason, or another kid with a pitbull.

So maybe Azreal Kennedy's ashes and his mom's were finally scattered together at Mount Morris Park, and he could be up in Jannah right now tapping houris while equality hangs off his lips and he waves a forty ounce of Kauthar high above his head…

22

Somehow I had lucked into witnessing the formation of the Daughters of Hajar. Though rooted in a local situation, this was no more about Morgantown, West Virginia than the 1848 Women's Rights Convention was about Seneca Falls, New York; nor will it end with Asra Nomani now being allowed to walk through her mosque's front door and use the main hall. Amina Wadud said that the events of this weekend would help "rescript the current history and face of Islam." Shortly after 4:00 a.m. on Thursday I got in my Skylark and drove ten hours with little naps along the way. In the car I flipped through my copy of *Rassa Shastra: Inayat Khan on the Mysteries of Love, Sex and Marriage*. Inayat Khan says that the sun needs the moon and the moon needs the sun, that kind of thing. And that some are meant for monogamy while others cannot be anything but polygamous: "No matter how happily placed in life, or how carefully guarded, these naturally seek variety in experience of sex." I'm no Sufi saint, but I say it comes and goes several times throughout a life. Sleeping in my car all alone in an unfamiliar part of the state with only a green Buick door between Mike Knight and the darkness, just one true heart would be enough to get me through it—but walking through the mall behind a pack of laughing high-school girls, I knew I could marry all four and treat them equally.

In Morgantown, I knew a little bit of how to get around from a time I walked up and down the hills between the homeless shelter and West Virginia University. Broke my heart to see that they tore down the Greyhound station and hadn't even cleaned up the mess, leaving a big mound of rubble for me to see.

I entered the Radisson Hotel's Rat Pack Lounge to hugs from Asra and Mohja Kahf and a round of introductions: there was Nabeelah Abdul-Ghafur, long-time New Jersey activist; her daughter Saleemah, former chief operating officer for *Azizah* magazine and currently at work on her book about "kick-ass Muslim women"; Samina Ali, author of the novel *Madras on Rainy Days*; Sarah Eltantawi from MPAC; and Asra's mother Sajida Nomani, president of Morgantown Muslims & Friends. I took a press pamphlet and sat by Asra's brother Mustafa. This is how you save the world; just meeting cool Muslims in a bar and learning that it's not all hopeless does more for me than a conference of lecture-pushing academics.

Asra was staying at the Radisson and gave me the key to her house, a substantial step up from my usual accommodations. I got there after 1:00 a.m. and set her alarm for 4:00 so I could drive back to the hotel for Fajr.

With hotel towels for rugs, we prayed on the grass outside. I don't remember who led, but it wasn't me.

Praying in a line with women and being led by a woman only struck me as unusual when I considered how it'd look to others, or how it'd look to the old Mike Knight of 1995 who'd be thrown into moral chaos if he brushed shoulders with a girl on the stairwell. I describe myself in those days as a Wahhabi, but what's a Wahhabi? You don't have to be Wahhabi to be a conservative gynophobe. I'm sure you could find self-described progressives who would react the same.

The two most common objections to a woman leading prayer involve the physical bending-over and such, that these positions could be degrading for the woman and distracting for the men. The books and imams told me that as long as there were girls around, no man could ever concentrate on Allah.

111

It's true if you make it true. It used to be true for me.

For a hormonally agitated seventeen year-old it made all the sense in the world. I decided that I was weak, which allowed me to drop all responsibility and become weaker. I progressed so far in the deen that I wasn't only concerned with tits and ass—I had moved on to the dangerous sexual power of bare ankles and forearms.

From that point it became easy to hate girls. Since they knew that I was only a man and could be no other way, it was their job to keep my thoughts clean; so who were they to walk where I could see them?

Looking back on it, I think I made shirk to my testicles; I feared them more than I feared Allah.

I've gone through some well-documented ups and downs to crawl out of that. Maybe I'm not qualified to write on Islamic feminism, being Captain Handjobs at the ISNA Convention and all; but if this oversexed manchild can pray with a woman and keep his gaze lowered, do you want to be the man who can't?

I was too tired for much else in the way of coherent thoughts, but after prayer Asra led us in a breathing exercise and noted loud zikrs from the surrounding birds and it all felt alright. Later in the day she brought us to Sky Rock at Dorsey's Knob, the highest point in Morgantown—which was something notable since the whole town was a pile of steep hills. I sensed that Asra had a feel for the history they were making, as well as the poetry with which one can approach these things. Otherwise, why have your strategy meeting on a big graffiti-tagged rock on top of a hill? Instead of driving, why march to the mosque chanting du'as? These details helped set the tone; the Daughters of Hajar wasn't a gang of unruly militants but a spiritual and Islamically grounded assembly reclaiming the rights accorded them some fourteen centuries ago.

The actual event popped off at the West Virginia University College of Law with two rakats of prayer in the parking lot. I stood between Saleemah and Sajida. Nabeelah served as imam. During our second rakat, Asra's son Shibli jumped in and made his sujdah in front of us.

Morgantown mayor Ron Justice gave his welcome, the media people took pictures and from there we walked to the Islamic Center of Morgantown, followed by the local newspaper, TV station, writers with the *New York Times Magazine* and *Wall Street Journal*, a documentary director and her crew, a photographer from *U.S. News and World Report* and a reporter for the Princeton University paper. During the walk Sarah gave me some new appreciation for MPAC, in that they received no foreign funding and would make no endorsements in November; up until then I had dismissed MPAC as just another acronym of the pro-Bush Saudi lobby.

Waiting outside the mosque was its appointed representative for the day: white female convert, Christine Arja in business suit and perfectly wrapped hijab. Besides the Daughters of Hajar, she was the only woman I saw there.

We made our sunna prayers and sat in the back. As the mosque filled up, the tension died down. Then the imam took his place at the minbar and seemed to know the character that he was meant to play, with a standard-issue khutbah that focused on there being a right way and wrong way to do things since Islam after all was a perfect way of life with every detail coming straight from the Maker. He made glaring eye contact with a few of us. As we stood up to make our rows, the imam reminded us that "the best lines for men are in the front and the best lines for women are in the back." Two brothers in the last row of men left a space open for me. I stayed where I was while one gave a dirty look and they sealed it up.

Though back at our shukran salat I prayed between two women shoulder-to-shoulder and feet-to-feet, at the Islamic Center I left an open space between Asra and myself. At one point during the prayer it dawned on me that I was the only Muslim in there (besides the imam) who was standing alone. Then a teenage boy came in and rather than join the last men's row, he stood by me. After the prayer we shook hands.

The media was waiting outside. The Daughters of Hajar took turns reading their statements to the cameras, the motif being that their feminism by no means made them anti-Islamic or less credible Muslims than the Islamic Center's board; they only wanted what the Qur'an and the Prophet gave them.

The emotional climax of the weekend may have come at the literary event, "Daughters of Hajar: A New Generation of Muslim Women Speak," at the Garlow House next to Morgantown Public Library, where the women read from their works. Standing in back working a camcorder for Asra's father while he watched after Shibli, it struck me hard that something had started here—a scene, maybe, though I hate words like *scene*. At any rate, whatever brought these seven women together was bigger than the Islamic Center of Morgantown.

Mohja was in the middle of owning the house with her performance when, while introducing a piece which commits the apparent sin of portraying Muhammad's beloved Khadija as a human being, an older woman in powder-blue hijab stood up and announced that she'd had enough. You're insulting the Prophet, she said. Mohja pleaded that she meant no disrespect and kindly asked the woman to hear the piece before judging it. She then somehow shook off the tension and went on with the show.

If Mohja had reacted differently, that woman might have stormed out and never heard another word of this Islamic-feminism stuff. Instead, the heckler stayed and took part in the question-and-answer session, which opened up a whole mess of issues and enabled a healthy exchange between the readers and audience. It also helped the largely non-Muslim crowd to get a first-hand sense of what's happening in Islam today.

"Progressives" or whatever you want to call them have no better representative than Mohja Kahf, who in that critical moment reinforced what for me had been the point of the whole weekend: that you can question and challenge all you want while maintaining a love for the community and sincere compassion for those you may offend—and it's actually an Islamic thing to do so.

The next morning it rained so we prayed Fajr in the hotel lobby. Before leading, Samina explained the subtle differences in Shi'a salat. Forget about gender issues—this time it was just cool to pray behind a novelist. After that it was breakfast, a round of goodbye hugs and my long drive back to upstate New York.

I sometimes forfeit my religion to those that would make it ugly. If presented with a side of Islam that I don't like, my gut instinct is to say, "Fuck Islam then, you can have it." Chalk it up to a punk ethic or just intellectual laziness. But these women are stronger than that. They hit the books. They can fight tradition with tradition, Qur'an with Qur'an. They are Muslim and Feminist, with emphasis on both. They come from all backgrounds: Arab, South Asian, African-American, American-born and immigrant, Sunni and Shi'a, artists and activists and professors, mothers and daughters. And they preserve Islam for those who, when assuming that the Islam they were taught was the way it has always been and the only way it could ever be, may be tempted at times to give up.

Like me.

SAC, DETROIT

SAC, CHICAGO (100-33683)

July 31, 1957

W.D. FARD
SECURITY MATTER - NOI
OO: Chicago

     As a result of a recent inspection of the Chicago Office, it was suggested that a concerted effort be made to determine the whereabouts of W.D. FARD, reportedly the founder of the Nation of Islam (NOI). According to speeches and writings of ELIJAH MUHAMMAD, the National Leader of the NOI, "Allah" came to Detroit, Michigan from Mecca in 1930 in the person of one W.D. FARD and taught him for 3 years concerning Islam. According to MUHAMMAD, FARD was arrested by the Detroit Police Department in 1933, and shortly thereafter was asked to leave Detroit by the police department. MUHAMMAD claims that FARD continued to teach Islam in Chicago until 1934, at which time FARD disappeared and nothing about him has been heard since this time.

     The files of the Chicago Office indicate that W.D. FARD, as WALLACE DON FARD, FBI # 56062, was arrested as WALLACE FARAD by the Detroit, Michigan Police Department on May 25, 1933, their number 45138, on a charge of INV. No disposition was given.

     The Identification Record for FARD also indicates that he was arrested by the Los Angeles, California Police Department as WALLIE FORD, their number 16448, on November 17, 1918, on a charge of ADW. No disposition was given.

2-Detroit   (RM)
2-Los Angeles (RM)
2-San Francisco (RM)
1-Chicago (100-33683)

SMC:dcd
(7)

Walter
87-2892-22,23
25-97-4426
77-6336 (Nw)
87-2033

SEARCHED   INDEXED
SERIALIZED   FILED
AUG 5 1957
FBI SAN FRANCISCO

100-43165-1

1

Through the first half of 2004 I had been squatting illegally in dorms at Buffalo State College. A $10,000 bill for unpaid tuition kept its hold on my registration but Residence Life had never turned off my electronic fob-key, nor did they replace me in my room at Moore Complex so I just came and went, slept in my old bed and sat around playing video games with the same freak roommates like nothing had changed. At twenty-six years old I was still having all the stupid fun of college life, but without the classes. When the spring semester ended I took to sleeping in the Commuter Council's lounge in the Campbell Student Union since I knew the code to the door. The lounge was great because once they closed the building you could crawl out of the room and have that whole place to yourself—live off the vending machines, waste time on the Internet and download songs, sleep on a couch, meander down the halls and explore rooms that you can't access during the day. It beat paying rent for a place.

I had a job working relief at group homes for developmentally disabled adults but the hours were inconsistent—sometimes I'd pull a ninety-hour week and then not be needed for a month—and I blew all my checks at the Elmwood Kinko's to ship my books out to Alternative Tentacles in California so I could almost break even on three dollars of every six for a copy sold. At least the frequent off-time allowed for road adventures. My standard of living was pretty low but my lifestyle was good.

Then I picked up a regular shift doing overnights. Wasn't a bad gig: for the six hours each night before the residents woke up, my job basically amounted to mopping the kitchen and bathroom floors. I'd take out the trash and stare at the big van in the driveway, thinking if I had a van like that it'd be my house and my mosque. Then the residents got up and we had breakfast together. After helping them get ready for the day, I'd go home.

I was trying to save up for my summer adventure: a foolish bus jaunt all over the continental United States going through July, August and some of September. Greyhound had a thing called the Ameripass in which you could pay for a certain time period of unlimited bus-riding; I'd get the pass for sixty days and live like a wandering-bum Qalandari to see if I could really find that American-Islam thing—"Walk through North America like Master Fard, me and my squad" (Brand Nubian, "Straight Outta Now Rule"). I'd visit a mosque in every town, meet all sorts of confused Muslims, party with Wahhabis and Progressives and everybody, get on a bus when I needed to sleep and wake up six hundred miles away, hajj myself to what may or may not have been the grave of W.D. Fard in Hayward and wrap it all up with another ISNA convention in Chicago. Tried calling Lawrence Nixon a mess of times to see if he'd really come along, but he never answered the phone.

I had my notebooks filled with places I wanted to see, and bought an ankle-length jalab from the Muslim store on Hertel Avenue—I'd be wearing shorts through the summer but needed to cover up at mosques and such, and Hujwiri allowed for the holy traveler to take a patched cloak on his journey. My jalab didn't have patches but my friend Jain had given me a Sex Pistols patch that I could stick on with safety pins.

I'd be set on food: for the last few months I had been hoarding Subway "Sub Club" stamps. Subway had that deal where if you bought a six-inch sub they'd give you a stamp, and if you bought a foot-long they'd give you two stamps, and once you had eight stamps you could buy a small drink and they'd give you a free six-inch. Every day I'd buy a foot-long and pay for whoever else I was with, just to get the stamps. The kids working at the Elmwood/Forest Subway knew what I was doing and they'd sometimes give me ten or more stamps with a single sub. By the third week of May I had over two hundred stamps. If I kept to the sunna of W.D. Fard and ate only one meal a day for my trip, those stamps would make my food budget just a little more than thirty dollars for the whole first month.

During an overnight I got a call from Ben at Autonomedia; he had finished his second reading of *The Taqwacores* and was interested in doing something with it. He hoped to get a promo batch of 250 copies out for *Clamor Magazine's* Allied Media Conference in June, after which we'd talk about a real run in the fall. So now I had a publisher, which helped me through another round of scrubbing toilets at 4:00 a.m.

After punching out at 8:00, I drove to Forest Avenue, parked and walked to campus. Passing a closed down, boarded-up club called Hysteria, tired enough to vomit but too tired to sleep, I noticed a yellow Hurley hoodie bunched up and abandoned on the sidewalk. Had some grime but it was alright and the tag said Large so I put it on. A new hoodie and a book deal, all in the same day—maybe the tide of momentum had shifted and everything would turn out alright. Even Zainab the Pakistani-Bengali-Alabama sayyeda called and said that her parents gave up on finding a husband for her. "It's up to you," her father told her, "But no white boys that are six-foot-three." I asked what that was about and she said that when she told her parents about me, the first thing her dad wanted to know was my height.

Roughly two hours before my last shift, I pulled into a parking lot on Transit Road to see if I could get a quick nap. I pushed the seat back and picked up Rabindranath Tagore's *Gitanjali* to wear down my eyes when suddenly I was sharing the parking lot with two police cars. They pulled up behind me with their highbeams on. I stuck my head out and looked back but only saw white light. The cops got out and walked to my car, one on my side to talk and the other waving his flashlight in the passenger-side window.

"What's going on?" asked the talker.

"Just hanging out before work," I replied. He took my license, which I knew would cause trouble since nobody in Buffalo had ever heard of my hometown nearly two hours away, and my car definitely had the looks and smells of homelessness. So he called me out.

"How 'bout you put your hands on the car." His buddy rummaged around the front seat and brought out my Tagore. "What's this you're reading?"

"He's a poet."

"What kind of poet?"

"He's like the William Blake of Bangladesh."

"You read a lot of religious-type things?"

"Tagore wrote more romantic-type things. Like love poetry."

"You have any dynamite?"

"Nope."

"Guns, drugs, anything in there?"

"No, sir."

"WHAT'S WITH THE BRICK?" chimed in the one doing the searching.

"It's from the childhood home of Zelda Fitzgerald." Our dialogue then missed a beat as he thought it over. I got the feeling that he had never heard of Zelda Fitzgerald.

"So it's like a memento?"

"Yeah."

"Just so you know, your car is disgusting."

"Yes, sir."

He looked in the backseat while the other pointed his flashlight at the pavement and told me to stand by the light. They didn't find any dynamite but did collect the last remnants of my fireworks shopping spree in Indiana: a few bundled packs of bottle rockets and a smoke bomb, all illegal in New York State. "We're going to dispose of these," he said, "and cut you a break." At least I had already shot off the good stuff.

They returned my license and let me drive away. One of them followed me through the first few lights and then turned around.

That'll teach me to be vagrant in a suburb like Amherst but it didn't matter—soon I'd hit the road and all of Erie County would cease to exist until September. I worked my overnight, sure to mop those floors the best I could.

Since I'd be riding terrible buses and doing the streets for sixty-plus days I figured I'd go back to my mom's house and live a good life while I could: eating real food, sleeping comfortably and watching more TV than I had in the previous six months. The only time I went outside was to check the mail. I removed myself from the world, save limited dispatches by email or phone: talked to Asra Nomani about how she tried taking her struggle to CAIR, which went after Nike for supposedly putting Allah's Name on a sneaker but could give a rip about women's rights in the mosque… talked to Azreal, who said we'd go to Baltimore together; I had been planning to meet Warith Deen's national representative there on the 25th, and Azreal knew Gods that we could crash with along the way. Then Daniel Pipes said that he'd be up to meet if I found myself in Philly again. Pipes was, to use the words of the day, a *neo-con* and *Islamophobe* who occupied a Bush-appointed seat at the U.S. Institute of Peace and kept a close watch on any professors who taught remotely pro-Palestinian perspectives. Mohja Kahf was on one of his lists.

It was disturbing to see myself as someone that Daniel Pipes would have dinner with, but I almost wanted to check him out just to make a big fiasco of it. If I brought Azreal, the three of us sitting around a table in a fancy restaurant could make for another sitcom episode: you'd have Pipes in a suit and tie trying to be all dignified *Washington Post* on us, preaching the virtues of the Patriot Act with Azreal the lithium-shaikh in a t-shirt and gym shorts showing the scars on his legs, telling Pipes that he was John Kerry's running mate. I'd just be sitting between them, trying to smooth everything over and making "Oh man, I'm fucked" Zach Morris faces to the studio audience. My life was getting strange enough for a scene like that to fit. I had been cleaning toilets for $8.50 an hour and had the business card of a *Wall Street Journal* writer in my wallet. This was the same time that *The Village Voice* was calling Khalida, Mark Wallace drove down to Power Hill to see her mosque for *The New York Times*, *The Los Angeles Times* ran a story on *Muslim WakeUp* and *The New York Daily News* ran a story on Mohja's *Muslim WakeUp* column "Sex and the Umma."

The first batch of books from Autonomedia came on my last Thursday at Mom's house. I brought the big brown box inside, cut it open and there they were in two stacks protected by paper stuffing. I took one out and felt the smooth cover.

The Taqwacores.

They used the same photo as I had for my Xerox/Kinko's edition of me sitting in a garbage dumpster with an old-school typewriter.

The dumpster was by the loading dock at Porter Hall, a huge dorm building at Buffalo State College. The typewriter was purchased at Amvet Thrift Store down a short ways on Elmwood for a few dollars or so. After the photo shoot I dumped it in Butler Fountain by the library.

Anyway, I had a box of books. Real books, with real spines and covers and a publisher's logo on them. They even had bar codes.

If every couple of years or so I could feel what I was feeling at that moment, I'd be happy mopping floors for the rest of my life. I could be a rotten old man with stringy white hair yellowed from not washing it, living alone in a crumbling apartment in miserable Buffalo... Allah could even put me back at my old place on Herman Street where I couldn't sit outside without smelling the sweet, burning dog-food smell of someone making crack, if I just had a shelf of books with my name on them.

The night before hopping on the bus I took some empty pop bottles back to Wegmans and then drove to the Borders Books by Eastview Mall. Found Asma Gull Hasan's *Why I am a Muslim* with her smiling on the cover in jeans and a V-neck top. The inside jacket's blurb began with "In the wake of 9/11," which was a little annoying—but to the media world, everything a Muslim did was in the wake of 9/11: from the Daughters of Hajar and their Islamic Feminism to a gay-friendly mosque in Philadelphia to this Asma Hasan girl tearing up her knee on a snowboard to me throwing eggs at trucks on the I-90.

Mom offered to make pork-steaks so I could have one last decent meal before hitting the road but I whined at her that I wasn't going to embark on conquering America's Islam with pork-steaks in my stomach, so we had spaghetti instead. I was all packed up. I had my sixty-day pass for unlimited Greyhound rides, a pocket-sized Rand McNally atlas, notebooks and pens, some white t-shirts, a baseball cap from Abdullah the Butcher's House of Ribs in Atlanta, a tube of toothpaste, and the scar on my leg from hopping a fence to see Mohammed Webb's grave. Mom drove me to the Greyhound station in Geneva, on the outer edge of downtown and right by Seneca Lake. It scared me at first to find that the station had been torn down, but a new one stood right across the street. I was still sad to see the old one gone; it was my hang-out when I was fifteen, I'd just go in there and read the Qur'an in bad lighting while grubby lowlifes leered at each other.

And then I put myself on a bus heading down 5 and 20, my first destination being Fayetteville more than twelve hundred miles away but who knew where I'd end up besides Allah. It was Allah who willed everything up to this point and nobody knew why He willed things to turn out a certain way, but He did, and for some secret reason it seemed to work out for me.

So mash'Allah, I laughed my ass off.

We made a stop in Buffalo and continued on the I-90 to Cleveland. The bus was half-full but some goof came all the way to the back and sat next to me. You look like a nice guy, he said. He appeared to be in his early twenties and was skinny but seemed as though he'd have a sinewy strength to him.

"You watch the news?" he asked.

"Not really."

"You don't? You need to know what's going on. You know what's going on?"

"What's going on?"

"War, man! That's our country out there!"

"I hear you," I said. "Where you from?"

"Oklahoma, man. You know about the snakes n' shit?"

"Snakes?"

"Yeah man, like cobras. They have snakes in Iraq, all kinds of snakes. They've got poisonous spiders that'll kill you with one bite."

"Damn."

"My brother's over there."

"In Iraq?"

"No, Afghanistan. He's in Afghanistan so I know how it is over there. Over there they give you a pill every day so you don't go crazy."

He kept going and all I had to do was nod my head and say "absolutely" or "hell yeah." He said that if there were ten of him in Iraq, it'd be a different story. "They won't even see me, I'm like a thief in the night. I don't need a weapon, either. Nature's a weapon. You know what I mean?" I said that I knew what he meant. "This is what George Bush died for, you know? This is what Abraham Lincoln died for. It's in the Bible." He showed me his pen that he received as a bonus when he worked as a door-to-door salesman, I gave him a little bag of potato chips and then he walked back to the front.

As the bus made stops in every little town and passengers came and went, the poisonous-spiders guy stayed on. During the ride to Memphis he passed some guys on his way to the bathroom and howled "SKEEEEET!" out of nowhere. Everyone laughed but the kid had his best Manson freak-out eyeballs going and he said something like, "DON'T MESS WITH ME, I'M TRYING TO MAKE IT TO WORLD CHAMPION. THAT'S MY LIFE."

"Skeet?" said some girl. "What's he talkin' about, *skeet*, is he the Ying Yang Twins?" Through laughing at the guy we had all turned into a community and he kept it up for us, glaring back and shouting that he had been in "every jail across the U.S."

As long as he stayed up front I was cool. The back seat was like the penthouse of the bus: it was the only place you could lay down and be right by the bathroom (though that wasn't always a plus). I curled up and fell asleep. When I woke up it was dark, the bus was pulling over into a rest stop filled with tractor-trailers and my man was standing in front, the very front of the bus, right by the driver and staring us all down.

Flashing blue and red lights came up behind the bus and on its side. The bus door opened and the man got off.

"Stand over here," said someone outside. We looked out the windows but couldn't see anything.

A woman who was riding all the way from Albany, New York to Little Rock, Arkansas with her two young daughters explained to me that the guy must have been on meth since he had all the symptoms of her ex-boyfriend. Her twelve-year-old asked who made meth; Mom replied that Hitler did, to keep his troops awake.

"Who's Hitler?"

"Oh, someone that you'll never meet." Then our whole half of the bus had a roundtable discussion on meth. You can make it with anything, the mom told us. Kerosene, bleach, rat poison… all you do is boil it until it rocks up.

I fell asleep again and dreamt that I was driving a beat-up old car through the various rooms of an Islamic Center. In the passenger seat sat Minister Louis Farrakhan. We were looking for a place to park without being disrespectful to the mosque, but it seemed like every room we came into was a prayer hall. So we kept driving through all these wide doors hoping to find a suitable room but with maze-like repetition we just found the same prayer halls over and over again, with gray or pink carpeting and clean white walls. Finally we decided that we'd just have to park the car in a prayer hall and be done with it, so we did, and as soon as I got out of the car I was jumped by the Islamic Center's security. As they wrestled me down I screamed that I was with Minister Farrakhan. Go ask him! He's right over there! They ignored me and pulled my hands behind my back so I called out for Louis himself but he had his back turned and it looked like some social event was going on, like he was suddenly mingling at a party, and then I woke up.

2

It was morning when we hit Memphis. We had a two-hour layover so I left the protective shell of the Greyhound station and walked around town. Memphis had a nice feeling to it but upon closer examination turned out to be all upscale shops and trendy restaurants, like the South's answer to Seattle or Toronto. None of the restaurants opened before 11:00 a.m.

Back at the bus station I dug through my bag and took out Henry Miller's road book, *The Air-Conditioned Nightmare*. At one point he mentioned the "stir" caused by Swami Vivekananda ("hailed as the greatest spiritual leader of our time") at the 1893 Parliament of World Religions in Chicago.

"The story of this man who electrified the American people reads like a legend."

In Chicago, Swami became a celebrity surrounded by rich friends and lavish gifts, but in Detroit he gave it all up and went back to being just a wandering holy man. I left my Henry Miller at the Memphis station with hopes that maybe someone cool would find it.

The bus came into Fayetteville a little after midnight and Mohja Kahf was there to pick me up. She had arranged for me to be featured at the next gathering of her Ozark Poets and Writers group, but I owed her for a lot more than that.

When I had first written *The Taqwacores* and thought that it'd never find acceptance from Muslims, she was the one who offered encouraging words and honest criticism—real criticism, from one writer to another on the art of storytelling, whereas some would just look at whether the characters were sturdy in their religion. For me, Mohja's the sign that we can honor the Creator and still be minor creators ourselves—and she may be the only one that can pull it off, because I hold no interest in seeing the same calligraphy of Allah's Names over and over again and you can only talk about Rumi so much. Mohja Kahf shows me that it's not betraying your deen to be obsessed with Leonard Cohen. I hate to tag her with a label like "progressive" because to me she's bigger than that whole crowd.

On top of that, Mohja Kahf has helped with my understanding of the Islamic Society of North America. She grew up an ISNA child and can look back to when its headquarters were in an old farmhouse, back before the Plainfield fortress.

In the car she had a copy of the *Northwest Arkansas Times* with me in it sporting a five-day beard and stolen Buffalo State Dining Services hat, looking like I had arrived on someone's front stoop to take his daughter to the prom in my van. The article described my bus trip as a quest for "the Islam that will enter no official history book."

At home she made an Arab lentil dish and showed me the new *Poets & Writers* magazine with Samina Ali on the cover, then my room for the night. After thirty-four hours of curling into unnatural positions on Greyhounds, I had a bed!

The next day Mohja drove me around Fayetteville and stopped at the newly built mosque. "The door by the dumpsters is probably for the women," she said. It was. Then we picked up her ten-year-old daughter Banah and her friend and drove off to a Confederate-era cemetery.

There was a family plot blocked off with an old iron fence. The stones were weathered and crumbling away. Mohja turned to her daughter and asked, "What do we do at graves, Banah?" and Banah knew that what you do at graves is recite al-Fatiha for their souls. They said it together, Banah leaning against the fence, and I said it in my heart. Human beings were just human beings, and who knew what was going on in those graves?

That night we had dinner at an Iranian restaurant where I got to meet the eclectic group of artists that Mohja hung out with, and then we went to the Ozark Mountain Smokehouse for my reading. The local TV station was there to do a piece on me. We sat down at a table and they attached the microphone to my shirt.

"So," the reporter asked, "is it hard being Muslim today, with the war in Iraq?" He threw me off with that one. I just looked at him and didn't know how to answer. My gut reaction was to say that I had no idea, since nobody who'd see me walking down the street would assume that I was Muslim unless I had the right kind of hat on. There are Hindus, Sikhs and even Christians who could say more about anti-Muslim prejudice in this country than I ever could.

For his next question, he wanted to know how I felt about Americans getting their only impression of Islam from these guys in Baghdad chopping people's heads off. The whole interview ran less than five minutes and all he wanted to know about me personally was how I came to Islam.

They stuck around for a bit to film me reading my piece on the Five Percenters and then bailed. I didn't feel like I had read well, though people reacted at the right spots. I had a better time listening to the other writers read their works—besides the featured writer, these meetings consisted of an open-mic thing where people put their names in a jar and then came up to read when their names were pulled.

When it was all done people came up to buy my book. One of Mohja's students was there and told me that she had written a paper in which Hanif Kureishi represented "straight Islam" and my work represented "queer Islam." A hat was passed around for people to donate money to the featured writer; between the hat and selling books, I pulled in a hundred dollars, which meant worlds for my traveler's budget.

At one point I found myself standing next to a poet who'd read a long piece on voodoo mythology, and I told her about my Louis Farrakhan dream. She said that it was of great significance that in my dream, I was the one behind the wheel. "The fact that Farrakhan was riding shotgun instead of driving," she explained, "means that it's your journey, not his." And she said that his abandoning me once we left the car means that in the end, I'm on my own.

Mohja's friend Kelly asked if I'd like to meet the man who had testified on Intelligent Tarref Allah's behalf. He was having a guys' night out in a bar across the street, she said, so we all hiked over and it turned out she was married to him: Ted Swedenburg, Professor of Middle Eastern Studies. First thing he said was that he liked my Five Percenters shirt. I sat at his end of the table and we talked about Intell (Ted said he still had a box full of paperwork from the case and continually received letters from incarcerated Gods in similar battles).

Kelly then told me that she knew a guy who wore green all the time because he believed himself to be Khidr, the Qur'anic mystery man and initiator of prophets, the Green Man who bewildered Moses and remains a subject of debate. Some say that Khidr was a prophet while others call him an angel or another kind of creature known only to Allah. Peter Lamborn Wilson wrote that when you mention Khidr's name, you should offer the greeting of *as-salamu alaikum* since he may be in the room with you. He has been called the patron saint of travelers and a guide to those wandering in search of God, so I wanted to track him down if I could. Kelly said that one could usually find this guy outside around campus playing the *saz*, a stringed Turkish instrument.

They turned the TV up once the 11:00 news came on and there I was with my scruffy and sloppy self. The only piece of the interview they used had me blaming Islamic fundamentalism on political and economic factors. Basically, it was nothing that Ibrahim Hooper wouldn't have said.

Talking to the media is like playing Yahtzee. When you shake that cup you have no idea what the dice are doing or how they'll look when they spill out.

Next they showed the old footage of Saddam Hussein when he was freshly captured and being examined for lice. The whole segment on this American Muslim writer was just a lead-in to their story on Iraq, where it was already June 30th and Bush had transferred Iraqi sovereignty from his right hand to his left.

We took my stuff from Mohja's car to Ted's. I thanked her profusely for all she had done on my behalf and then went to Ted and Kelly's house filled with artifacts from their travels: a round table covered with Islamic calligraphy, Bollywood movie posters, paintings of local Sufi saints of South Asian villages. Ted showed me his Noble Drew Ali button and his bootleg tape of Fun'Da'Mental videos. Fun'Da'Mental was a hip-hop outfit from the U.K. whose kifaya-wrapped member Aki had been called "the Asian Chuck D" and "the Pakistani Johnny Rotten."

As Ted drove me to the bus station with his big dog (named Malik Fahd) in the back seat, we got to talking about W.D. Fard. Ted told me that he had always thought of Fard as a Druze or an Ismaili. At any rate, Fard had a chance of being Arab. In 1930s Detroit, Ted explained, if Arabs weren't at the auto factories they were door-to-door salesmen. "You look at that portrait of him and you think, he could have been Arab or he could have been Pakistani, or whatever you'd want him to be." I remembered Fard's FBI file describing his complexion as "swarthy" and "olive."

The bus station was closed but one of the characters sitting in front with his bags said that one was on the way. So Ted dropped me off and I sat on the ground to wait. A redneck-looking guy asked me where I was headed and I said Jackson, Mississippi (home to the country's only specifically Islamic museum, the International Museum of Muslim Cultures). He could read on me that I was living hobo-style and advised, "if you go to Jackson, man, don't do the streets. Believe me, man, don't do the streets." I looked at the way he stood and the way the words came out of his mouth and reasoned that he was drunk. He swaggered off for a second, then turned right back around. "Don't do the streets there, man. Believe me on that one." He'd look away and think about it and then just say it again: DON'T DO THE STREETS IN JACKSON, WHATEVER YOU DO. Then he asked if I had a ticket and I told him about my unlimited sixty-day pass. "What are you gonna do with that?" he asked.

"I'm going everywhere."

"Shit, you'll see shit out there that you'll never see again." He nodded to approve of his own point, and then repeated it slower. "You will see shit out there… that you'll never see again." He walked away, bummed a cigarette off his girlfriend on the bench and then came back. "Shit man, if I had one of them I'd go up the east coast, up the west coast, come back and do it all over again… I'd go to Colorado, I'd go to Oregon, North Carolina, South Carolina, I'd go to Florida… "

"That's the plan." We started breaking down each state or region in the country and how cool it'd be to go there. For each place the guy said that it'd be the most beautiful thing I had ever seen, or ever would see, and that I'd see shit out there that I'd never see again.

The bus took us to Ft. Smith and when the bus driver was unloading luggage, my drunk buddy gave him so much hassle that they wouldn't let him on the bus to Little Rock. I watched the poor guy from the window as we rolled away, leaving him at the Ft. Smith station with his girlfriend and their duffle bags in the middle of the night. I got to Jackson a little after 5:00 p.m. the next day. The museum was closed and I'd have to spend the night in Jackson if I wanted to see it. I remembered the drunk telling me more than once not to do the streets in that town. It couldn't have been worse than doing the streets in Chicago, but he had said it a mess of times and even if he wasn't wearing green or playing the saz, maybe Allah had sent him my way as a guide; so I got on the next bus.

3

When I told Zainab that I was coming she booked me a room for four days at a hotel and said not to worry, she'd pay for it. I arrived at Birmingham around two in the morning and walked a couple miles to the place while some guy followed me, talking about his drug habit and how he had a good woman who kept him alive… even though she threw him out of the house now and then, if it weren't for her he'd be face-down in a shitty Alabama gutter somewhere. As with that drunk at the Fayetteville bus station I was in a state of mind to take every fuck up that came my way as some instrument of Allah's mercy and guidance, so the fact that I was hearing this "if you have a good woman, don't let her go" stuff might have been an ayat.

She came by the next morning and it felt like I had a girlfriend, though we both knew that this wasn't going to work. With me nine hundred miles away all the time she could play the perfect desi girl for her parents and then hide in a closet to talk to me on the phone… but you can't run that game forever, insha'Allah.

I thanked her for the room and she told me it was hard finding a motel in Birmingham that wasn't owned by desis who knew her father. She came back during her lunch break and we walked downtown. I wanted to hold her hand but was afraid she didn't want to—she'd tell me later that she did want to but was afraid of the "Desi Police," especially while walking in the medical sector.

One evening I got to meet her brother at the UAB campus. She told him she was running out of lies to get out of the house and see me; he advised her to tell their parents that she was going to the MSA party. That night the three of us went to see *Fahrenheit 9/11*.

The next day was a Friday and Zainab didn't go to mosques but her brother drove me to one on a hill where the khutbahs were all about the importance of sending your kids to the Muslim school. I didn't have any long pants to wear but had packed a jalab and completed the Muslim Costume with a kifaya and kufi. I looked nuts. To make it worse, my beard was coming in.

The khutbah was exactly as lame as Zainab's brother had predicted, but afterwards I got to shake hands with a guy named something-Rasheed who played second-string linebacker for the San Francisco 49ers.

For most of my stay in Birmingham, Zainab was either at work or trapped in her parents' house so I passed the time reading Khaled Hosseini's *The Kite Runner* (Mohja had given it to me) about the friendship between a

Sunni boy and Shi'a boy in Afghanistan, and Asma Gull Hasan's *Why I am a Muslim.*

After mentioning the names of Allah and Muhammad, Asma doesn't leave a *subhanahu wa ta'Ala* or *sallallaho alayhe wa salam* or even a SWT or PBUH. She explains that she wanted to avoid confusing the non-Muslim reader. "I encourage Muslim readers to say these blessings to themselves as they read along," she tells us, "as I did while I was writing."

Zainab told her parents that her clinic would be open on the 4th of July, a pretty high-risk lie. She showed up at the motel wearing her blue scrub just to be safe. We went to a fireworks store, which I'd usually love but the place was packed with families and all walks of life and the whole thing lost its outlaw appeal—it was like seeing your favorite punk band show up on TRL to get hugs from junior-high girls. But I had a good time just riding around town with her, listening to her CDs. She had one with Jeff Buckley doing a cover of Nusrat Fateh Ali Khan.

We drove to the big statue of the Roman god Vulcan, which used to hold a red light that would shine when someone died on the road but people found that disturbing and replaced it with a spear. Once we pulled into the parking lot, Zainab spotted some South Asians and immediately pulled out.

"They know my father," she said.

"Who are they?"

"I don't know. But if they're Indians in Alabama, they know my father." So we went back to the room and watched a *Rocky* marathon on TV. She had to go home around the time that she would have been getting out of work, but came back later with the excuse that she'd be watching the fireworks with a friend.

It was hard to appreciate all the exploding gunpowder and things with *Fahrenheit 9/11* still in my head, but afterwards it was nice walking downtown with this girl and having sweet couple-type conversations. She talked about the day I'd ask her father if I could marry her and I said there was no way that was happening. She said it had to. I asked if that was a Southern thing or a South Asian thing and she said it was both.

When she dropped me off at what she thought was the bus station, it turned out that I was a block away. So I walked with my head down and my heart sunk, mad at the bus and mad at the world. I didn't want to go back in that station with all the losers and mean people while missing my sayyeda. She had softened me so bad I felt like I had never even seen the grimy noisy insides of a Greyhound station.

Usually I can embrace bad times and hardships on the road for their literary merit: you run out of gas money or food money, it'll just add to your story. Wash your hair in a public fountain and you're king of the underground. But this time I didn't care about writing a book or riding buses or any of it, I didn't even care about W.D. Fard.

The bag on my shoulders was heavy and I turned to walk inside the station when I heard her yell my name.

I looked up and she was standing across the street.

I walked over and dropped my bag and we hugged. The top of her head was hot in the sun and I studied the tints of red and golden brown in her million black hairs.

"Where are you going next?" she asked.

"I don't know. There are a few places in Georgia I need to check out, and I'm going to Miami."

"I have rich family in Miami."

"Really."

"They might have invited George Bush to their house in 2000, but I'm not sure."

"That's crazy."

"*You're* crazy," she said.

"Yeah, I guess I am."

"No, you really are. The craziest thing I've ever done was have a boyfriend."

It occurred to me that I could walk the line for this girl. Maybe we'd never see each other again; maybe she'd decide one day that it'd just be easier to do what her parents want and marry the damn doctor. We had been there once already. Maybe I'd be careless with my heart and fuck it up. But if this was the end, she at least gave us the corny movie ending before I finally got back on my loser coach and left her there.

4

At Miami's Greyhound station in the middle of the day I was trying to find out which metro to take to Opa-Locka so I walked up to a guy with his shirt unbuttoned and flapping in the wind, his hair blowing all around—he almost looked like a movie hero—and asked him where to go. He said the 42 bus but I had better watch out because he was gutted once in Opa-Locka. Since his shirt was already open he showed me the scar on his stomach and demonstrated how the guy stuck him and pulled the knife in an upward motion.

"But that got me mad," he said, "so I kicked him—BOOM! And when we fell down, my elbow was already on him, like that—BOOM! An' I wasn't going to let him up. I had him on the concrete and I wore his head out."

"Damn."

"I could've sued the State of Florida for it—did you know that? If you're attacked by somebody that ain't got nothing that you can sue him for, you can sue the State of Florida."

"Oh, shit. Really?"

"Yeah." He walked to where he had laid his duffle bags down and picked up a long plastic tube. He dug in his pocket and took out a bottle-rocket, then stuck it on the end of the tube. "Think I can shoot this off?"

"I don't know."

"Think I'll get in trouble, shootin' this off at a bus station?"

"Where I'm from," I told him, "you can't shoot those off anywhere."

"Where you from?"

"Buffalo, New York."

"New York?" He jerked his head back and crinkled his eyebrows. "Shit, in New York havin' one of these is worse'n having a gun or even some good trippies. All 'cus of 9/11 they'll think you're part of a Saddam Hussein or somethin'." He studied his bottle-rocket resting on the end of the tube. "Man, with my luck it'd fly off into somebody's windshield. I don't want anybody suin' the State of Florida 'cus of me." So he put his bottle-rocket back in his pocket. When the 42 bus came we shook hands and he said maybe I'd see him again sometime.

Opa-Locka was called "the Baghdad of Miami-Dade County" which was tragically humorous since both this Baghdad and the other one were Bush-occupied territories at the time. Florida's Baghdad was the brainchild of an eccentric aviation genius named Glenn H. Curtiss. Curtiss had started with motorcycle engines, moved on to produce the first engines for dirigibles and is credited with around five hundred inventions. In 1926 he set out to build his "dream city," inspired by *The Arabian Nights*. Started out upscale but had turned into an impoverished ghetto.

Going down Ali Baba Avenue on the 42 bus, it was like I had gone to Morocco with its horseshoe arches, glazed tiles, crescents and colors. Everything had them—even the police department, regular peoples' homes, auto body shops, supermarkets and the golden wall surrounding a junkyard. The houses were topped with domes and used to have minarets, though they had crumbled away. The streets all had names like Aladdin, Ahmad, Beder, Caliph... Alexandria Drive, Baghdad Avenue, Cairo Lane, Harem Avenue, Port Said Road... I got off at Sharazad Boulevard and walked down the palm tree-lined street towards City Hall which looked like a big Turkish mosque with long pointy minarets and a pile of domes, sharp crescents on top of everything. In July it was easy to forget that this was only the Baghdad of South Florida, not the real Baghdad, and it was easy to picture Jeb Bush rolling down Sinbad Avenue in a Bradley tank.

I was on my way to the Keys. Got to the southernmost point in the United States, Key West, a little before midnight, walked behind the Holiday Inn and found its private beach. I hid my backpack between two beach chairs to avoid looking like a vagabond to hotel security, though I was the only soul out there besides a white-haired man who popped up out of the darkness and asked if I minded him shooting off some bottle-rockets. I told him to go ahead so he set them down on the sand, lit the fuses and disappeared. They whistled and screamed. For a few seconds it was pretty cool. Some drunk people hooted and clapped from their balconies, then went back into their rooms and I was alone again. I waded in the warm Gulf of Mexico for a minute, then picked up my bag and walked a few miles back to the Greyhound station.

The station was closed so I lied down in front with my backpack as a pillow, piecing it all together. To the seeker of Master Fard, Key West offered a footnote: in 1958 the FBI tracked down Wallace Dodd Ford's former common-law wife, Hazel Barton here at Sun Crest Trailer Park (lot 7). I wanted to check it out but couldn't find any sign that the place still existed.

Hazel (then Mrs. Clifford Evelsizer) told the agents that Wallace used to send her money for their son from Detroit and Chicago, except for one six-month period in which she didn't hear from him. He later told her that he hadn't written because he had no money. She told him to write whether he had money or not. The last time she ever saw him—1932 or '33, when he showed up in Los Angeles with an out-of-control mullet, white sheets over the seats of his car and a new lifestyle of eating just once a day—he gave her a box of self-threading needles. Hazel gave it to the agents.

She also told them that she found a letter in his trunk one day, addressed to one Fred Dodd, and was sure that he had used the name when he lived in Portland. From what Wallace told her, they couldn't marry because his Portland wife refused to grant a divorce. Hazel couldn't remember him ever espousing any unusual beliefs, certainly nothing about white devils; as far as she knew, he was a white man from New Zealand. She had even helped him write letters to his parents back home.

Finally, Hazel told the agents that she had her son's name legally changed from Wallace Dodd Ford, Jr. to Wallace Max Ford, and that Wallace Max Ford died while serving in the Coast Guard in 1942.

Around the time that federal agents were interviewing W.D. Fard's ex-girlfriend, Imam Muhammad Abdullah journeyed from Fiji to Chicago to meet with the Honorable Elijah Muhammad at his mansion. They had been corresponding for some time; about what I don't know, though Zafar Abdullah believes his father was trying to bring Elijah toward *al-Islam*. At any rate I doubt Elijah had any idea that his pen pal was the One… and when Muhammad Abdullah stood at the mansion's front door, I doubt Elijah's bowtie-wearing bodyguards recognized this bearded desi imam as their long-lost Savior from that famous retouched portrait. They let him in and led him upstairs to Elijah's chamber—I'm picturing it as in the Malcolm X movie—and when Elijah turned to look at him, he knew.

It had been twenty-five years since he drove the Master to the airport, but he knew. Eyes don't change. Your face ages and you can disguise yourself with gray hair or a beard, but those eyes are the same as when you first learned to walk. So Elijah knew who he was looking at and his whole world shattered all over again. The Master smiled, patiently waiting for Elijah to formulate a reaction. Maybe it took a while before either of them said anything.

If this was how it went down, at some point they agreed that Master Fard would remain hidden from the community; so Elijah kept him around as "internationally renowned Muslim scholar" Muhammad Abdullah, personal mentor to Wallace.

In the years that followed, Wallace would fall in and out of line with the Nation's teachings. He'd side with Malcolm in the schism, then reconcile with his father; and after Elijah's passing he turned it all around with Muhammad Abdullah standing behind him.

The bus took me back to Miami, the town where Cassius Clay won his first heavyweight crown and then told the world that he would now be called Muhammad Ali…

Lying flat on my back in the last seat on the bus as we rode up the coast of Florida, I looked up to see the clouds roll across my window like I was watching it on a video screen. It's easy for Americans to look at their lives in terms of movies, that's how we're taught to see the world from day one. Master Fard, his life could make an epic summer blockbuster. If I had millions of my own dollars I'd sink it into his story and get it told the right way. Who could play him? You'd need someone who could be simultaneously charming and creepy, a morally complicated monster—Christopher Walken, maybe—and there'd be no issues with the actor's ethnicity since Fard was everything at some point and the makeup people could always work on him. Between Vero Beach and Palm Bay it started raining hard. I sat up just in time to see the top of a telephone pole spark into a big round ball of white and blue flames.

5

SAPELO ISLAND, GA—I was riding a five-dollar rented bike up and down the island's dirt roads through palm tree forests, chasing big buzzards and searching for the two-centuries old Behavior Cemetery; legend had it that your behavior at the graves affected how their spirits would treat you. One story said that people who "weren't supposed to be there" had found the cemetery and ended up surrounded by rattlesnakes.

The night before, I had walked eleven miles from Darien to Meridian to catch the morning's first ferry. It was about four hours of walking down a long country road in complete darkness with every other house hosting three or four big barking dogs. A couple of houses had their dogs untied so they'd follow me maybe three quarters of a mile, twenty feet behind me and barking the whole time. I figured that running or making eye contact would make it worse so I just trudged on, muttering under my breath that they thought I wouldn't kick a dog, but I would… I'd kill a goddamned dog if I had to, I'd wrestle it down and bite its neck like Jack London did in that one story. The dogs all tired of the chase sooner or later and left me alone and I kept walking. I walked until I had a shadow, and then until the roosters crowed and I could read signs without a flashlight. I made it to the ferry a little after 6:00 a.m. with big blisters on my toes that exploded when I pressed on them.

My mission centered on Bilali Mohammad who was taken as a slave to the Bahamas and came to Georgia in 1803, ending up on Sapelo Island in a tabby house made from a mixture of water, lime, sand and seashells. He was the author of a thirteen-page Arabic manuscript believed to be a treatise on Muslim jurisprudence and the first Islamic writings of North America. Bilali's descendents still lived on Sapelo in a community called Hog Hammock (population: 70). Though they had since gone Baptist, Bilali's legacy crept through here and there; the island's two churches were built facing east and segregated by gender.

I sat on the front stoop of Stanley Walker's trailer as he relaxed from cleaning three hundred pounds of fish. His thick arms didn't come from the gym but a naturally hard life. Sapelo Island people were rugged, with their straw hats and beat-up old pickup trucks and bumpy dirt roads, and old trailers and a pump that would only give you gas two days a week. Stanley told me that people would still say "I'll see you tomorrow if Allah spare me life," and then pointed me to the home of his mother, Cornelia Bailey, who served as the island's historian.

I sat at her kitchen table while she attended to her little grandson and told me that Bilali had a lot of secret chapters to his story, and you can't say that the story is even over yet. Cornelia was directly descended from Bilali and said that Muslims had to practice in secret back then, so who knows how long it lasted after him—but Bilali never hid anything, he even taught Islam to his kids. The historian who wrote that Bilali prayed three times a day didn't know what he was talking about, said Cornelia, "because nobody was there to witness him praying before the sun came up or at the end of the night, and those people weren't Muslim so they had no idea."

We talked about his writing. She said his thirteen-page book was at first thought to be a plantation record, but were "actually the teachings of an old man he knew in Africa" and still available at the archives in Athens.

I asked her about the legend that Bilali was buried with a Qur'an. She didn't know about that and had never heard of him owning one; where would he have gotten it? When he was brought across the ocean in the bottom of a boat with his hands shackled, did he have a Qur'an on him? Maybe he was a hafiz, she considered, and transcribed the Qur'an in America. But she did know that he had prayer beads and rugs.

"There was a great deal of Islamic history in Georgia," she said. "Elijah Muhammad was born in Georgia, did you know that?" I nodded. "But did you know," she asked, "that there are white Muslims too?"

It was Cornelia that told me I could rent a bike from behind her son's trailer. Five dollars would get me one for the whole day. "Find one that fits your frame," she said. There was something to walking all night down a country road and then riding a bike all over Sapelo Island that seemed a big Fuck You to the people paying for Bally's memberships so they could walk nowhere and ride bikes that don't move. I had a map of the island showing where Behavior Cemetery was but it didn't help much so I went up and down the same dirt roads, passed the same garbage dump twice and scared the buzzards each time. Even if I found the cemetery, I wasn't sure that I'd find Bilali Mohammad; Cornelia said he left Sapelo Island for Darien as an old man and may have died there.

When I finally spotted tombstones through the palm trees I parked my rented bike and walked. The cemetery was surrounded by a fence. I decided to respect the barbed wire and recited al-Fatiha for the souls. When I rode back to the docks, thinking that after the ferry I'd have to walk all the way back to Darien, I met up with a man who had come to the island to work on people's air conditioners. He said he'd drive me the eleven miles, so I guess good behavior paid off.

6

Malachi Z. York has been known at times as as-Sayyid al-Imaam Isa al-Haadi al-Mahdi, Chief Black Eagle, Chief Black Thunderbird, Supreme GrandMaster Nayya, Dr. Malachi Z. York-El 33°/720° ©™, Malachi Zodoq York-El, Supreme Being of This Day and Time and Imperial Grand Potentate, an extraterrestrial from the planet Rizq (in Illyuwn, the 19th Galaxy) whose father was assassinated in a conspiracy between Hosni Mubarak and Mu'ammar Qadhafi and whose grandfather was the Sudanese Mahdi... now he's just Dwight York #17911-054, tossing salad for serial killers in an orange jumpsuit.

The story began in 1967 when York founded Ansaar Pure Sufi in Brooklyn. He changed its name to the Nubian Islamic Hebrews (Ansaru Allah Community) in 1969. His followers loitered on New York subways wearing white robes and turbans, handing out fliers that denounced W.D. Fard as an agent for both the Nazis and CIA. York even had a paramilitary unit called the SOI (Swords of Islam). After Bilal Philips' exposure of the group in his book *The Ansar Cult* and a rumored confrontation with Louis Farrakhan's enforcers, York took the money and skated. He moved to Georgia, paid $975,000 for 476 acres in rural Putnam County and reformed his hustle from the safety of a protected fortress. To get the Moozlems off his back he stripped the cult of its old Ansar style—the new product would blend Native American and ancient Egyptian aesthetics with Fardesque tales of Motherplanes and distant galaxies. Wearing a feathered headdress one day and costumed as King Tut the next, York filled his compound (now called "Tama Re") with forty-foot tall pyramids and gaudy sphinxes but also claimed descent from the Yamassee of the Creek Nation and said that he came to Earth on a small drone plane called SHAM that had been launched from a larger ship called Markabat or Nibiru. I'm not sure how it all gelled together but the old Ansars bought it and stuck with their man. The group was renamed the Nuwaubian Nation of Moors and later the Yamassee Native American Moors of the Creek Nation. Meanwhile Malachi's son Jacob York (also known as Yaquwb Abdullah Muhammad) made a name for himself in the music business as executive producer for Junior Mafia, Lil' Kim and Cam'Ron.

It looked like business was alright until local hospitals noticed several births by underage girls from Tama Re, some as young as eleven, all refusing to name the father. Then the police received letters from Tama Re that sparked what has been called the biggest child abuse case in Georgia history.

In May 2002, over one hundred state and federal agents ambushed

Malachi Z. York outside the Milledgeville K-Mart. He was arrested and indicted on seventy-four counts of child molestation, twenty-nine counts of aggravated child molestation, one count of rape, four counts of statutory rape, two counts of sexual exploitation of a minor, five counts of enticing a child for indecent purposes, and one count of influencing a witness. The youngest victim was four years old. York pleaded guilty and was sentenced to one-hundred-and-thirty-five years in prison.

I took a bus to Roanoke, Virginia to meet up with my friend Samia who'd let me crash at her Virginia Tech dorm and drive us down to Tama Re. Samia was Sudanese and had grown up in Saudi, where she was good friends with one of Bilal Philips' daughters, who'd listen to headphones under her hijab during class. Samia was in D.C. on 9/11; she saw the plane pass overhead so close she could see the nails in its wings. When it crashed into the Pentagon, she said, everything around her shook.

We left for Georgia early in the morning and Samia got us a room in Madison around midnight. Before leaving the hotel the next day we stocked up on free muffins, juice and little boxes of cereal. It was only twenty miles or so to Eatonton. We arrived at Tama Re a little after eleven and were stopped at the front gate by a security guard who said the place wasn't open.

"I'm doing research for an article," I told him from the car, "and would like to talk to a representative of the community."

"You can talk to me," he said.

"I'm doing an investigation of W.D. Fard, and—"

"Well, for him you should talk to the Nation of Islam."

"I'm looking for everyone's perspectives... you know, the Five Percenters say one thing, Warith Deen says something else and I know that Dr. York portrayed Fard as being a double agent—"

"I'm sorry, sir. We're not open."

"When will you be open?"

"One."

"We'll see you at one then." As we left he got on his walkie-talkie.

With two hours to kill we drove down to Milledgeville to see the K-Mart parking lot where York was seized by the SWAT teams. Then we found the Uncle Remus Museum, though it was closed. Out in front they had a statue of Brer Rabbit. Samia and I walked around the museum's backyard and I spotted a big rock on the ground with sign reading, "BLACK STONE FOUND IN PUTNAM COUNTY... POSSIBLY AN ASTEROID." Since I may never see the other black stone, I kissed this one.

We drove back to Eatonton, where another security guard told us that the day's tour had been cancelled. "But we were just here and he said to come back at one," I said. He said he was sorry but the tour was cancelled. Samia got out of the car and said that we had come a long ways just to check out the place and he again said he was sorry but couldn't help us. I told him that I was writing on the Nuwaubians.

"You should go to our website," he said.

"Sir, I feel that the true measure of a group isn't what their website says but how they treat you at the front gate."

"Well, I don't know what to tell you." With all the ancient Egypt stuff they had, Samia told them that she was legit Sudanese and wanted to see their pyramids but it was nothing doing. Then a car leaving the compound stopped at the gate. The driver told the guard that he was going to Madison and the guard nodded.

We gave it one more try. I pulled Samia's car up to the front gate and got out to talk to the guard.

"Who's running the place?" I asked him.

"Excuse me?"

"York's not here, so who's in charge?"

"I can't tell you that, sir." Then a stocky man got off his riding lawn-mower and walked up to us looking tough.

"MOVE YOUR CAR!"

"I'm trying to talk to this guard here, I'm doing research on the Nuwaubians and Master Fard and—"

"MOVE YOUR CAR, YOU'RE BLOCKING THE GATE!" He looked like he wanted to do something. "MOVE YOUR CAR, SIR. NOW!" We got back in and pulled out.

7

Chicago is going to be your new Mecca.

—Noble Drew Ali

But since Master Fard fled the Motor City for the Windy City with police trouble on his back, Five Percenters referred to Detroit as D-Mecca and Chicago as C-Medina. I hit Chicago first, getting off the bus around one or two in the morning. I didn't have much of an idea where I was walking but ended up at the same old Thomas Jefferson fountain. And then I saw that I was on holy Wabash Avenue.

The Shriners' huge Medinah Temple was built at 600 North Wabash in 1912 and is now registered as a historic landmark; an even decade later, America's first Ahmadiyya mission was established at 4448 South Wabash (now named Masjid Al-Sadiq after its founder, Dr. Mufti Muhammad Sadiq). When T.H.E.M. in his turn fled Detroit for Chicago, he and Clara and the kids moved to 5830 South Wabash. For what I was into, it may have been the most cosmically significant street in North America.

So I got to where 600 N. Wabash should have been and came to a massive brick building covered with arabesques and arches, and topped with copper domes on the corners—and a big "BLOOMINGDALES" splashed across the side. I went around and found the main entrance to the store surrounded by Arabic shahadahs and geometric forms and it looked like the front of a mosque in Isfahan, except for the alarmed glass doors listing the store hours and lit-up dinnerware on display in the windows.

I kept walking north until the neighborhoods got worse and more and more characters came at me. I was offered some things and asked for some other things and then a dude who looked like he hadn't slept in a few years jumped out of nowhere in a dirty Pepsi t-shirt, yelling that he was too tired to think and he had no thumbs: "I GOT NO THUMBS MAN, I WAS BORN THAT WAY!" He held out his hands for my inspection and he turned out to be legitimately thumbless. He kept going his way and I went mine.

All those guys seemed to crawl out of sight as the rest of Chicago woke up. I found my way to North Milwaukee, walked a long way and bought an orange juice at Burger King just to rent a place to sit... but when I finally got out of my booth I spotted a framed cityscape drawing by Wesley Willis, dated 1992! He had drawn that Burger King and the taco place across the street with CTA buses driving past, and now it hung on the wall in a cracked glass frame.

I continued on N. Milwaukee to find the Buddy Collective where Rogue Nation would be playing as part of the Total Liberation tour. Their singer Omar X is a Muslim vegan who thanks Allah SWT in his liner notes. The band collectively dedicates their album *The Sedition* to "the children of Palestine, Afghanistan and Iraq who are resisting the foreign occupation of their homes." Rogue Nation's label, Uprising Records, is run by the guy from Vegan Reich who himself embraced Islam.

The show was supposed to start at noon but there were no signs of life, so I kept on moving. For the rest of the day all I could do was walk and when I couldn't walk anymore I hopped on a CTA to find the grave of Noble Drew Ali.

8

The suburb of Alsip is home to a lot of ghost and poltergeist stories, perhaps because so much of the town is occupied by graveyards. I headed for Burr Oak Cemetery, the biggest one, and resting place to Noble Drew Ali (peace be upon his mention) who had heard Allah's voice in the forests of North Carolina and emerged to save his Moorish people. On the long walk until finding a hole in the rusty mesh fence I thought of how he may have gone to Chicago due to the presence of a troublemaker at his Canaanite Temple in New Jersey, a half-Russian/half-Syrian silk salesman named Abdul Wali Farrad Mohammed Ali... which made it interesting that Chicago police martyred Noble Drew Ali in 1929 and Wallace Dodd Fard surfaced in Detroit in 1930...

It was another big cemetery and I wasn't sure that I could find Noble Drew Ali before dark. Down the lanes I spotted a parked van that could have been the undertaker's but with the luck I seemed to have in these situations, I could expect it to belong to Ali's great-grand-nephew.

Behind the steering wheel sat a middle-aged black man. I asked if the cemetery had a directory so I could find an individual's plot and he said "Buddy, the place is closed and I'm just here to look out for people like you." Then he asked who I was looking for. I said Noble Drew Ali and he took a look at my Five Percenter t-shirt with crescent and star, big #7 and the words "IN THE NAME OF ALLAH AND JUSTICE." He nodded and said he'd take me to it.

We stood at a flat plaque with Noble Drew Ali's face on it, with a 7 and 2 shaking hands. I sang a Fatiha over his bones and sang it for everyone else in that yard too, and even the ones in nearby Lincoln Cemetery (which included the man known as "Noble Drew Ali Reincarnated") and Glenwood over in Thornton where Elijah and Sister Clara slept.

After I left, the undertaker closed the front gate even though I had come in through a hole in the fence. My feet were still killing me. I rode the CTA back downtown and didn't know how I'd spend the rest of the night until remembering my unlimited bus pass—so I hobbled to the Greyhound station and by midnight had fallen asleep on a shuttle bound for Detroit.

The Moorish Science Temple had a story in which Noble Drew Ali met with Woodrow Wilson at the White House and demanded the return of his people's flag. The President's counsels opened a big vault and went through all sorts of old flags until finding the red Moorish National... and then Woodrow Wilson told Noble Drew Ali that his people would never follow him, that it'd be like "putting a pair of pants on a mule." The details in these stories change as they resurface in new places. Elsewhere it was Roosevelt, Fard and putting pants on an elephant.

It was in Detroit, which Henry Miller called a "Mecca of futilitarian salesmen," that the Master had been seized by police outside his hotel room for questioning in the blood sacrifice of James Smith. Smith was bashed in the head with a rear-wheel axle, then laid out on an altar and stabbed in the heart. It all went down in the home of Robert Harris, who claimed he had Smith's consent to kill him because in death he would become "savior of the world."

Harris, Fard and Fard's minister Ugan Ali were all thrown into the psychopathic ward at Receiving Hospital—Fard had, after all, told interrogators that he was the Supreme Being on Earth while Harris claimed to be King of the Order of Islam. Harris was found unfit for trial and committed to Ionia State Hospital for the Criminally Insane. Ugan Ali was released after agreeing to give any information he had that could help destroy the group. With disciples protesting outside the hospital and police fearing a race riot, Fard was released on the condition that he'd leave Detroit forever.

Of course he didn't; at least not right away. They got him again a few months later for "disturbing the peace." During his second round in the interrogation room, Fard confessed that the mosque was just a get-rich-quick scheme. The cops let him go with a more serious understanding that he'd never be seen in Detroit again.

That was 1933 and this was 2004 and for better or worse, I sat on a bus saying *labbayk Allahumma labbayk* to myself.

9

One of the NOI offshoots claimed to possess a book entitled *Wallace Fard Muhammad vs. Albert Einstein*, which contained a transcript of their debate at a Detroit radio station.

According to the group, there was no information in the book regarding its author, copyright or a means of contacting the publisher (Malik Publishing Inc). As the story goes, their copy of the book came from a sister who had gotten it from a brother who told her that it was taken from a phonograph recording that was owned by a ninety-year-old man who had since died.

The meeting of Fard and Einstein was said to take place in early 1933 at WCNB Detroit 1440 AM, on a program called "Religion in Brief" with host Keith Brandon.

KEITH BRANDON: Gentlemen, it is a great pleasure to have you two here tonight as guests on Religion in Brief. It serves us here at WCNB, as well as the public, as a great opportunity to probe in activities and lifestyles, philosophies and religious outlooks of you two gentlemen who are contributing much energy to certain sections of our nation. Mr. Einstein, to our scientific advancement in the Principles of Relativity; and Mr. Fard to the minority of our nation with what I've heard you say on many occasions in the past, "Knowledge of Self." Mr. Einstein, could you give our listeners a brief rundown on yourself?

ALBERT EINSTEIN: Yes, I'd be glad to. First, I'd like to say thank you Mr. Brandon for inviting me on your show tonight. I feel comfortable and it is a pleasure to be here. At this stage of my work, I am involved in certain experiments, which cover the scope of "atomic enlightenment" as well as developments for this country in case of nuclear warfare. Second, Mr. Brandon, they refer to me as being a scientist, opening up new channels to the principles of relativity. Now I say, my work includes the science of matter and energy, and of the interaction between the two. Thus, I would rather be known to the world as a theoretical physicist in the mathematical view of relativity.

KEITH BRANDON: Very interesting. Mr. Fard, could you give the listeners a brief rundown on yourself?

W.D. FARD: Salaam-Alaikum. For you, Mr. Brandon, Mr. Einstein and the listeners elsewhere and abroad, my attribute is Fard Muhammad Ibn Alfonso. I extend my thanks first to Allah, God, for enabling me to be here tonight. Your offer, Mr. Brandon, is greatly appreciated by me, may Allah bless you. A little about myself: I am SON OF MAN, as it is written; seeking to save that which is lost, and restore again that which has gone astray.

KEITH BRANDON: Thank you gentlemen. We'll be right back in 60 seconds.

Einstein and Fard go on to discuss Spinoza (Fard reminds both Einstein and Keith Brandon that Spinoza was a "mere mortal"). The show ends with Einstein asking Fard if he speaks Arabic.

"Would you know how to say my name in Arabic, Mr. Muhammad?"

"Yes, in Arabic you would say *Yacub!*"

Then Keith Brandon jumps in and thanks everyone for listening.

The transcript has been circulated online, along with a letter that Master Fard wrote T.H.E.M. from the "South West Part of N. America," on December 18th, 1933 at 4:00 a.m. The letter first reprimands Elijah for his "terrible mistake and unofficial movements." Fard then instructs Elijah to study his assignments, go to Milwaukee and inquire about a Joe Bey at 8ᵗʰ and Center Street—interesting in that Bey was the usual surname for members of Noble Drew Ali's Moorish Science Temple.

The letter is sprinkled with grammatical and spelling errors. "Have patient," it says.

Fard tells Elijah, just look at me.

"I have all the hard luck," he says, "and confronting more hard luck by my own people; don't you see they are poison [sic] by the devil and so badly poison that they can't see me walking among them every day and eating with them."

The Master reminds Elijah to "stop in these little towns on your way home and leave little wisdom everywhere." You are doing fine, he says. And he gives Elijah some homework: if light travels 186,000 miles per second, and the sun is 93,000,000 miles from Earth, how long does it take for sunlight to reach us? Fard's hint: divide the distance by the speed.

"I shall have big time with you when I see you," he writes, "but now do not be bashfull [sic] to study, for the wise always go to the bottom to secure real cure; write to me every day and tell me all about your study."

The letter ends, "I am going with you, from W.D. Fard."

The uncle of Mr. W.D. Fard lived in the wilderness of North America and he lived other than his own self, therefore, his pulse beat seventy-eight times per minute and this killed him in forty-five years of age. How many times did his pulse beat in forty-five years?
—*The Supreme Wisdom Lessons of Master Fard Muhammad*

Looked to me like Fard was genuinely trying to uplift his Moozlems; why else would he assign them math problems? Elijah quit school in fourth grade but Fard had him at thirty years old dividing out the time it takes light to reach Earth. And it was pretty fatherly how Fard could begin his letter scolding Elijah only to reassure him at the end.

I called the NOI offshoot and spoke to a sister who said that they had obtained the letter from Elijah's brother, "Supreme Minister" John Muhammad. She then told me a neat story about Master Fard and John: when the Savior left Detroit in 1933, he made a point of giving each of his followers a copy of the Qur'an. Fard put a picture of himself in the copy that he gave to his personal typist, who happened to be John's wife. John became upset that he wasn't also given a picture so he went to Fard and asked why.

Fard told John Muhammad that he didn't need a picture since he'd remember him; his wife needed the picture because she'd forget. And as Allah would have it, years and years later she abandoned the Nation of Islam while John stayed strong. Even at ninety-some-odd years young, he'd still bear witness that there was no god but Allah in the form of Master Fard Muhammad.

I asked if their newspaper, *Muhammad Speaks* was an official NOI publication, since Warith Deen used to call his version *Bilalian News* and Louis Farrakhan put out *The Final Call*. She laughed and said that the Nation was so divided, who knew what was "official" anymore? But *Muhammad Speaks* wasn't affiliated with Warith Deen's Sunni Muslims, Louis Farrakhan's NOI, Silas Muhammad's LFNOI, Royall Jenkins' UNOI or even Supreme Minister John Muhammad ("we disagree with his claim to be a minor prophet"), as a Muslim needed no leader besides Allah.

We talked a little about Warith Deen Mohammed; she called him a hypocrite and blamed his Sunni swerve on resentment over Elijah not always being there for him as a boy.

10

It seemed that all of D-Mecca's holy sites were gone: Fard's Muslims originally held meetings at 3408 Hastings Street but a freeway ran through it now, and the original Muhammad's Mosque #1 was at 11525 Linwood but the building had since been torn down. A "Masjid Wali Muhammad" stood at 11529 Linwood so I figured I'd check that out.

As I limped down the sidewalk past a cluster of middle-aged black working-class heroes, one looked at my Five Percenter shirt and said peace, so I said peace back and then he asked if I was Five-Percent. I said I had built with them and he told me I could find those guys building down on Jefferson all the time. I walked up Woodward, took a bus and then walked some more until finding Linwood Avenue. In front of the Linwood Citgo station a black street sign read "Honorable Elijah Muhammad Boulevard." From there it wasn't too far to the mosque. I put on my jalab and kufi and went up the brother in front who sported a suit with long necktie and asked him if this was a Nation mosque or Warith Deen mosque... he said it was a Warith Deen and I went on in. The actual mosque part of the place was upstairs. I put my shoes on the shelves and went in to make two rakats out of respect for the building... then I was back downstairs with some old codgers asking them about the mosque, whether it was named after any of Elijah's sons or grandsons and one of the guys said no, it was named after "an old Muslim of a long time ago." I got us all to talking about W.D. Fard. Somebody said that a guy showed up in California claiming he was Fard, "but he was too young to really be him."

A flyer on the wall announced listings for Warith Deen's radio show. It said that in Detroit you could catch him on 1440 AM.

That night I rode a bus to Milwaukee (known as Cream City to the Five Percenters), just for a place to sleep. Once we got there I waited around for a minute and got on the next bus to Chicago.

11

Back in C-Medina on the morning of July 15th, my limping was really bad but had a rhythm that seemed to threaten normal people on their way to work. It was also my third consecutive day wearing the Five Percenter shirt. A truck driver at a red light yelled "PEACE, GOD!" as I passed him. I turned to look and he gave me the peace sign.

Beyond a few scattered Allah Schools, Five Percenters really don't have anything like mosques or temples, so finding Gods in most cities is a matter of luck. To me it fit with the attributes of a Poor Righteous Teacher: a physical house has its advantages but also leads to an Executive Committee, a Board of Trustees, community elections and sermons centered around giving donations and none of that offers anything to a God who can build just as easily on a street corner or in a public park.

I was going down Lake Street when a God saw my shirt and gave peace.

I returned it and turned to keep walking but he asked where my sword was. I asked him what he meant and he built on Master Fard's *Supreme Wisdom Lessons* where it said the Devil had to study for thirty-five to fifty years before calling himself a Muslim Son and wearing the flag, but he'd have to add a sword to it. "That goes back to Muhammad," he told me, "you know—the *original* Muhammad. It means that if you reveal your secrets, I can cut your head off." But then he said that I wasn't the devil, I was a righteous so-called Caucasian. He said he'd never call another man the devil because we all had that potential in us. "I can be the Devil," he explained, "or I can be God. You can be the Devil or you can be a Righteous Man." I nodded and he kept adding on. "The only reason you can't be God is because you didn't make me. I made you, you were grafted from *me*. You're the living germ." He asked if I knew my degree.

"Wisdom Equality," I answered.

"No, that's your *physical* degree. Do you know the degree of your people?"

"Can't say that I do."

"Six thousand years."

"Yacub's People," I said with a smile.

"True indeed." Then he warned me about wearing the flag out in C-Medina since there were Gods that would quite literally take my head off. "There's a lot of science going on here, but also a lot of chaos and confusion… I've got to watch my own back out here because of some so-called Five Percenters that are really Jive-Pretenders living savage." He said that within the Five Percent existed another eighty-five percent that were still not applying their knowledge—the real Gods were only five percent of the five percent.

He said that was how they were in Brooklyn, Brooklyn had a few warriors. I told him I had only built in Harlem and the Gods there were nothing but peace. "True indeed," he replied. "That's how it's supposed to be. That's why I build like a Mecca God, not a Medina God. Who'd you build with out there?"

"Azreal." Then the God flashed a big smile. You can't say Azreal's name to someone who knows him without getting a smile out of it. Then I told the God of my life's quest to find the truth of Master Fard and he said that was peace too but maybe Fard was only a mystery or "spook-god" and he may have only been a face for Elijah to use in spreading the message, "just like Shakespeare was only a face for the Moors to tell their stories."

"Why chase after a mystery?" he asked. Why chase after a dead end?

Before parting ways we introduced ourselves (his attribute turned out to be Jura Shaheed Allah) and exchanged math. He said he'd call me later and cautioned me again about sporting the flag, mentioning one C-Medina God in particular who was giving out warnings and causing lots of trouble. "It's a dangerous place," said Jura Shaheed Allah. "Watch yourself out here."

Then I got on a CTA bus to find America's first Ahmadiyya Anjuman, a worn-out eighty-year-old mosque near the southern end of Wabash Avenue. Two blocks from here, Master Fard had been arrested for preaching just two blocks away, on September 25, 1933. The next morning a judge let him off, citing his right to free speech, and Fard left for Los Angeles.

I put my kufi and jalab on but the mosque was closed. An elderly African-American man walked by and asked what I'd call the things I had on.

"This is a *jalab*," I replied.

"What about your hat?"

"It's called a *kufi*."

"Really? I thought it was called something else."

"Depends on where you go," I told him. "In Pakistan it might be called a *topi*."

"Oh. Well, I'm not a Muslim but as-salamu alaikum."

"Wa-alaikum as-salam."

Half an hour later I was walking back towards downtown when the driver of a fire engine stopped and waved me over.

"Where you coming from?" he asked. He was an archetypal old Irish fireman.

"Buffalo, New York," I told him. He looked at me like he had thought of something.

"Get in." So I ran around and climbed aboard to sit with a mess of firemen and they all agreed that I would have been dead if I kept walking around the bad part of town. "We'd rather pick you up now," said the old guy, "than ten minutes from now." He added that I had the fresh-out-of-town look all over me, with my big backpack and disoriented expression. They dropped me off at Chinatown and said the train there would take me safely back downtown near the bus station.

Between that Five Percenter warning me not to wear his flag and these firemen whisking me out of Chicago's South Side, I figured that Allah had put some kind of protective hedge around me. I wasn't one to push it so I got on a bus and bailed for St. Paul, Minnesota. The next day I'd sit in Rice Park under a life-sized statue of F. Scott Fitzgerald and watch two kids throw each other's shoes into the fountain. A round white-haired man in a green polo shirt came up and put his arm around Scott like an old pal, saying it was a shame since Scott hated St. Paul and now he'd be stuck there forever as a dumb monument. I asked him why Scott hated St. Paul so much and he said that Scott saw everyone there as a bunch of rich snobs and they thought of him as the college dropout and town drunk. I told him how in Key West around that time they'd be having a big Hemingway festival with writing competitions, look-alike contests and boxing matches but where was the Fitzgerald festival?

"Screw Hemingway," said the guy.

I walked to Zelda's Café at the public library and tried to figure where I'd go next with my unlimited Greyhound pass. The St. Paul's station had a 4:40 bus to Seattle, which the Five Percenters called Morocco.

I prayed a silent Fajr on the bus en route to Fargo, North Dakota, which I didn't think had a new Five Percenter name. Just sitting in my seat with hands folded over my stomach I'd nod my head up and down and that was my prayer. I wasn't clean. You can't really make wudhu on a bus, unless the wet-naps in the restroom count as water (and even then, I wouldn't snort them up my nose). Another interesting detail: for someone who barely prayed at all, I seemed to make more Fajrs than anything else.

I'd never seen anything like the mountains and wild buffalo of Montana, but crossing it on the I-90 made me feel closer to home. . . I knew a girl in Syracuse, New York who took the 90 to work every day, so I knew we'd be on the same road at the same time, just three thousand miles apart.

12

We got to Morocco around 7:30 a.m., some thirty-nine hours after leaving St. Paul. I hoped I'd have time to walk around town and check it out—I even had the address of the local Jerrahi order in one of my notebooks—but a bus for West Asia (San Francisco) was leaving in just ten minutes so I hopped on it.

I transferred buses again in Portland, home to W.D. Fard's alleged "Fred Dodd" years that we'll never know much about. Got to West Asia around nine and walked around until I was limping again… walked from downtown to Haight Ashbury, which turned out to be a mess of trendy dumps and even had a Gap on the corner. I called my friend Keith who was doing the same Greyhound thing and had ended up in San Francisco. We met up and then had dinner with Jawad Ali, co-creator of e-zine *MuslimWakeUp*. He took us to Rotee, whose menu was full of witty comments ("In Pakistan, breathtaking legs or breasts usually refer to chicken tikkas… relieve your conscience by trying a whole leg or breast that is lightly marinated in spices and lemon juice barbequed to perfection.").

Not only did Jawad pay for dinner, but he let us crash at his place, just as I had again reached that point of road-weariness where access to a shower and a couch to sleep on were like gold.

The next day Jawad drove us to the Alternative Tentacles headquarters where we met up with Jesse Townley and made off with a load of swag—hats, shirts, coffee mugs and AT work jackets. Jesse gave me Wesley's *Rush Hour* CD, thought to be his best besides the *Greatest Hits* comps. I also picked up the Crucifucks' *Our Will be Done* at Jesse's recommendation. The Crucifucks guy had a voice. The last song on the CD, "The Savior," was about Qadhafi's baby that Reagan killed.

As we drove to Oakland Keith spotted a sign reading "BLACK MUSLIM BAKERY" so we had to check it out. Inside the walls were covered with huge portraits of Elijah Muhammad along with newspaper clippings and pictures of someone else that I think was a local leader. I took a picture of Keith and Jawad standing in front of the beverages, a giant W.D. Fard looming from the wall behind them.

We sat in front of the place with our tofu burgers—the Nation encouraged healthy eating, give them that—and Jawad told Keith the story of how an NOI old-timer once pointed him out to Louis Farrakhan as an example of Master Fard's skin tone.

Then we went to the next stop of the Total Liberation tour down on Telegraph. On the way we found another Your Black Muslim Bakery and this time I got a big bag of granola for five dollars. It'd come in handy since we'd arrive at iMusicast to find a mess of punk kids with vegan patches on their bags and t-shirts with stuff about non-human liberation. As they passed around my granola bag I learned that they were all in the bands that would be playing that night. I asked if Rogue Nation would be there and they said probably, as far as they knew. I was concerned because the tour's website didn't have them slated to be there but they were advertised on the flyer... but then again, the flyer said the show would start at noon and here we were at six just standing around the parking lot doing nothing...

The show finally started around eight with a kid in cut-off fatigues on stage talking about how blowing up a McDonald's was cool but there were other ways to liberate human-animals. The audience was basically comprised of the various bands. Then a white punk guy with tattoos on his neck came up and started rapping. Made for an odd scene, with him trying to get these dozen or so vegan kids to throw their hands in the air and such, especially since he rapped about Islam in a few songs. Then in a heartfelt spoken-word he cried of having "the same blood type as Magic Johnson" and not being able to do anything with his girlfriend because she was afraid to touch him.

The guy's name was Naj.One, aka Foeknawledge. I went up to him after his set to buy one of his DIY CDs and ask if I had really heard right about the Islam-Allah stuff. He said he was Muslim and asked if I was, we exchanged salams and then he introduced me to three or four other Muslims, one of them a rotund white guy with bushy blond beard. I was quick to explain my Five Percenter shirt by saying I had built with everyone from them to the Sunnis to the Shi'as—then Naj stepped in and said that he was Shi'a and I replied that I was all about Shi'as, I had built with them in Muharram. Naj said that someone had stolen his turba at the last show; my first reaction was to say "Who steals a fuckin' turba?" but I guess it was in his bag and someone had stolen the bag. I gave him my turba from the grave of Imam Ridha.

I asked a girl who looked to be one of the tour's organizers whether Rogue Nation would be playing. She said she didn't know since nobody had heard from them. If they showed up she said she'd love to pencil them in but at the moment it didn't seem promising. I guess if things had any more structure and reliability than that, it wouldn't be punk.

There was no vacuum of Muslim voices, however, as Amir Sulaiman and Abdul Shahid took the stage. Amir tore the house down with his spoken-word piece "Dead Man Walking" where he spewed that he knew about "shahadah, Qur'an and homemade bombs" and then Abdul Shahid (voted "best unsigned MC" by readers of hip-hop magazine *The Source*) took the mic and gave props to the people of Palestine, Bosnia and on down the list...

Naj.One's real name (or at least his convert name) was Harun. I told him that it was kind of surprising to see all these Muslim rappers at a vegan punk show and he told me about the Taliyah al-Mahdi movement: "We're getting ready for the Time," he said. "We're all Shi'a, we're all vegan and we take kung-fu and it's pretty... *yeah*." He seemed unsure of how much he should tell me and could read the shock on my face.

"Where is it based out of?" I asked.

"We're everywhere."

13

> There's a million ways that we are lost and found.
> —Time in Malta, "The Wayfarer"

In terms of the Islamic experience, Maria in Denver could be my female parallel; after converting she went hardcore and wore not only regular hijab, but the full niqab, with her whole face covered and even matching gloves. But you can only keep that up for so long before burning out on it, and here we were at a Buddhist stupa.

(Another thing about Maria that resonated with me: she once rented a house from the nephew of seven-time NWA heavyweight champion Harley Race.)

We left Denver with her husband Gabriel, who I kept thinking of as a Five Percenter because white Five Percenters were always named after angels, and their son Bilal, the coolest three-and-a-half-year old ever, who used thobes for pajamas and was obsessed with trains, four Muslims on our way to a Buddhist stupa… *five*, maybe, since Maria was about seven months pregnant and fetuses were supposed to be Muslim too, making sujdah in the womb.

I've always had a thing with Buddhism, even as an extreme Sunni. During my stint in Pakistan I wanted to check out the Buddhist ruins in Taxila but never had the chance. I was diving into the Qur'an every day and found the same idea that occurs to everyone at some point: since Allah sent prophets to every nation, maybe Buddha, Confucius and other holy figures outside the Semitic world were the appointed messengers for their people. I'd ask scholars about it but they'd shrug me off with "Allah knows best" and try to get me to learn my Arabic.

Salman Rushdie once wrote that Islam was the least "huggable" religion; in comparison, Buddhism looks pretty huggable. The stupa's official handout described it as a "monument to peace, kindness and compassion in our world." I've never heard anything in Islam described that way—it's all about serving Allah, following orders and spreading the proper system. In Islam, peace and kindness are meant as byproducts of obeying laws. In cases when compassion disagrees with faith, compassion usually takes a backseat. For people like Maria and myself, Buddhism seems to be at the far end of the spiritual spectrum from all the junk that we've put ourselves through. On the back covers of Buddhist books, the baldheaded authors are always smiling like they've found the Big Secret of Eternal Deep-Down Joy… while at Maria's I had been reading *Death & Dying* by Ahmad H. Sakr, PhD, who sneered like he had just beaten Tito Ortiz in the octagon.

So we were walking up the foothills toward this Great Stupa, which looked beautiful when you first saw it from far away, then looked like an alien fort… and as you got closer it looked like a gaudy prize you could win at the carnival. At the bottom of the steps leading to the Great Stupa stood a bowl for offerings with a sheet reading "FINANCIAL DONATIONS ARE A POWERFUL WAY TO MAKE A CONNECTION WITH THE SPIRIT AND VISION OF A SACRED PLACE." People had left a lot of loose change in there but all sorts of other stuff too: beads, watches, visors, keys, two student IDs from the University of Wisconsin—one belonging to a guy and the other to a girl. I wanted to take the guy's ID; you never know when something like that could come in handy.

We went up the steps to the Great Stupa, where I took off my shoes and almost felt like I was at a mosque. I stood in the doorway. From outside I saw maybe a dozen people sitting on mats with their legs crossed and backs straight in front of a giant stone Buddha that was still under construction—the unfinished head was covered in plastic wrap and surrounded by scaffolding. I couldn't go in there—it was like some magnetic repulsion held me outside. So I sat with Gabriel on the steps and said that even if I couldn't handle all the formal trappings of Islam as a "way of life," I had enough in me to still be bothered by statues. With our backs to the stupa we looked out at the mountains and Gabriel noted that we were actually facing qiblah. Mash'Allah that it'd work out that way. Then a couple approaching the stupa stopped and bowed right in front of us. "Don't take it personal," said the man.

Like Time in Malta's Todd Gullion once told me, "with all religions you gotta weed through the crap to get to the jewel." Maybe Islam's jewel was that we had no statues, that I'd never see Muslims contemplating a plaster Muhammad-head.

Bilal circumambulated the Great Stupa a few times and befriended some Buddhists along the way. Then we went down to the gift shop for ice cream. The store must have had thousands of books—the crap you had to weed through, I imagined. There were also posters and gimmicks for sale like a beggar's bowl for sixty dollars. As we sat outside with our Ben & Jerry's and two college boys walked by with their Frappucinos, I was glad for having skipped on the "suggested" ten-dollar donation. The Great Stupa experience had left me feeling great about Islam; but when Bilal ran around the house yelling, "GOD IS A MORON!" I still thought it was funny.

Maria had also taken me to a mosque in Saudi Aurora. On the way we talked smack about Career Progressive Asshole, Farid Esack—Maria had helped him get a speaking engagement and then he sent her the rudest email she had ever gotten.

She had also tried bringing in Career Sufi Asshole, Hamza Yusuf (may Allah SWT elevate his status in this world and the next) but he had some rock-star demands like an outrageous speaking fee, first-class airfare for him and his three bodyguards and a quality hotel. The shaikh's not crashing on anyone's couch.

I didn't know about Hamza Yusuf but I once had dinner with Farid Esack, in December 2002 at a mutual friend's house in Washington, D.C. I was sitting between Farid and Farid's buddy Junaid, who after hearing my conversion story replied, "So you're like John Walker, then." Junaid with a smart-ass smirk said something in Urdu to Farid and they laughed like junior-high kids. Farid then turned to me, struggling hard to keep a straight face, and asked "Michael, why are you Shi'a?" No sooner had the words left his mouth than they both erupted in giggles. Earlier I had told Junaid about my interest in Imam Husain, and Junaid must have just told Farid, and for some reason Farid must have found it hilarious. They kept it up through dinner, laughing to each other and going back and forth in Urdu even when others at the table asked that they stick to English on my behalf. Since coming to Islam in 1994 I have sat in on many, many all-Urdu conversations—and never once did I feel uncomfortable or suspicious that negative things were being said about me until I sat with Farid Esack.

Farid at the dinner table is like Farid in his books: he pontificates, he gets a little wordy, he comes off as well-intentioned but incredibly arrogant. The man can't speak as anything but a lecturing academic and you can tell that he loves it. But in this "Battle for the Soul of Islam" and "the Wake of 9/11," Farid may be one of the good guys. I wish that little egomaniac all the luck in the world.

14

Instead of her gray hooded sweatshirt reading, "THIS IS WHAT A RADICAL MUSLIM FEMINIST LOOKS LIKE," at the mosque Maria wore a black abaya. I wore my jalab with an Alternative Tentacles ski cap. She entered through her door, I went through mine. Then I found more of my inner Sunni coming out. During our congregational Maghrib prayer I realized that with all the radical changes of the progressive movement, eventually some-one will lead a prayer in English—and I want none of it. Might be for the wrong reasons, though: I like not knowing what the imam says.

When the imam recites, I don't want to think about the meaning—I can't cloud up the moment with intellectualization or the chance that he'd say something I could question—just let me relax my brain and feel like the words are holy, that Arabic is so brilliant that no other language could capture the thoughts of Allah Subhanahu Wa Ta'Ala... *Subhanahu Wa Ta'Ala*, shit I don't even know what that means because Allah's message is so over my head. I know that the first word means something like "glory" but it can't just be glory, it's some variance of glory that you can't express in English, right?

When I recite al-Fatiha in a mosque or graveyard I don't think the words in English. With Fatiha's literal meaning concealed in words that I don't understand, the dot under the *ba* in *bismillah* takes on all the wisdom and wonder of Allah's whole universe. You can say that I exoticize the Arabic, but most of the Islamic world does the same thing. 75% of Muslims don't speak the language, but they pray in it. Allah doesn't speak Urdu.

So keep it in Arabic or I'll leave disappointed.

I walked down to Ogden Theatre on Colfax and stood among the cool kids waiting to see Sonic Youth. Sometimes while standing in line for a show you can spot that one desperately lonely guy who's not there to see a band or anything, he just wants to be around people... but being there, surrounded by all the people he'd want for his friends or girlfriends, he has no idea of how to talk to them so he just leans against the wall with his hands in his pockets and hopes that it's the night for a miraculous change in his life. For some reason I saw myself as that guy for that night. Not sure why; sometimes you just choose to be sad.

In two days, Time in Malta would be in town opening for Sick of it All. Time in Malta's singer Todd Gullion grew up punk in the 80s, veered towards political punk in the 90s, did the whole punk-house thing, eventually went straightedge, began studying religion and took shahadah. The band's album *Alone with the Alone* was named after Henri Corbin's *Alone with the Alone: Creative Imagination in the Sufism of Ibn 'Arabi*.

The same night of the show, Asma Gull Hasan would be downtown signing copies of *Why I am a Muslim*. She called and said that Jawad had told her to read my article about hitting on Muslim girls at the 2003 ISNA convention.

"So I'm like, why wasn't he hitting on *me?*"

I didn't know that she was there. She then told me that her booth was the one with big photos of her mom standing beside George W. Bush.

15

Afternoon of July 28th I went to the museum where Maria worked. Between the outerspace stuff and wildlife stuff it ended up being my big ayat-Allah (sign of God) for the day. I was heading back to her house when Todd Gullion called and said he was in town so I walked over to the Bluebird on Colfax to meet him and the band. Todd and I went to an Ethiopian restaurant across the street where we talked about the chance that Prophet Muhammad lost his mantle on the way from Mecca to Medina—before the hijra he was just a pacifist street preacher, almost a seventh-century Quraish hippie, but once he arrived in Medina and became an authority figure it all went downhill with the Qurayza massacre and marrying a child and all of that. If Muhammad was really human and could experience everything that humans go through, why couldn't he let the power corrupt him? The moral of the story could lead to an Islamic context for anarchism: not even prophets can govern their fellow man.

Todd looked at it in the most beautiful way: that maybe, if Muhammad did in fact fall, it was only to turn attention back towards Allah. Since Jesus was so mythologized into a perfect life and nobody knew of the mistakes he had made, it was easy to prop him up as divine—but knowing the full atrocity of Muhammad-as-Statesman allowed us to keep him human.

Then we talked about the Taliyah al-Mahdi, those kung-fu vegan Shi'as I had run into in Oakland. Todd had some insight on the movement. He said the driving force behind it was a partnership between that Muttaqi kid from Vegan Reich and a yahoodi convert named 'Isa Adam Naziri, who might have been the bass player. Todd said that some of their writings were alright.

Meanwhile:

> These *jihads* do not have to be serious ones either. I daily face a
> *jihad* not to overspend on my shoe budget. Actually, I face a *jihad*
> simply to maintain a shopping budget at all!
> —Asma Gull Hasan, *Why I am a Muslim*

Maria drove me to the Tattered Cover bookstore at 7:00 p.m. The self-described "Muslim Feminist Cowgirl" showed up in a denim skirt-and-jacket ensemble. I thought that she looked like an attorney (turned out she was, with her dad's company).

So she did her thing, basically summarizing the book, telling stories about how kids called her "Asthma" when she was younger.

Asma's a bit of an optimist; I don't know if I can write chapters like "Being American Makes Me a Better Muslim" but at least someone's giving it a shot. She might have been taking it too far: during her talk she described the U.S. as the only country that was helping the world's poor Muslims. Hanging around after the event, I heard her dismiss Afghan freedom movements of the last fifty years as opposing "what they *perceived* as colonialism." I'd later learn that this girl has served as official greeter for Laura Bush at the Denver airport.

She then complained about how she had to do most of her own publicity and promotional stuff, as opposed to someone she knew that had a bigger publisher—

"I guess I'm just a working-class writer," she moaned. I wanted to ask if she had made her books at Kinko's too. Then she drove me in her dad's Mercedes to the family condo, explaining that her parents were at their house in the mountains. "I *am* a princess," she confessed. At fundraising dinners, Dubya would head straight for her mom. And her mom's cousin was Salman Ahmad from Junoon, the biggest rock band in Asia. They played at the wedding of Asma's sister. Asma told me that Salman's mother made him become a doctor first, and then after that he could be a rock star or whatever he wanted.

I played around on the computer while she got dressed for the show—it took Asma so long to find "punk clothes" (which ended up being a pink jacket, white t-shirt with a pink star on it and a matching Louis Vuitton purse) that we missed Time in Malta's entire set but did manage to catch five or six songs by Sick of it All. We stayed in back, by the door. You could kind of tell that it was Asma's first punk show but she seemed to enjoy herself. Then she and her brother-in-law took me and Todd to a coffee shop and we talked for a couple hours. Asma said that she liked George W. Bush because of his "outreach to Muslims," which meant that he hosted Ramadan dinner in the White House.

"I'd rather he skipped the dinner and just stopped bombing people," I told her.

It was an interesting assortment of personalities at our table: we had tattoo-sleeved Todd who toured the country in a rented van opening for Sick of it All, sitting across from Louis Vuitton-sporting Asma Gull Hasan who had been on *O'Reilly Factor*. We all got along fine and I felt like the Beyonder character from Marvel Comics' *Secret Wars* series, who rounded up the superheroes and supervillains and threw them together on a distant world just to watch what would happen.

16

> Singin' Hi Jolly, Hey Jolly, twenty miles a day by golly
> Twenty more before the morning light
> Hi Jolly, hey-I gotta be on my way-I
> told my gal I'd be home by Sunday night
> —"Hi Jolly the Camel Driver," campfire song

Riding through New Mexico, the isolated shantytowns in the shadows of red-brown mountains reminded me of those Afghan refugee settlements on the margins of Islamabad. I pretended that I was all alone in the desert, knowing that I would be soon enough, and that I was an American Berber wearing my t-shirt kifaya with the drawstring from an old pair of sweatpants, hoping to find Colonel Qadhafi out there in his tent writing poems or at least some billboards with giant Qadhafi faces—no people anywhere, just massive painted Qadhafi expressions like Easter Island statues in revolutionary aviator sunglasses staring out at nothing, saying nothing. Qadhafis scattered everywhere guarding the deserts with a father's militant love—surveying the Awbari, the Marzuq, the Ramlat Rabyanah. I was on my way to a graveyard and imagined that the tombstones would have no names—in the desert, even Qadhafi billboards wouldn't need his name on them—and if I came across a lonely tattered holy man out there you know he wouldn't have a name, he's just a marabout, a saint who took himself away from the cities to spare mankind all his old hurt.

I had a chance to call Cihan Kaan when our bus overheated on the way to Flagstaff and pulled over. I spent at least an hour and a half standing beside the I-40 with all the other passengers. Interstate 40 was the road that had swallowed up historic Route 66, which itself had been partly composed of Hi Jolly's camel trails. Cihan asked if I'd find myself in California. I said sure and he said he'd hop on a plane and meet me out there. He had just wrapped up his film and wanted to session with me about a screenplay.

Another bus came to get us and we abandoned the first one. Got on the I-10 at Phoenix and arrived in Quartzsite around midnight. Quartzsite didn't have a Greyhound station, though—its Pilot Travel Center was just a fifteen-minute snack-and-cigarette break so if I got off there I'd have no idea when the next bus was coming.

I asked the lady at the checkout where I could find Hi Jolly's grave. She said she didn't know but thought it couldn't be far. I asked an old man and he thought it was somewhere across the road. I went into the men's room, wiped a toilet seat clean and reached into my bag for *Why I am a Muslim*.

"An American Odyssey," it said on the cover. American Odyssey. I wondered what *that* was like, then threw my ruck on my back and walked away from the only things in Quartzsite that I had going for me: the parked bus and the truck stop.

In the parking lot I noticed that those things flying over me weren't birds but bats. Across the highway I saw a gem prospector's tent still lit-up and open so I went in and asked him where I'd find Hi Jolly. He said he had never heard of it. I knew he was full of shit—Hi Jolly was on all the postcards and had a huge yearly festival in his honor, and he was right on that road! The prospector was a creepy dick anyway. Who sells rocks in a tent at midnight?

I went around behind his camp and walked across a quiet lightless sand-lot of scattered RVs. (Suggested soundtrack for the moment: "Mohammed's Radio," by Warren Zevon.) This town attracted lots of gem-hunters; the name was Quartzsite, after all. Hi Jolly himself spent his last days as a prospector. I spotted a faint white triangle in the dark distance and walked towards it. As I got closer I recognized it as a six-foot-tall pyramid, the pyramid from the postcards.

It was topped with a copper camel and stood as the centerpiece of a dusty cemetery roped off like a wrestling ring.

The plaque read, "THE LAST CAMP OF HI JOLLY" and then told his story. Someone had left him flowers and a toy camel. I observed that all the surrounding graves were facing the same way but I didn't know which direction it was. There was no grass to sleep on so I used my jacket as a mat and lay in the dirt and stones on the dark side of Hi Jolly's pyramid.

Back at Maria's in Denver I had been reading one of her old conservative books that cited Ibn Taimiya as saying that jinns hung out at graves, so people that spent too much time in cemeteries were usually close to the devil. In that nameless graveyard, when I preceded al-Fatiha with *aoudhu billahi mina shaytani rajeem* I made sure to think hard on it so Allah would send angels to drive him away. Then I said my sura, lying on my back and looking up at the stars.

Even in the middle of the night, Arizona was hot. The stone pyramid was warm to touch. The big rigs at the Pilot Travel Center were far enough away for their rumbling to be almost therapeutic. I feel asleep and slept hard.

Since this monument was all my business in Quartzsite, here's the tale:

His name was Hajj Ali and he came from Syria to head the United States Calvary's experiment with raising camels for use in the desert. The "Camel Corps" project was approved by Secretary of War Jefferson Davis, who'd later spearhead another failed venture: the Confederate States of America.

Hajj Ali arrived on the coast of Texas in 1856 with thirty-three camels. The U.S. government had ordered thirty-two but one was born on the way. They named it Uncle Sam.

The project didn't do so well and the camels were auctioned off to circuses and zoos or let loose into the desert. There's even a legend that Uncle Sam's descendents are still out there, running wild. Hajj Ali stayed in Texas, ran a freighting business up and down the Colorado River and later moved to Arizona as a prospector. He died in Quartzsite in 1902. In 1935 the Arizona Highway Department dedicated his monument. In 1976 the Camel Corps served as a loose basis for the slapstick comedy *Hawmps!* —with Gene Conforti in the role of Hi Jolly, Oxford-educated and sporting a monocle, saying *mash'Allah* when the cowboys fall off their camels and issuing weird proverbs like "May the breath of a thousand camels be always at your back."

I woke up early but couldn't find the strength to open my eyes, so I just lay there feeling like a dead man. When I finally checked the time it was 6:00 a.m. Now I could tell that the stones were facing west. One of them wasn't even stone, but wood and fraying on top, so weathered that I couldn't make out the name.

The sign in front of the cemetery explained that Hi Jolly's "proper Arabic name" was Hajj Ali, and Hi Jolly was only what the cowboys called him. It also said that his "Greek name" (followed by a question mark in parentheses) was Philip Tedro. They didn't know what that Greek-name business meant, but I did—because my proper Arabic name was Mikail Muhammad and Michael Knight was only my Irish name.

I said another Fatiha for my crazy-convert brother, then crossed the road to sit and bake in front of Pilot Travel Center. The next bus came in five or six hours.

17

W.F. Muhammad was the master of the great escape… his exit was flawless.

—Abraham Apollo, Internet poster

I went to Santa Cruz to take a vacation from my Muslim-American Vacation and hang out with old kufr friends. We ended up going out for ice cream with a bunch of people that knew my friend Tom's girlfriend Cindy, and I met a girl named Tess whose parents had recently flown her to Fiji. I started asking her for details on the Indo-Pakistani population there but she had no sense of what I was talking about.

"She's just nineteen," Cindy reasoned later, "and happy to have been somewhere."

While in Santa Cruz I called the number I had for Hayward's Ahmadiyya Anjuman. I wanted to find out the deal with 1540 C Street, which was listed in online directories as both "Masjid Imam Muhammad Abdullah" and "Ahmadiyya Anjuman Isha'at Islam." The imam informed me that his community was not located at the above-mentioned address. We got to talking and he told me that he knew a man who claimed to have introduced "Master Abdullah" to Warith Deen Mohammed, but that guy had since left the country. I told the imam what I heard from Zafar Abdullah, that his father met Warith Deen through T.H.E.M. himself. He replied that he only heard what he heard, and he didn't think that Master Abdullah was Master Fard since Abdullah was so much younger.

In the Bay Area I spent the first half of the day riding buses and BARTS before ending up at the Masjid al-Jame (Fiji Jama'atul Islam of America), founded by Fijian Muslims allegedly at Muhammad Abdullah's suggestion. The outside was plain white, the parking lot out back surrounded by a white picket fence with minaret-shaped posts. Christmas lights hung above the marble courtyard. The bathrooms were outside. I made wudhu and put on the complimentary slippers. Nobody else was there.

Inside, the prayer hall was filled with wall-hangings and decorations. Salat lines ran diagonals across the room. There was a definite feeling to the place having been tied to a homogenous immigrant community.

I approached the case of books by the wooden minbar and found a stack of pamphlets containing Ya Sin and al-Fatiha, the two suras most often read for the dead and dying. The back cover mentioned that the book had been donated by Sahidan Bibi, Mr. and Mrs. Mohammed Sadiq and family, in loving memory of Haji Mohammed Hanif. "All readers are requested to offer dua for the departed soul," it read, "and for all Muslim brothers and sisters." The suras were printed in both the original Arabic and transliterated Roman letters. I took one.

When you have a mosque all to yourself it can feel like a mansion, with the marble floors, wide rooms with wide windows, soft carpeting and beautiful chandeliers. There was a time when I'd devote my Friday nights to the Islamic Center of Rochester, just lording over the place. I'd spend at least a portion of the night reading Qur'an and praying, but I'd also watch TV in the classroom or scrounge up spicy banquet leftovers in the kitchen. Sometimes I'd stand on my head in the mihrab. During one of the last visits, I jumped off the women's balcony onto a mattress like I was wrestler Mick Foley.

I sat with my back propped up against the Masjid al-Jame wall and tried to fathom that Muhammad Abdullah had been in that room, which meant that maybe W.D. Fard had been there. I could have lost my mind on that but brothers began coming in as the time neared Asr. One brother who looked like he might have been the imam came in wearing a brown robe with gold trim like Dr. Shafiq used to wear at the Rochester mosque, but then the real imam came in with his bushy black beard and towering black Jinnah cap. After prayer I approached him to mention that I was from New York and doing research on Muhammad Abdullah, but before I could even finish my spiel he pointed to a white-bearded baba-ji in tan shalwar kameez. I gave my salams to the uncle and he said it back. Once I mentioned Muhammad Abdullah he gestured to a quiet corner of the mosque and sat me down.

He had known Master Abdullah both in Fiji and Hayward.

"We called him Master because of our respect for schoolteachers," he said. "In Fiji, we respect the teachers more than anyone. If you have a doctor, lawyer and schoolteacher, the schoolteacher will be the one that we respect." Uncle sat with his legs crossed and fiddled with yellow plastic zikr-beads as he spoke. "Muhammad Abdullah was a very nice man, very humble man... "

"His son Zafar told me that he was involved with this masjid," I said, "and he had advised the Fijian community to build it—" The uncle said it wasn't true since Muhammad Abdullah and family were all Ahmadiyyas and "out of the fold of Islam." In fact, he had never known of Muhammad or Zafar ever stepping foot in that mosque.

He was, however, friends with Zafar and had welcomed Muhammad into his home on many occasions in Fiji.

"Even with him having his beliefs," he said, "he never tried to argue or disrespect the other people." He couldn't say whether Muhammad Abdullah and W.D. Fard were one and the same: "To tell you these things when I have no knowledge… I fear my Creator too much for that."

I found myself dwelling on the uncle as I rode the BART to San Francisco International Airport. He feared Allah too much to talk out of his ass. Maybe most people didn't fear Allah enough. I looked around at the other people on the BART. None of them really looked like they feared their Creator. Maybe they talked out of their asses all the time.

And at the airport I rode the Air Train from terminal to terminal as mortal douchebags got on and off and it didn't seem like any of them feared their Creator either. I called Asma Gull Hasan and we talked for twenty minutes. Did Asma fear the Creator? She seemed too bubbly to be contemplating Jahennam.

But look at me, saying what's in people's hearts when I don't know…

After almost two hours of riding air-train laps around the airport I got a call from Cihan Kaan. His flight had finally come down so I told him to find the Air Train's red line and I'd be in the very last car.

We crashed at Jawad Ali's place and the next day borrowed his neighbor's bicycles to go exploring. Rode the BART to Hayward, brainstorming about a *Taqwacores* movie and what it'd take to pull that off, and then biked to 1540 C Street. It was just a regular house.

The colors were out of place—bright blue with red and purple in a neighborhood of earth tones. 1540 was the upstairs half. We went up and knocked on the door. I looked in the mailbox to find an electric bill with a very non-Muslim name on the envelope.

We walked around back to find a junkyard of old treadmills and weight benches, thousands of ceramic flower pots, abandoned refrigerators and ratty couches. So that was it. Zafar had told me that 1540 C Street wasn't a mosque but just his father's old home; the address found its way into Sunni and Ahmadiyya masjid directories because so many people came seeking knowledge from Master Abdullah that it basically functioned as a mosque. There wasn't much to do but have Cihan take my picture out on the front steps. Then we rode to the Zaytuna Institute that had been founded by the ex-surfer Mark Hanson (who converted when he was seventeen and became Hamza Yusuf) and some other guy. The only part that really had anything going on when we were there was the bookstore, which was run by a white hijabi girl who said either *mash'Allah, subhana'Allah wa Ta'Ala* or *al-hamdulilah* in every sentence and wouldn't make eye contact when we asked her questions.

She was another crazy convert, I just knew it. She took her whole Hamza Yusuf Bookstore role a little too seriously. The desi girl stocking the shelves had a good vibe to her, no pious hostility or anything—and even though she wore hijab, it somehow seemed more casual than what the white girl had wrapped around herself. Damn converts with shit to prove, they always go so far and try so hard—

On the way back Cihan told me a story about two kids in medieval Persia who made a pact that if they grew into important men, they would use their knowledge and influence for the good of humanity; one of the kids ended up being Rumi and the other became Hassan bin Sabbah, leader of the Assassins. It was only a twisted-up version of the "three schoolfellows" legend about Sabbah, Omar Khayyam and Nizam ul-Mulk, but it worked for me.

"So which one are you?" I asked. We pondered the issue for a minute and mutually decided that Cihan in his Sufi love would be Rumi while I would be Sabbah who said, "Nothing is true, everything is permitted"—but then there was the question of who'd get more tail in 2004.

"You know Sabbah would be landing all kinds of girls," said Cihan.

"Jewel didn't mention *Sabbah* in her poetry book," I countered.

18

That night Jawad showed me the Muslims for Bush website, established by Ali Hasan (Asma's brother) and Seeme Hasan (her mom, who also founded the Hasan Foundation "dedicated to bringing better understanding between developing countries and the United States, through creative arts and performing arts"). The site featured a photo of George W. Bush standing between Ali and Seeme, another shot of Dubya with his arm around Seeme, and then Ali with a grin like he was rolling on Ecstasy. Ahmed Nassef had interviewed the guy and asked him what he thought was President Bush's greatest achievement: the Patriot Act, invasion of Iraq or invasion of Afghanistan. Ali answered it like a serious question and said Iraq.

According to the website, Ali Hasan was an "avid snowboarder" and considered himself a "budding comedian."

Seeme, meanwhile, was "often cajoled by her friends and family to run for Senate."

And to think, I took Seeme's princess to her very first punk show.

19

Friday afternoon I'd check out Oakland's Masjid Waritheen where Muhammad Abdullah gave that historic first khutbah. Jawad, his girl Reima, Cihan and I all went in his car. On the way to the bridge I spotted an old building with the word TAKAHASHI splashed across its red brick, which reminded me of Fard's buddy, the Japanese subversive Takahashi, leader of the Black Dragon Society. What if the Nation of Islam had been a Hirohito-backed insurrection? I thought about flags. The NOI flag had a white star and moon on a red field. Imperial Japan's flag had a red sun on a white field.

Masjid Waritheen was a large pink building and used to be a church. A Sister Clara school operated next door and the Elijah Mohammed Cultural Center stood across the street.

We got there during the imam's khutbah. I looked at the scenery around him. The old church balcony loomed over his head and there were double-doors behind him, where the mihrab would usually be. The front of the mosque was the back of the church.

This was Imam Fahim Shuaibe, whose name I remembered from the 1976 *Bilalian News* article—on that amazing long-ago Friday afternoon, Fahim performed the adhan. He was there from the beginning. Or at least the end of the beginning, or the beginning of the end... Allah knows best.

I closed my eyes and tried to sense whether the Man in Question had left any aura to the room. If I couldn't feel anything in the air, maybe I had the wrong guy.

The atmosphere was alright, however, with no crazy-convert or Salafi seriousness. We laughed at Fahim's jokes. I even heard the voices of my Muslim sisters with their *Allahu Akbars*. Fahim spoke of Satan, not Shaytan. And when he recited Qur'an it sounded like a gospel song that just happened to be in Arabic. Made me think of how his adhan might have sounded (with "melodious strains," as *Bilalian News* put it).

After the prayer I exchanged salams with several brothers and then greeted the imam. He led me to his office, sat me down and we went to it.

Were Imam Muhammad Abdullah and Master Fard Muhammad the same person?

The imam said yes without a pause.

According to Fahim, Muhammad Abdullah made his first appearances in the NOI sometime between 1957 and 1959 when Warith Deen was a minister in Philadelphia. "Around Malcolm's time," he said. And it was in 1959 that Elijah made hajj to Mecca.

Fahim knew Muhammad Abdullah during the two years or so in the late 1970s that Muhammad ran the masjid. Muhammad claimed to have met Fard in the 1950s and said "he was an old man even then."

Muhammad Abdullah didn't talk much, Fahim told me; "his words were strategic." Fahim said he had many private meetings and moments with the man. One of the last times they were together Muhammad kept looking at Fahim, "like staring, like 'I wonder if he knows who I am.'"

Once when it was Fahim, Muhammad Abdullah and Warith Deen together, Warith Deen said that around Savior's Day people still sent him birthday cards for Master Fard; and then he joked, "but I'll just send them to *him*," with a point to Muhammad.

I asked Fahim if W.D. Fard had ever claimed to be Allah in Person. He told me that when Warith Deen was excommunicated from the Nation for denying Fard's divinity and his mom tried bringing him back into the fold, he asked her, "Did he ever tell you that he was God?" Clara replied that Fard wouldn't even let her call him a prophet, "He said even that was too much."

Fahim said that when Elijah Muhammad went to prison for draft evasion he began an exhaustive study of religions, just devouring books in his cell all day like Malcolm Little would in later years. It was then that Elijah reformed Fard's doctrine. Being a practical man, he weeded out most of the esoteric or mystical elements and placed the focus on moral self-improvement.

Muhammad Abdullah never actually said that he was W.D. Fard, relying instead on "signs, symbols and hints" for Warith Deen to uncover. "If you're truly committed to secrecy," said Fahim, "you never reveal your plan; you just go ahead and carry it out." It was always symbolic with Fard. Fahim even allowed that Fard wasn't born in 1877, but there might have been some mysterious meaning to that number; a clue that still needs to be deciphered. Maybe I had it: 1876 was when the British Empire started shipping South Asian laborers to Fiji, giving birth to the oppressive conditions that would in turn spawn Fard and his revolution.

Fahim said that there was one brother who knew more than him, and he was about to introduce us. So he left the office and came back with Abdul-Latif Rahman, a stocky older man with dark, dark skin and big heavy hands. At first I thought he had an accent but then realized that he didn't have his teeth in. Abdul-Latif had joined the Nation in 1969 and rose to the rank of lieutenant in the Fruit of Islam. As a member of Warith Deen's community he served as driver and personal security for Imam Muhammad Abdullah.

So I asked him if Muhammad Abdullah was W.D. Fard and he said sure, Muhammad Abdullah looked like Fard. "I asked him once or twice," Latif told me. "I asked him, 'Are you Fard?' and he said, 'No,' but in a joking way… and then I went to Imam Warith Deen and asked him, and he said that he was. So I went back to Imam Muhammad Abdullah and told him, 'Imam Warith Deen says you were.' Then Imam Muhammad Abdullah just said, 'Okay,' but that was in a joking way too."

I asked Abdul-Latif if he really believed that Fard was Allah during his time in the NOI: "I did, but I didn't… it wasn't in my heart. I went along with the program."

He was with Muhammad Abdullah every day and knew a lot of things. "I won't tell you everything," he said. "Some of it's personal." But he did tell me that Muhammad Abdullah was extremely smart, a "very wise man" and had been in touch with Warith Deen since the imam was maybe fifteen or sixteen years old.

"Here's the key," he said, leaning back to support the weight of his words. "Here's the key to all of it: you know what a Mujeddid is? Imam Warith Deen was the Mujeddid. You know who the Mujeddid was before him?"

"Elijah?" I guessed.

"No. Fard was the Mujeddid, and then Warith Deen. They were divinely guided. This isn't a fairy tale. This isn't a made-up story. I've seen them both get revelations. I've seen Imam Warith Deen get into trances and Imam Muhammad Abdullah used to get into them too."

Warith Deen and Muhammad Abdullah, according to Abdul-Latif Rahman, were a lot alike. They even had the same speaking style. "They really enjoyed one another, they were so happy to talk to each other… they'd go out and eat food, they had fun together… you know that Fard named him, right?"

"Yeah," I told him. "When Clara was pregnant with Warith Deen, Fard wrote his name on the door." And Warith Deen was their seventh child, the special one that Fard predicted would be a great leader.

"Fard named him. And Fard was his teacher. He knew what he was doing because God was in the picture. Fard was so unique, so smooth that he couldn't have done it all himself. Imam Fard couldn't have done it on his own." I don't think I had ever heard someone say *Imam Fard* before.

"Did Elijah know that Muhammad was Fard?" I asked.

"Sure he did. Elijah was in touch with him the whole time." Fard/Abdullah only subtly nudged Elijah towards *al-Islam*; he knew that the future lay with Warith Deen.

"Did Minister Farrakhan know?"

"Farrakhan went to his house and knocked on his door, saying 'Are you Fard? Are you Fard?' but Imam Muhammad Abdullah wouldn't even open the door to him, he turned him away." 1540 C Street, Hayward. I had knocked on that door too.

"Why did Fard disappear in 1934?"

"His mission was complete. He did his mission. This mission that you're on right now—when it's complete you're gone, right?"

"Do you know anything about where he came from or where he grew up?"

"He grew up in Fiji, I think. But his mother was Abyssinian, he told me that, and his father was Indian or.... " He mumbled the rest and his words drifted away, so I couldn't catch what he said. I asked him what Muhammad Abdullah did after retiring from the role of imam. "He went here for jum'aa sometimes," he said, "and he was a teacher somewhere. He taught around California." Abdul-Latif used to go to the house in Hayward and Muhammad's wife would cook for him.

Once it was time for Asr salat and Muhammad told Abdul-Latif to go ahead and pray. So Abdul-Latif made wudhu and then went to do his Asr. When he was finished he turned to find the good professor sitting in a chair behind him, following the prayer.

"He'd be sitting since he was up in age, then, and you know an old man can do salat in a chair if he has to… but I was leading him in prayer the whole time and didn't even know it until after."

When we shook hands he asked if I was married. I said no and he bellowed, "GET A WIFE THEN, AND YOU'LL BE HAPPY!" like a good uncle. I then caught up with Jawad, Reima and Cihan at the Elijah Mohammed Cultural Center's café across the street. Jawad ordered grilled catfish and I got a burger. Abdul-Latif came through, got his own burger and fries and immediately upon sighting Jawad proclaimed, "YOU LOOK LIKE MUHAMMAD ABDULLAH! THAT'S THE KIND OF COLOR HE WAS!" We all sat together listening to him go off about how great the seven heavens will be—"You can get around up there, they'll have cars but they're better than the cars we have here, and there's girls, maybe a girl that you liked down here and you can say 'Hey, baby' but I made a pact with my wife that we'd hook up again on the other side… "

And then he said that the white-black stuff all came from Satan. "Are you a white man?" he asked. I didn't know what to do but nod my head. "No you're not!" he snapped. He held up his plastic fork and compared it to my arm. "*This* is white. You're not white! Show me any part of you that's white." He examined the palms of our hands and laughed because his were lighter than mine. "There's no such thing as a white man," he said, "and there's no such thing as a black man. When you talk like that it's only the devil's talk."

20

I wouldn't want to be a prosecutor against Fard in the hereafter…
I believe he could pull a few things out of a hat.

—Warith Deen Mohammed

Riding our borrowed bikes down Mission in Hayward, Cihan and I passed a big mosque and agreed that if you're on a holy journey and just happen to encounter a mosque on the road you absolutely have to check it out. We went in and I made two rakats right in the mihrab on the imam's prayer rug, half-enclosed by blue tiles with kufic *Allahs* in the patterns. Then we walked out.

For years I had been shooting off my mouth about all the hypocrisies and contradictions of Muslim kids that would have sex and get sloshed but never touch bacon, but I had my own static. I was the guy who'd waltz in and make a sincere nafl prayer with no wudhu, but then bounce out only ten minutes before the adhan for Asr.

Cihan and I found our way to the Garden of Mercy, the Muslim section at Chapel of the Chimes with all the graves facing qiblah. I had gotten Muhammad Abdullah's location from the front office—2N/4E/D3—but there were no visible markers to make any of that useful. Cihan felt that our difficulty in finding the physical grave seemed to fit in with the rest of Fard's story, that it'd be just like him to make us chase him until the very end. I built on that in my own head for a while and I could have seen Fard making a big sport of it, loving his role as fox in the fox hunt; but then as I looked at all these other peoples' stones I realized that I was meant to read their names too—

Many of the headstones mentioned nationalities. I noticed a lot of Afghans and Pakistanis with either flags or outlines of their countries on the stones. I spotted Idris Hasan (1928–2001) from the Fiji Islands. There was Aisha Ting Chao with her name in English, Arabic and Chinese characters but no birth/death dates. I passed a stone marked SHABAZZ and knew that Rasheed (1949–1999) was either a black convert or the son of a black convert since Shabazz was the name of Fard's lost tribe. Then I saw Jacques Pierre Baston/Sa'id Muhammad (1970–1993) and James Abdullah Olivier (1944–2001). A few stones mentioned occupations, like Engineer Abdul Majeed Tarrar, but Shivari Arora's stone featured Spongebob SquarePants, Winnie the Pooh, Dora the Explorer and Bob the Builder. It also had a photo of her dressed as a fairy princess with wings on her back and a crown. The dates read 12/27/1998–2/4/2004. Nearby, Aisha's grave didn't give her last name but noted that she was born on March 19ᵗʰ, 1999 and passed away on November 4ᵗʰ, 2001.

We made for a jamaat, them and me.

Muhammad Abdullah was nowhere to be found so I asked a thick-accented Hispanic landscaper if he could help. He took my yellow post-it bearing the location, looked around and then left to get three more thick-accented Hispanic landscapers on a golf cart. It was kind of surreal to watch these guys dart across Muslim graves trying to find me Master Abdullah, but it worked out. I thanked them for their help and they went back to whatever they were doing before. Cihan sat in the shade of a tree some fifty feet or so away. I took out the Ya Sin that I had gotten from the Fijian mosque and said my *subhana k'Allahumma wa bihamdika wa tabara gasmuka...*

The stone read, Professor Muhammad Abdullah.

Born June 15ᵗʰ, 1905 in Ehsanpur, Pakistan.

Died June 18ᵗʰ, 1992 in Hayward, California.

I would have put his birth earlier, maybe around 1891 as it said in Wallie D. Ford's file at San Quentin (and then he could have been the twenty-three-year-old Fred Dodd who married in Portland in 1914), or closer to 1900 as police thought in Detroit.

I called Jura Shaheed Allah out in C-Medina to help me break down the years using the Five Percenters' system of Supreme Mathematics:

$$1891=1+8+9+1=19=1+9=10=1+0=1$$
$$1900=1+9+0+0=10=1+0=1$$

Both *born* 1, which in the Five Percenter system represents the attribute of Knowledge.

Elijah Muhammad, however, put Fard's birth in 1877 while Warith Deen and this tombstone had him born in 1905:

$$1877=1+8+7+7=23=2+3=5$$
$$1905=1+9+0+5=15=1+5=6$$

In the Supreme Math, 5 represents Power or Refinement. 6 is Equality.

Anyway, after celebrating a real or imagined 87ᵗʰ birthday, W.D. Fard had three days to think about the adventure his life had been. And then it was over.

The FBI, which initiated an investigation of Fard in 1942 that was to last more than thirty years, could not substantiate or verify his name at birth, birth date, place of birth, port of entry, exit, or present whereabouts, despite exhaustive inquiries. There are even indications that bodies were exhumed in the search for Fard.

—Prince-A-Cuba

Master Fard Muhammad sneaked into America and used a name that made it hard for them to identify him. Because he did not wear a turban, he looked like an American… He was wise because he knew how to hide his identity, to do his job, and sneak out.

—Warith Deen Mohammed

Was this god the Pope of Rome? The Archbishop of Canterbury? The leader of the Parsees? The Brahmins? The Bahais? Mirza Ghulam, leader of the Ahmadiyya Movement? Or John Walker, a.k.a. W.D. Fard, the slightly cockeyed man who came from Greece. [He] was a Greek who came to this country at the age of 27 years of life, and who served 7 and 2 years in jail, in America, for stealing a truck load of junk in Gary, Indiana; and for raping a 17-year-old, so-called white girl. This man died in Chicago, Illinois, at the age of 78. Your Captain Raymond Sharrieff knows this. Do you?

—Khalifa Abdul Haamas Khaalis

That is the beauty of Truth: it must be discovered from moment to moment, not remembered. A remembered truth is a dead thing. Truth must be discovered from moment, because it is living.

—W.D. Fard to Albert Einstein, 1933

There was no reason to believe that he ever really said it; and if he did, I don't know that he said it to Albert Einstein on a Detroit radio show. But a man who had over fifty aliases and nearly as many nationalities, whose birthday fell somewhere in a thirty-year span and who had in the course of one lifetime been a pistol-brandishing café cook, convicted drug dealer, door-to-door silk salesman, prophet of Allah, Allah in Person, Supreme Ruler of the Universe, Mahdi of the Muslims, Messiah of the Christians, Chief of the Voo-Doos and Head of the Japanese Army could be said to have found his truths by the moment.

Fard used to sell his followers new names to replace their old "slave names." In his absence, however, no original names could be issued, so applicants that had been approved prior to Fard's disappearance were granted the surname of "X." The policy later extended to new members of the Nation. X represented the Unknown, as in the black man's true name that his ancestors had lost in slavery—but on an esoteric level it expressed the loss of Master Fard, the Savior.

I could see Fard standing with me in the grass: suit and loose tie, hands in pockets, maybe wanting to shrug like it still hadn't hit him that I wanted the man to say something...

He didn't have to say whether these Pakistani bones at our feet comprised the real deal, or admit that I finally caught him... but he could at least say that I had come closer than anyone who ever tried, or that I seemed to want it so bad, worse than any other Fard-hunter to come down the pike. He could say that the last chapter in his story was mine and then leave me to write it.

Instead he just lowered his gaze, maybe so I saw him from the same angle as in his NOI portrait. And he looked like the kind of guy who could, as the stories went, wander all over the Middle East and Indian subcontinent, venture to every corner of Africa, study wildlife deeper in the jungle than any man before him, explore China and Japan, cross the Bering into Alaska and the Yukon, reach the North Pole and spend twenty years in America before revealing himself... the man who studied in London for a diplomatic career in the Kingdom of Hejaz, spoke sixteen languages and wrote ten, knew the language of the birds, knew the language of nine-foot-tall black Martians and could tell you the history of the world going back 150,000 years. The man who was sent by twenty-three wise scientists into the wilderness of North America.

Like that Five Percenter told me in Chicago, there was no real Fard. He was only a face. You might as well pick the story that suits you. Warith Deen Mohammed believes that Fard was a Muslim and believed in the Qur'an from the very start. "Master Fard," he writes, "let us know that by having his picture taken with the Holy Qur'an in his hands." Warith Deen needs his story, worked out in such a way that makes sense for him and his community.

My story says that it took a long time but the Master found his way back. After watching the decades unfold from his *ghaybat* in Fiji, he feared for the consequences of being called Allah by thousands of people; so as Imam Muhammad Abdullah he crept back into the Nation he created and saw to its unraveling. In my story, it was Muhammad Abdullah who led Warith Deen to challenge Fard's divinity... and Muhammad Abdullah who persuaded Elijah to make hajj... and I imagine that he even met Malcolm and Cassius, if only once.

It was a good idea for Fard to return in disguise. If Elijah had put his Savior back in the limelight, the FBI would have licked its chops and gone to town on him. If Warith Deen paraded him out after Elijah's death and all the strife of Malcolm and the Khaalis family and announced "here's Master Fard, he disowns the whole thing and says you can all go fuck yourselves," it'd spark another round of holy war.

When the police banished him from Detroit in 1933, Fard told his teary-eyed followers that he'd come back someday and save them. Standing at his grave seventy-one years later, I'd say that he kept the promise—and he died a submitter to the same One True God that Malik Shabazz found in Mecca.

I sat down and read Ya Sin. It had been a long time so my reading was filled with clumsy stops and starts.

Then the images came like Allah was running a movie-reel through my head. I thought of the ones who had once been called "Black Muslims" approaching a gentle Pakistani imam with their confusion and anger and fear, asking whether Master Fard was really just a man that could die like any-one else... and then I thought of his face as he heard them, the secret sadness behind his eyes... just to picture him I'd feel all the bad feelings in his gut and wonder how he stuck through it, how he managed to stay at that mosque in Oakland and teach Islam at 1540 C Street in Hayward, how he kept from just hopping on another plane and putting it all behind him again...

But by then, he was at least in his seventies. I don't know what runs through a man's mind at that stage of life.

I again imagined my phantom W.D. Fard standing beside me, the mug-shot W.D. Fard, and he still hadn't said anything.

Cihan got up from where he was sitting and walked toward us. Fard and I looked at each other. Fard had that early 1900s immigrant charm about him like in those movies of Italian or Jewish kids growing up tough and working-class in the Bronx...

"As-salamu alaikum," said the Master with a slouch and hands still in his pockets.

And then, *poof.* Peace be upon him. "Now," wrote Warith Deen in *As the Light Shineth from the East,* "we can get the full value of the great thing that happened to us in 1930, July 4th."

21

Cihan had his heart set on going to Slim's to see Stiff Little Fingers, and Jawad and Reima were down. Todd Gullion was back in West Asia so I asked him if he'd want to come too; at first he was into it but then backed out because Time in Malta had broken up just that day and he didn't want to be anywhere near music. When we went out I wore my Time in Malta t-shirt—partly for a tribute to the deceased band, but partly because I had only three shirts in my rotation.

Stiff Little Fingers, punk legends going back to glorious '77, came out looking like ordinary middle-aged dads with dad-haircuts but when they start-ed playing all the punks just ate it up. At first I stood outside the margins of the pit, watching it as it went down: the kids with their mohawks and spikes smushed together in front, shoving into each other, waving their fists or point-ing fingers to the ceiling, singing along to these dudes who could have just as easily been their high-school math teachers. But you couldn't deny Stiff Little Fingers; I think they had the magnetic of Supreme Truth on their side. When we all sang along to a chorus like "BE WHAT YOU ARE" with its holy repeti-tion, the show felt like that Friday's second jum'aa. I snuck into the action and got shoved around from all sides. Sometimes I struggled to stay on my feet. Most everyone was cool—a few times I watched a kid get knocked to the floor, only to have all the surrounding punks help him or her back to safety—but there was also a tank-sized fat asshole of a skinhead with his black boots and red suspenders barreling into people like he wanted to hurt them, and a wiry little skinhead piggybacked on him to make a human battering-ram. While the rest of us became a kind of thousand-armed collective mush, the fat skin-head did a good job of keeping everyone out of his personal space.

After Stiff Little Fingers walked off the stage I made my way to the steps leading outside. They returned for a double-encore but I walked out during the first song, just to look at everyone else hanging around outside Slim's and feel the cold air and the life of Harrison Street as a punk show reached its emotional closure. There were couples sitting on the sidewalk, huddled together usually with the guy leaning against the building and the girl leaning against the guy... and I saw the skinheads again, standing by the door with a posture like they had been hired to work security.

They made me think about my old man who used to shave his head, used the term "blue-eyed devil" enough times for Mom to remember it over twenty years later (though she had forgotten the context) and responded to my Islam with "You don't like niggers, do you?"

But at least he had the defense of schizophrenia: after watching the "Gay Hitler" skit on *Saturday Night Live,* my father was convinced that the Nazis had kidnapped Chris Kattan and "forced him to be gay, to inject homosexuality into the Jewish blood." Another time he just said that *SNL* had turned into a "bucket of shit" because their writers "insist on portraying people as homosexual that were not so."

Insha'Allah, maybe Dad's illness will clear him on Qiyamah.

I met up with Cihan and he told me that Jawad had taken Reima home because she was falling asleep. Our ears were ringing with the proof of a good show. At one point, Cihan said it was one of the best punk shows he had ever seen.

Then we talked about various girls that were there and it came out that most of the time I can't really hit on girls. To just invite a girl to your house you must become the con man who believes his own con, and I can't be that guy because I think it out too much. It's the same with being a writer. Getting someone to buy your book is a bunko game—you're promising answers that you don't really have, like selling the Brooklyn Bridge.

Mostly Cihan and I rambled on about how great the band was for building in their cipher with no gimmicks or posturing. They just got up and played their music and then headed home to their families, you know? We talked about the skinheads and considered whether they were regular punk skins or the white-power kind. I can't even tell anymore but we quickly forgot about those guys. There's something to good punk rock that I don't think you'll find in any other genre quite the same way—while most shows are about celebrating the people on stage, punk shows only celebrate the crowd. Maybe that's why people costume up for these things.

At 4:03 a.m. I was the only one awake, sitting at Jawad's computer to get all this down when I got a call from Zainab. She said that she couldn't handle me anymore and it had nothing to do with the ham. But she reminded me that I'd be okay without her.

"I'm going to be stuck in Birmingham," she whispered—whenever she called me at night she'd whisper and I knew that she was hiding in her closet with the radio on—"getting a PhD in something that I just kind of… *fell into,* while you'll be living some amazing life."

I couldn't find a good way to react, though I ran over a few options in my head. No reason to fly off the handle on her. No reason to beg her not to break my heart, though I wanted to. All I could say was good night. The mighty Hujwiri told travelers to say clear of those "sensual things" and I should have listened…

22

My psyche was fragile enough from the wear and tear of thirty-some days and 13,000 Greyhound miles (enough to go from Boston to Seattle four times). Now I felt like someone had placed a sewer rat on my stomach and then trapped it with an upside-down bowl so escape would mean burrowing in and chewing through my intestines.

After arriving in Santa Cruz with Cihan we headed for the beach and walked in the tide, past girls on towels and little kids building sand castles. The whole time I trudged about thirty feet behind Cihan, with my rolled-up long pants and Alternative Tentacles jacket and Five Percenter shirt and black-and-gold kufi and nasty beard, carrying my big World War II rucksack and my shoes, poorly fed, poorly rested, miserable over a girl, just seconds away from stabbing myself. It was a fairly cinematic moment, I felt, so I started making crazy faces for Allah's holy cameras. Then we went inland less than fifty yards and I spotted the cave used in the 1996 film *Glory Daze*, a punkish independent thing back before Ben Affleck was really Ben Affleck. I threw down my rucksack and then myself while Cihan went off on his way. He was there to see the roller coaster from *The Lost Boys*.

In *Glory Daze*, this oceanside cave was where Affleck's character supplicated his ex with pleas of poet-love and she just replied that he was scaring her and needed to grow up. Then she ran away and some kids laughed at him. And there I was, in the same spot completely by accident—or mash'Allah, if you prefer.

Staring at my turned-off mobile phone with my ass in the sand, I was in no place to issue a statement on sexual liberation. Maybe dating *should* be haram—why not let the parents or whoever figure it out for us, then make our own kids and do the same for them. No reason to lose sight of everything over some girl and our screwed-up Muslim romance. We had already made each other insane enough times.

Cihan stayed in Santa Cruz because he knew a girl there. I got on a bus for Eugene, Oregon. Maria's husband Gabriel had told me about a mosque there that let guys live in it.

Just a bunch of filthy slackers, as the story went, and the whole mosque smelled like them. Maybe that was what I needed—to flee from the sensual things and hide in a masjid until it stinks like my stink. And I knew that I'd find no sensual things in the mosque, since these masjid-squatters were said to have commandeered the former women's section.

During the fifteen-hour bus ride I closed my eyes and thought of girls that I had done wrong and others that had damn near killed me. There was Miss Drunken New Year's Eve when I was fifteen, getting my first kiss and five minutes later a scared hand in her pants. There was the twelve-year old Muslimah that the imams set me up with a year or so later, the one I was supposed to marry. And there was a girl who, if I were Yusef from *The Taqwacores*, would have been my Lynn—the girl of my post-Sunni transitional time, the one that caused me to pray three hundred rakats over a kiss. Then I thought of the girl that would be my girlfriend for nearly four years, the kufr girl that couldn't understand when I said I'd name a son Husain.

There were random hook-ups that never went anywhere and dumb crushes that never went anywhere. My memory was clogged with faces that I'd never see again. But I couldn't picture that Alabama sayyeda. She was still too fresh for the parade.

The bus rolled into Eugene around 6:30 a.m. Again by accident or mash'Allah, the street that the mosque was on ran right by the Greyhound station. I walked more than twenty blocks before finding what looked like a couple of ugly green tool sheds that had been built as add-ons to each other. Even before seeing the stenciled letters reading ABU-BAKR AS-SIDDIQ ISLAMIC CENTER I knew it was the place. The parking lot hosted an abandoned car, busted washing machine, overflowing dumpster, collapsed picket fence and a basketball pole with the net and backboard missing. The lawn had gone long enough without mowing for the weeds to reach knee-high. By the front door I observed a small hill of cat litter and some empty cans of tuna with the lids still attached. The door was locked so I walked around to the side past monstrous tangles of ivy and weeds taller than the ones out front, these must have been shoulder-high at least... and I went up the moss-matted concrete steps to pull on an old doorknob but it was locked too. Then a skinny Arab akhi pulled up in his jeep. I must have looked like a sketchball just sneaking around the place so I walked over and gave salams. He got out and led me to the front door, which turned out to have been unlocked the whole time, only jammed. The bathroom was right there. I went in and did my business, emerging from the stall to find my brother taking a shower. Between us stood a yellow mop-bucket on wheels, the kind I had at my old overnight job but this one was caked with dust. I averted my eyes from my naked brother to the rust-stained linoleum floor, the sophisticated network of cobwebs overhead, the wastebasket with garbage piling up.

The main prayer room had no mihrab, just a thirty-year-old microphone on a stand. The walls were drab off-white, the carpet an unvacuumed cream. The adjacent room had ping-pong and foosball tables, couches, a TV and junky old VCR (first encounter I've ever had with the brand "Quasar") and some posters of holier sites. The door marked "WOMEN'S PRAYER AREA" led to a room of couches draped with bed sheets and a fraying rug with salat lines marked by duct-tape.

My brother left after his shower and ABU-BAKR AS-SIDDIQ was all mine. I went into the kitchen to brush my teeth. There were no pipes under the sink, just a pail with water spilling over. The refrigerator didn't have much beyond some vegetables of unknown age, but the long horizontal freezer yielded a collection of goat parts in plastic grocery bags. I took out the head and carried it into the mosque library, where the shelves were packed with leather-bound Arabic books. There were Qur'ans in zipped-up leather jackets and fancy boxes, complete sets of the famous hadith collections, classic books on fiqh and audiotape lectures starring Jamal Badawi. I cleared off the desk and set down my frozen goat head. We stayed in the library long enough for the plastic grocery bag to hang off his face a little looser. When I picked him up again he left a reddish puddle on the desk.

I stared him in the face. He had little hairs around his mouth, his front teeth jutted out and his eyes were frozen solid. At first I played with the idea that he was an Eid goat and his death was something holy, but then realized that Eid was six months ago. So I put him back in the freezer and went to the bathroom for istimna to Muslim Cowgirl's smiling book cover. In post-ejaculatory haze I wondered how I'd feel if I had a daughter who posed on book covers with no hijab so some scumbag can istimna to her—and for just a second I really understood. You can slip into that anti-sex trap so easily that you don't even notice—all you have to do is nut. When the poison sperm is out of you, look at the object of your desire, whatever it was that got you all worked up and distracted from the things that really matter—the Zuhra that was so beautiful she'd get angels to drink wine and worship idols. That girl can own you but once you bust, you might hate her for it.

Remember that scene in *Malcolm X* when Malcolm walked down the street and all those prostitutes kept coming up to offer their holes, and Malcolm wouldn't even turn to look at them? He just kept his gaze forward, jihad against the testes. I used to relive it in my head while walking the halls at DeSales High School. Girls—just normal teenage girls—would smile and say hi but I'd grit my teeth and keep moving without a word. I loved it. They were only sluts and slam-pigs for all that I cared, and I'd show them how little they were. I'd show them what a man I was—a *real* man, not one of those boys that'd stick it in them. I was a real man because I could keep it in my pants. Who are you to wear a tight shirt and smile at me? What are you trying to do?

I thought that maybe I'll end up an old conservative who speaks his conservatism with the authority of experience. I could visit Islamic summer-camps to tell kids that there's a wall around their sheltered little world and I had lived life outside the wall, and they'd take my word that it's not worth it. The ISNA teens would eat that up and I could probably sell some lecture tapes. Wasn't such a big leap.

When I was nineteen my best friend Tom decided that I needed to see some porn. "It'd be good for you," he said. I had stayed away from vaginas not for any admirable reason but simply for them scaring the hell out of me. At nineteen I was like a little boy. So we drove down Monroe Avenue and I spotted a good friend of mine walking out of Show World with a brown paper bag.

Nadeem was one of those Salafi-bearded RIT students that hung out at the Islamic Center of Rochester, the guy that'd sometimes be there when I showed up at night. He used to tell me the most beautiful hadiths that I could never find in my Sahih Bukhari. I don't know where he got them, but they were good. "BROTHER NADEEM!" I yelled. Tom stopped the car and I got out to chase him, calling his name but he wouldn't turn around for anything. I knew it was him. After three or four times he stopped and looked at me.

"Oh, hello."

"As-salamu alaikum," I said.

"As-salamu alaikum, brother!"

"Wa alaikum as-salam, how are you?"

"Al-hamdulilah, brother Nadeem, how are you doing?"

"I am not Nadeem. I am Nadeem's brother."

"Oh. I did not know that Nadeem had a brother."

"Yes, yes. I heard you calling 'Nadeem! Nadeem!' and I thought, 'insha'Allah is someone calling my brother?' So I turned around."

"Oh," I said. "I'm sorry." I knew it was Nadeem, and he was stroking his black beard nervously, but all I could do was say salam and let him go.

Tom and I couldn't get into Show World because we were under twenty-one, but it was a mind-blowing night for me anyway.

In college I eventually dropped Islamic misogyny for the American version. At the end of spring semesters my friends would drive past dorms yelling THANK YOU FOR YOUR DAUGHTERS! at middle-aged dads loading up their minivans.

In early 2001, I began work on a novel about my college years. I called it *The Furious Cock*. In 2002 I'd print up xeroxed copies and hand them out on the Buffalo State campus. A few record and bookstores on the Elmwood strip agreed to carry it. My female characters had names like Jizz Gomper, Candy Maker, Nikki Scabies and Monica Bukkake. You know what *bukkake* is? It's a genre of Japanese porn that involves up to a hundred men ejaculating on the same girl's face, or her drinking their collective semen from a funnel. The main idea of *The Furious Cock* was that there's something seriously wrong with too many guys—being both young and male should be a disorder in the DSM-IV—but I had failed at getting my point across; readers told me that the sex stories were funny. The only thing that I really got out of it was a girl who gave me head in my car and then said, "Now I get to be in your book."

"You're like the antithesis of Malcolm X," another told me, "because you started out Muslim and *then* became a pimp."

A shaytan lives in every scrotum. I can ejaculate him out of my body but he always grows back. And he lives off whatever I give him; the shaytan of the balls craves Islam and porn just about the same. Muhammad Knight in his Wahhab days was afraid to look at girls, but a few years later he'd be feeding strippers. The way I lived it I'm not sure one was more messed up or wrong than the other.

Sometimes the shaytan jumps out of mean men in mean ways; for example, I'm a Nazi's rape-child.

Dad used to say that you can make a girl so afraid of you that her fear turns into love. You can tie up a girl for so long that untying her breaks her heart. When Mom was nine months pregnant with me, and Dad made her sprint around the block, he didn't do it by swinging a belt at her. He knew that all he'd have to do was walk out the door and Mom would chase after him.

"Woman is the Nigger of the World," he told me when I was fifteen. "You see, the black man is not the true Nigger of the World, because in some places the black man is king. But the woman is a nigger wherever she goes." And now I march with the Daughters of Hajar. I'm a Radical Muslim Feminist with the authority of a self-hating sack of shit.

I made ghusl in the shower and dried off with a roll of paper towels. Emptied and refreshed, I sank into a couch and was awakened at around 2:00 p.m. by the sounds of an African-American man and his Caucasian wife walking around. As I sat up, the woman scrambled for her hijab and went into her designated section. The man introduced himself. "I'm sorry to wake you," he said. "Have you made Zuhr?"

I hadn't so we did it together. He invited me to lead, which scared me at first but I got through it okay. After prayer I told him that I was just passing through. He replied that Abu-Bakr As-Siddiq was that kind of mosque, a bus-stop masjid for a bus-stop town. He told me that he and his wife used to live in the mosque before moving to Portland. Said he liked Eugene better—

Portland Muslims were tense from all the FBI scrutiny. Eugene Muslims were naturally chill, "maybe *too* chill since we don't even have an imam."

Neither of us had grown up in a Muslim house, so we shared the obligatory stories of how we arrived at the deen—

> I'm just an American boy raised on MTV
> and I've seen all those kids in the soda-pop ads
> but none of 'em looked like me
> so I started lookin' around for a light out of the dim
> and the first thing I heard that made sense was the word
> of Mohammed, peace be upon him
> —Steve Earle, "John Walker's Blues"

I left out the part of my story where I quit praying and pissed on a Qur'an in my mom's backyard. He looked at me like I was really his brother while those little things cut at me silently from within. That's life as a munafiqeen.

My old apostasy essay still floats online. It will always be there. You can also find it on page 361 of Ibn Warraq's *Leaving Islam* anthology. Prometheus Books sent me a free contributor's copy addressed to "Professor Knight." People still ask about it; Muslims write me trying to win one back to their team, Christians ask if I had ever considered Jesus. A Hindu once emailed his congratulations. I wish they'd just leave me alone.

I'm not an apostate, not anymore—*la ilaha illah Allah/Muhammadu Rasullullah*. My story with Islam is like one of those terrible relationships that never really end, though we consistently bring out the worst in each other. Even as a Muslim I entertain a few unacceptable ideas, and when I sit in a mosque like this, either alone or with a true brother, I still feel that empty little pit.

One of my unacceptable ideas is that Prophet Muhammad did horrible things that can't be brushed aside with a simple "it was okay in that time and place." There are a few ways to look at it, but I reconciled the issue by realizing that those ugly moments in Muhammad's life—the wars and Qurayzas and mean stuff—had all gone down after Khadija died. The man had a broken heart and it messed him up, made him hard. That I can relate to.

The moment of this realization was fictionalized in an unfinished, unpublished novel titled *Ben Majnun:*

> Ben thought about that as he held a warm naked girl in his arms
> who had love for him that wasn't only lusting or crushing or puppy-

something and it wasn't the kind of love that'd make her bound to his bed forever. What she really had for Ben could best be called a ridiculous extreme of compassion.

Somebody had that for the Prophet, even when he'd run down from mountaintops and tell her what crazy voices were saying to him. I'm going nuts, he'd cry, I'm really losing it this time and Khadjia would just bury his head in her bosom and hold him tight. What would it be like to not have that after so long?

If Rasullullah's downfall was that he felt sad and lonely over a girl, Ben could see a little Sunni in himself—

On their way out, my new brother's wife said they needed to buy more tuna for the cat. He said they didn't have time, or something—I'm not sure what the issue was—but anyway they were having a little tiff over it so I intervened with an offer to go buy the tuna myself. The cat's the landlord, I told him, and I owed him rent. So they left and I walked to the store. Bought two cans of salmon and gave the cat one. He gobbled it up fast and then sprawled out on the sidewalk. I sat out in front and watched him for a while, though he didn't do anything but lift his head to hiss at me. I didn't hiss back. There was a hadith or something about being nice to cats, right? One woman was perfect in every aspect of her rituals, but Allah sent her to hell because she wouldn't feed her cat; and then another woman was kind to her cat, so she went to heaven even after stink-palming Uthman.

I washed my shirts with a bar of soap under the wudhu faucets and hung them over the bathroom stall doors. In the library I found a few books in English; read a commentary on Ya Sin, read a book on the concept of tawhid, flipped through some old Muslim magazines. Learned that Hasan al-Basri said man was only a group of days and when each day passed, he lost a part of himself. I tried calculating how many parts of myself I had lost to that sayyeda girl since the week of Thanksgiving.

W.D. Fard also followed the wounded-heart-sunna, going really weird after losing a girl. A year or so before making his master escape, he left his roles in Detroit and Chicago to go back to Los Angeles and see Hazel one more time. That was when he had grown his hair into a mullet and put white sheets over the seats of his car.

Nobody came for Asr, Maghrib or Isha so I did them alone but with all the formalities, which meant turning on the terrible sound system and giving out-of-tune adhans on the microphone. The mosque smelled, but for some reason I only noticed it at night.

And night was when I got lonely. I was itching to call this girl, and then

I was itching to call *any* girl. It was a real, physical itch—like the symptoms of a crack-fiend. But I was at the rehab center for that kind of thing, so I turned back to my Ya Sin book. The commentator said something about the Qur'an describing day as a "cover" over night, meaning that night was the original or normal state. It was 11:26 p.m. when I read that and dogs were barking outside.

If I was the skinny and bald-chinned singer of an emo band, my Alabama sayyeda could have been the Immortal Ex-Girlfriend who'd inspire a few albums' worth of terrible lyrics. The driving force of every emo band was its whiny, skinny frontman.

One thing I'll give the emo boys: they really do capture what it means to be young and have the blood running hard. They sing upbeat, poppy songs about high-school romances but get so epic and urgent on it, you really believe that their girls had broken them in half. And then you're propping up a seventeen-year old skater in his zip-up Etnies hoodie as your tragic hero, which isn't so bad if you remember that Shakespeare wrote about teenagers killing themselves over each other. But I was too old for all of that.

I woke up to a loud Fajr adhan, went into the prayer room and found the married brother from the day before. I joined his prayer, still only half-awake and having forgotten to make wudhu. As we sat afterwards he told me that his marriage wasn't completely working out. He still thought about what else was out there. He expected more from her, and more from himself, and their new baby was a stress. Then he thought about it.

"But it's also a source of strength," he said. "Al-hamdulilah." Then he told me how Allah first offered Islam to the mountains but the mountains turned it down, afraid they couldn't bear the weight, "so we all have something inside us that could crush a mountain, that's how strong Allah made us."

There's never anyone at the mosque, he told me while pulling up at the carpet. "It's usually just me, but that's why I like it. I don't think there's any kind of masjid like this place." After he left I put out the second can of salmon, fixed myself some ramen noodles and went back to bed.

One afternoon a Malaysian brother came with his autistic son to do exercises in the prayer room. I watched the dad as he coaxed his boy to do somersaults and such. He told me that I could crash in the mosque as long as I wanted.

That same night I sat alone in the library and called a friend in Los Angeles (which was called Love Allah in the Five Percenters' lexicon). Far and away the most sexually charged Muslim virgin I had ever encountered, she fiended for dick so bad she'd grind her teeth at night and had to wear a special dental device. She was tensed out and knew what she had to do but could never dream of actually going ahead with it. I have to confess that I wanted to grey-dog down to UCLA and solve her problem.

A week ago her mom brought home the first suitor. If he wins he has no idea what he's in for. And maybe he'll hate her for it.

With a shower, plenty of sleeping bags and blankets that had been left behind and a grocery store within walking distance, there wasn't anything else I needed. I could sleep on a couch, or in the prayer room with my head towards qiblah, or in the library surrounded by walls of books I could never read. I even found a way onto the roof and hung out there with my hot ramen noodles and a biography of Muhammad Ibn Abdul-Wahhab that had been published by a Riyadh university in 1979. The way that book put it, he didn't seem so bad. I wrote a few letters as it seemed that my circumstances put me in a unique position for that kind of thing. I wondered about those who lived in the mosque before me: where they came from, why they left, whatever became of them out there in Eugene and beyond. I knew that I'd have to leave too, that this place wasn't really my fort.

I had no interest in seeing an Abu-Bakr As-Siddiq jum'aa, if it even had a jum'aa. Sharing the mosque with any sizeable group of brothers would have killed it for me. So on Thursday I gave my salams to the goat head, said *khuda hafiz* to the cat and walked back to the bus station.

23

Rode to Boulder, Colorado, which didn't have its own bus station so they dropped me off at a Mobil. Zeshan picked me up and gave me one of his backstage passes to a three-day music festival out in Lyons. I had arrived in time for the second show, headlined by Joan Baez (who my father had once called "the female Robinson Crusoe of her time"). It was mostly hippie and bluegrass acts, which left me confused by the presence of one Ben Kweller doing his indie-rock/emo-pop or whatever it's called. He began his set on the third night with an acoustic cover of "Ice Ice Baby" to an audience of folkies who didn't get it. Ben won them over by the end, even though he messed up the words on three songs and a roadie made fun of him for putting up the collar on his denim jacket: "It wasn't cool in the '80s, and it's not cool now."

I later called Khalida, who was riding a train from Power Hill to Now Why. She told me that there were now seven progressive mosques across the country and I started us on a big argument about the scene.

I know that organized religion generally isn't cool. "Progressive Islam" is for people who know this but lack the heart to admit it, whether to the Community or themselves. They play the same "Is this okay with Imam?" game as conservative or traditional Muslims, just looking for new imams and scholars to give them softer answers. They're trying to change what's legitimate, but who needs to be legitimate? Progressives write their Islam with wash-off kids' markers.

Back when I first began writing for *Muslim WakeUp,* readers would post comments blasting Progressive Islam like it had anything to do with me. I did an article on my time at the 2003 ISNA convention and someone wrote, "Does Mr. Knight look forward to a pot-smoking/gay American Muslim culture... is this what 'Progressive' Islam is aspiring to achieve in the US?" Which is fine by me, but I could care less about calling it *progressive.*

"It's just a term for watered-down liberal chickenshits," I told Khalida.

"I don't think my Islam is watered down," she replied. Khalida used the term because it helped round up all the Muslims who believed in mosques being safe places for women and homosexuals. I couldn't argue with that.

Zeshan was a straight-up hashishiyyun, with baggies and bongs all over his house and a basement full of lamps. The only way he could afford to smoke as much as he wanted was to grow his own. Zeshan had thousands of dollars' worth of plants and equipment downstairs but he was in it for the love—he called weed a sacrament and explained to me which varieties took longer to mature, adding that they were more potent: "The more light it gets, the more light it gives you."

He also grew mushrooms, though he was hesitant to eat or even sell them because he had so much taqwa love/fear for the things. He had tried them a couple times but found the effects to be emotionally terrifying: "It just brought out a whole lot of shit that I didn't want to deal with." So he only grew shrooms out of awe for the fact that he could, like he had a special role in Allah's creation.

I knew that disciples of the Sufi saint Haydar spread cannabis leaves around his tomb and in Turkey, Lord Byron popped opium tabs with *mash'Allah* stamped on them—but I had never heard of a notable encounter between Muslims and mushrooms. One of Zeshan's books had a map showing worldwide psilocybe sightings; while North and South America were covered with dots, the whole Arab world had only two (both in Morocco). But southern India had some, as did central Africa, Indonesia and Malaysia. I called Peter Lamborn Wilson and he said that my best bet would be central Asia where Sufism met Shamanism, like Kazakhstan and on up to Siberia, and a patron saint of mind-altering substances "in a generic sense" would be Lal

Shahbaz Qalandar, one of those rare Kabir-types to earn deep devotion from both Muslims and Hindus. Peter said that Pakistan's Qalandari Sufis would use mushrooms if they knew about them. I also asked him about the Evanzz theory that *Shahbaz* was the root for W.D. Fard's *Shabazz*, which would fit with Fard being South Asian. Peter said it sounded alright but he wouldn't bank on the idea, adding that *shabbaz!* is a popular exclamation in Baluchistan.

He wondered why my interest in drugs and Islam was so mushroom-specific: "Why not something easier, like cannabis?" I didn't know what to tell him. In my other ear, Zeshan said that somewhere in the Americas, maybe six or seven millennia back, mushrooms were the center of a whole religion—either revered as a means of accessing God or worshipped as gods themselves. You could find Islam in there somewhere... I just knew it.

Before the advent of Muhammad, Allah sent a messenger to every nation in the history of the world; but did every messenger have to be human? When I held what looked like a vacuum-sealed bag of trail mix in my hands I told it, "You are Rasul, the Rasullullah." But not Rasullullah in the way that Muhammad was, because in this relationship *I'm* Muhammad. You're Rasullullah like Jibril.

I told Zeshan that I wanted to try shrooms and he said okay, if it was an easy dose in a proper environment—nothing stupid like tripping at a concert. He took me to Rocky Mountain National Park with two bags weighing in at a gram each.

The mountains were covered with pine-tree legions until the height at which trees couldn't grow, the alpine tundra. Zeshan balanced the steering wheel with his legs as he lit a bowl. "We're on the highest roads in the United States," he said. In the back of his jeep somewhere sat the mushrooms tucked away. I wondered what I'd find with them and then thoughts of my father scared the hell out of me. I already carried the genetic code for schizophrenia; maybe I'd set it off somehow. We got to our campsite and Zeshan inflated his raft. He said the right place for my experiment would be our own private island, far from campers and rangers so I could scream or do whatever I had to do. So we went down to the reservoir and Zeshan rowed us out. Between us sat a backpack with the weed and some peanut-butter sandwiches. The island was covered with trees and went roughly half the length of a football field. While Zeshan sat at a crumbling picnic table cutting up the shrooms we talked music. His favorite kinds were punk and reggae because both began as protest music, all about being poor and powerless and just spitting up your hate at the ruling class. Zeshan had been to Costa Rica and said the Rastafarians there were totally cool with him. I told him that I had been to Harlem and the Five Percenters were totally cool with me.

I grabbed a water bottle for the moment of truth. Zeshan warned that the shrooms could be bitter and tough to swallow. I said *bismillah* and had no problem. He said that was a good sign. Then I walked away to find a quiet spot. Sat on a big stone for a while. Rolled up my Dickies to wade in the reservoir. Paced back and forth watching ants in the dirt and sunlight wiggling on the water, waiting for something to not look right. Waved my hand back and forth in front of my face like John Cena. Nothing.

I found another picnic table and laid down on it. When I got back up I felt carsick and my legs seemed wobbly but weighted. My hearing seemed stronger, as I detected every scurrying critter on the island or in the water or birds a mile away and the sounds in my own mouth were amplified. Every movement seemed deliberate and slow. I took a piss on a tree and contemplated the fact of my penis looking like a mushroom, kind of.

I was happy but not in a stupid drunk-happy, I just had the calm contentment of an old man who had seen his troubles dulled away by the years… from a vantage point where I could smile at the huge chip on my shoulder I had as a young man, and know that I'd have to pass it along to another young man when it came his time… on and on it went through the cipher.

Zeshan came over to check on me. I explained the physical symptoms and he said everything seemed normal. He told me a quote by some obscure demo band called Spazztic Blurr: "IF YOU'RE SERIOUS, YOU LOSE." It struck me as the most brilliant idea I had ever heard. I hoped to someday slip Ibrahim Hooper some GHB so I could scrawl the quote on his forehead with a black Sharpie.

Zeshan rowed us back to the camp. On the way I took the second gram, since he didn't want it ("The only thing I have a tolerance for is pot"). My head rolled around on my shoulders but at no point was I ever "wasted" or saw things that weren't there—I only felt like my emotions had evened out and I had blossomed into the most normal, well-adjusted human being I could ever be. Though slightly less coordinated. I was never in a state of mind that'd make my prayer invalid, though prayer had become unnecessary and I don't mean that as any kind of blasphemy… on the contrary, I was overjoyed that Allah could make such a beautiful thing grow from heaps of cow dung. Maybe the Hindus were right and cattle really were sacred—Peter had told me that some suspected the Ṛg Veda's original Soma to be a mushroom.

We'd later sit around the campfire, Zeshan with his weed and me with my s'mores though I kept goofing them up. With only pine trees around I couldn't find a decent stick, so I picked up a huge one that was more like a complete branch. Then I couldn't get the marshmallows off the stick and onto the chocolate and the graham crackers just smeared everything around.

"It'll work itself out," I said, which Zeshan found hilarious.

We spent all night just talking and laughing and taking it easy—which doesn't seem a big deal, but it was for me. I didn't always know how to *take it easy* or really have fun or just relax and chit-chat with people, I was so full-throttle on one thing or another, be it W.D. Fard or a girl. When I was a little kid I couldn't hold a conversation about anything but pro wrestling. I ate, slept and breathed the WWF and to deal with anything else interfered with my one reason to live. As a teenager I gave Hulk Hogan's championship belt to Malcolm X but it turned out the same. And these days all I wanted to do was write. Addictive personality, you know? Anything can be a drug.

The mushrooms helped me to understand F. Scott Fitzgerald's alcoholism. As a writer you have to get in the mix with people and social situations but you're so introverted and insecure that you just sit in a corner waiting for the party to find you. How can you learn to write dialogue without ever talking to people?

"Why is this illegal?" I asked Zeshan, though I wasn't sure if I meant that in a U.S. government sense or the halal/haram sense. I told him that I couldn't look at shrooms or weed as drugs. Drugs are artificial things made in labs for profit. Hitler gave his soldiers meth so they'd stay awake—*that's* a drug. Zeshan told me that marijuana was technically considered a flower, but how does one rally voters to a "War on Flowers?"

24

Two days later I was on Fifth Avenue in Manhattan, mingling at a gallery showing by the SAWCC (South Asian Women's Culture Collective). I wanted to stop at the refreshments table and trade in my plastic cup of water for wine but something was holding me back, a weird mental block with no logical base—especially following the mushroom episode.

That same night I witnessed the second showing of *John Walker: the Musical* at Pace University's Michael Schimmel Center for the Arts. The show's official website promised a "rock and roll black comedy" full of "chases and hot girl fights, inventive dance numbers, shifting loyalties and sudden plot twists," the banner featuring a red, white and blue stars-and-stripes guitar with John's face as the sound-hole. It was the FCI Victorville John, clean-shaven and crew-cutted, looking like a regular Army grunt.

As the story went, a captured John Walker became the scapegoat of a demagogue named "Ed" (who spoke with a slight Texas accent and told his patriots, "BE SCARED ALL THE TIME"). Ed set up John's "escape" from U.S. custody to spark panic in the American people—and make himself over as Savior for recapturing the American Taliban. So we had John Walker running across the country with a tabloid reporter in search of a government agent who could help him. Everyone sang their own theme song (the reporter's was titled "I'm No Hemingway"), with music supplied by the "Taliband."

The whole thing was supposed to be funny but I couldn't laugh when it showed a teen John Walker listening to hip-hop and reading Malcolm's autobiography... or when he delivered a monologue about being a social outcast, or a song ("You Hurt My Feelings") directed at a girl he crushed over in high school... or when he told the story of his shahadah and how he changed his name, changed his dress and began studying under a strict Pakistani... or when his coddling Mom told him it was "you and me against the world" and that she'd stand beside him no matter what he did. While the audience giggled during her musical number ("I Support You"), I had tears in my eyes.

Then the reporter told John, "Not everyone is like you—they don't go to such depths to read and study and think—" and I almost ran out of the theater.

John was born in 1981, four years younger than me.

We both came from Irish-Catholic backgrounds and broken homes.

We were both sixteen when we took shahadah, sparked by Malcolm X and Chuck D.

I went to Pakistan in 1994 and was talked out of joining the war for Chechen independence.

John went to Yemen in 1998 and Pakistan in 2000.

We both made trips to Peshawar.

Nobody talked him out of anything.

He went to Afghanistan in 2001.

The kid was named after John Lennon and Chief Justice John Marshall.

Before belting out his rock-operatic "I'm Going to Afghanistan" (with burqa-clad backup dancers), John was introduced as a "21st-century teenage rebel." Earlier wheeled out by Ed on a gurney, bound and blindfolded in an orange jumpsuit, he was decried as "the worst American in the history of these United States."

The show ended with actor Brian Charles Rooney sitting in a cage while the whole cast sang "The Ballad of John Walker:"

John Walker came from California!
John Walker came from California...

I was in such a daze as we filed out that I made a wrong turn after City Hall Park and ended up going a different route than I had taken before. Soon I found myself in front of World Trade Center station, which was lit up like a baseball park. I went down the steps into the empty concrete plain that people took to subways and PATH trains but everyone was still quiet and respectful of the place—and there were still people having their pictures taken or looking through the fence at dark Ground Zero.

> Can the devil fool a Muslim nowadays?
> —Wu-Tang Clan, "A Better Tomorrow"

With some video game systems, if there were a lot of characters and action on the screen at one time everything would clog up and slow down as the console struggled to process it. My brain did that for me, overloading on the interconnectedness of countries and wars and years piled one on top of the other and how it all added up to one-point-eight million tons of concrete, steel, L.L. Bean office furniture and human beings tumbling down on itself. For enough people this was the whole of Islam's story, the first thing they'll think of when you say "Islam in America" and nothing will ever outweigh it.

For a second of inexpressible mental clarity, I understood. And then I lost it. I felt like I had smoked dope, the way it all came together and then vanished.

I called Khalida and that completed the cipher, Irish-white John Walker calling his Afghan heart. She was having an awful time at a party and for a second it looked like I'd ride a gray-dog to Power Hill so we could save each other, but then she went to a friend's house and crashed. I slept at the Port Authority station on spread-out pages of *Gaming Today*. Every twenty minutes or so a cop would come by and kick my foot. In my half-asleep moments I thought of various high-impact scenes from Spike Lee's *Malcolm X*: what they meant for me, and what I knew they meant for John. I wondered if he had also closed his eyes during the assassination scene.

And we both saw that movie with our moms.

The next day I'd go with Sara to see Face to Face play what I think was their last New York show ever. While I sang along to "Disconnected," jumped around in the pit with an Ahmadiyya girl and took elbows to the head, John Walker sat in FCI Victorville on the margins of the Mojave Desert.

25

Read! Read in the Name of your Lord who created. He created man from a clot. Read! He who taught with the pen, taught man what he knew not.

—the Qur'an

Greyhound bus drivers love to suck cock. They will suck you off until you come in their mouth. Big cock, small cock, clean cock, or dirty cocks. They will suck any cock because they are COCKSUCKERS. I would love to kick a bus driver's ass.
—graffiti found in the restroom of Greyhound coach #7241

These were the two worlds that I juggled all summer with varying success, but the Ameripass had just a couple of days left and then I'd be back in Geneva. Might as well end the marathon sprinting—so after taking a straight-shot express all the way from Denver to New York, I hopped back on and rode down to Houston. Just getting there and back would kill off the last week of my unlimited Greyhound pass and make my mileage count pass 20,000, which in the Supreme Mathematics would be Wisdom Cipher Cipher Cipher Cipher.

Houston had a mosque I wanted to see, a former bank that had been purchased by the Rockets' great Hakeem Olajuwon and turned into the Islamic Daw'ah Center. And I had a friend in town, a fauxhawk-wearing med-school dropout named Muna. And Houston used to be the playground for rich Saudis. And a Taliban envoy had gone there in the 1990s for some sketchy reason that I forget. And strangely, this would be the first time in all my Wisdom Cipher Cipher Cipher Cipher that I'd even step foot in Texas.

I got a message from Muna saying that she had been called into work. After getting off the bus all I had to do in Houston was walk downtown to Hakeem Olajuwon's mosque and then walk back to the station to get on a bus home.

With its stately gray stone and towering columns the Daw'ah Center looked like a former bank, or City Hall or courthouse or any important build-ing from a more noble age in architecture. The front door was locked and a sign said the entrance was in back but that door was locked too, until the receptionist (a middle-aged, rotund South Asian man with white hair and moustache) came and let me in. I left my shoes in the appointed cubby-holes and took the wooden double-doors to an airy, red-carpeted expanse that was surrounded by marble balconies and topped with a high arced ceiling, covered in intricate designs that may or may not have been part of the original bank. The only light came in through tall, sheer-curtained windows on the opposite wall—which I assumed was the qiblah wall until spotting a minbar on my left. That's how you can tell that this wasn't always a mosque.

Also: the stone balcony wrapping around the prayer hall wasn't the women's section. The women's half was side-by-side with the men, cut off by a wooden divider.

Other than that, it was a normal mosque. It had plastic folding chairs for old men. A huge copper plaque of Sura Ya Sin hung on the wall. I made my two nafl rakats facing sideways, which still felt wrong even though I knew it was qiblah. Then I walked back out to the lobby and spotted a sign reading "ABU BAKR AS-SIDDIQ." I couldn't help but smile, thinking of the Eugene mosque with its frozen goat-head.

Back at the Greyhound station, I was on my way to the gate when I spotted Muna just kind of standing around. She said she had decided to swing by to see if she could find me. I convinced her to skip work and her classes and drive me around Houston.

During the tour she told me that they filmed *Rushmore* in Houston and she had to pass by the school on her way to work, so I launched into my theory that Wes Anderson was secretly obsessed with F. Scott Fitzgerald: if you look at Scott in his time at Princeton, it perfectly matches the character of Max. Muna bought the shoes she had on because they looked like ones worn by Janet of Sleater-Kinney. And she told me that sometimes she felt out of place, being "the brown girl" at punk-rock shows. At one point we talked about Islam and I said I had lost the energy to care about religious things anymore. She seemed relieved by that.

Houston was really hot that afternoon, so when we passed the huge Mecom Fountain with its algae-laden pools and awesome jets Muna said she'd jump in. I told her she wouldn't so she found a place to park and we both went in. Just kind of sat in there for a long time, talking and playing with the water while these high-powered streams blasted up all around us. We waved at passing traffic and ducked when cops went by. I flipped off a bus, just loving the fact that I wasn't on it. Muna didn't want to go to the center of the fountain, where the biggest water-jet looked like it'd hurt, but I dragged her in and then she had no problem. I could have stayed in the water all day, but eventually we went back to driving and Muna found a park for us to do cartwheels and drip dry.

Before it was over we were lying in the grass while kids played around us and harmless lap dogs challenged each other. I had my arm around her and she put her head on my shoulder, and that was it and all anyone needed. I don't remember reading an ayat that says you can't cuddle in the park. If there was such a thing in the Qur'an, only a mean human put it there. Takbir.

She told me not to be a stranger. I said I'd be around but then wondered, when would I ever be in Houston again? I at least wanted to mean it and make it true. Muna was a cool person. To think you're never going to see someone again just brings up the whole stink of there being a time when no one will see anyone, since at the end of the party we're all going to our own private graves.... Schopenhauer said something about every parting being a small taste of death and every reunion a small taste of resurrection (I used it as my senior yearbook quote), but what if there's no reunion? Even with the millions of freaks that I had shared Greyhounds with, and the thousands that I'd say some words to or even engage in decent conversation there was something to the fact that those brief exchanges were all we'd ever have for each other. Or the guy in Chicago at whatever time of night it was, yelling that he had no thumbs—he had his walk-on and walk-off and that was all, unless he could make it to the next ISNA convention.

Anyway, it was healing for me to hold this girl. Healing from what, I'm not sure—maybe from Zainab, though it could have just been from the psychological torture of life on the grey-dog. I imagined a voice in my head saying MIKAIL, YOU ONLY WANT TO BE MOMMED and again I thought of the voice as belonging to Khalida; maybe since it called me Mikail.

I kissed Muna on the top of her head. She said she wished more people did that. After a few hours in the park she had to get home to her parents. She drove me back to the station and it overwhelmed me that this brief car-ride right here was the end of my summer—from Houston I'd just go back to Geneva, New York, to Mom's house and sit down at her computer to pound all this out into a book. Then it'd be another ISNA convention and from there, who knows. Maybe I'd go back to Buffalo and mop floors again.

I had been through the drill enough times in the last two months for them all to blur together into the same bus station and the same goodbye. We hugged and I lugged my bag out of the car. Gave her a sad smile before closing the door and then swung the bag on my back. I walked inside to the information desk and she drove home.

The itinerary said I'd get an hour layover in Birmingham, Alabama.

Isn't that a kick in the ass.

I should have figured. If you put enough energy out there, right? And leave it up to Allah, it'll turn out the way it's meant to. In this case it fit because I had seen Zainab once, and seen her twice, but Allah's the Supreme

Storyteller and He tells stories in three parts—plays come in three acts, successful movies become trilogies. Your standard plot triangle shows three escalations of conflict. This is Creative Writing 101—you think the Lord of all the Worlds doesn't have it down?

The Birmingham station was familiar by now, with the same drab yellow/off-white checkered floor, same greasy restaurant, same chairs with built-in TVs charging a quarter for fifteen minutes. Looking through the front doors at 19th St. North, it became a matter of principle not to go out and step foot in the real town—as long as I stayed in the confines of the Greyhound station, I wasn't really in Birmingham. This place fell under a whole other flag and set of laws.

I sat in a corner so I'd catch Zainab coming through the door before she saw me. I called her over. She had a sweet smile and gave no evidence of any tension or anxiety. I told her this was it, our final deaths out of each other's worlds. Zainab said no but knew I was right. She said something like "maybe I'll do my post-grad in Buffalo" but neither of us really believed it. When they called my bus I got up, gave her a one-armed hug and told her to have a good life. I walked to the gate without looking back.

I felt lousy but climbed aboard and knew that once I left Alabama I'd never need to be there again, and once I passed the Kentucky border into Ohio I was back in the North, while hitting Cleveland would put me in the Home Stretch and passing Buffalo meant the Nitty-Gritty. I put my bag under my seat, as I had every other ride of the last two months, but the driver barked "GET YOUR BAG OFF MY FLOOR!" At first I just pushed the bag's straps out of the aisle, because I thought that was what got him. He said it again like an even bigger dick than before: NO NO! GET YOUR BAG... OFF... MY FLOOR. So I put it in the overhead area and cursed him under my breath.

The bus broke down, as would my bus to Columbus the next day. We sat on the side of the road for two hours before another bus came and got us. At the Columbus station we all stormed the information desk and the Customer Service guy began sweating bullets. I wanted him to print me a ticket to Geneva because my pass would run out on the 28th—if all these bus failures caused me to be on the road when the pass expired I'd be fucked, so I wanted a guarantee that I'd make it home—but he refused and said I'd *probably* be alright.

"WHAT IF ANOTHER BUS BREAKS DOWN?" I shouted with twenty people in line behind me.

"SIR, ARE YOU TRYING TO HEAR ME?"

"NO, I'M NOT TRYING TO HEAR YOU! I'M TRYING TO MAKE IT HOME ON THE GODDAMN PASS THAT I PAID FOR!"

People started complaining about things that had nothing to do with the two-hour delay or their missed transfers—one lady said that since Greyhound merged with those other bus lines, all the little courtesies began disappearing, and someone else mentioned all the routes and stops that Greyhound cut as of August 18th. Then we shuffled towards our respective gates and waited in huddles of luggage and fury. It was nothing new to me; that summer I had heard the exclamation, "THIS IS THE LAST TIME I'M EVER RIDING GREYHOUND!" at least once in over a dozen cities.

Greyhound creates a culture of zero respect. The company doesn't respect its drivers, the drivers don't respect the passengers, and the passengers don't respect each other. The passengers in turn don't respect the company, and the company could care less about the passengers because we have no choice but to ride those lousy coaches. Negative feelings float in the stale air and eat into everyone, finally manifesting in anonymous prose like "GREYHOUND BUS DRIVERS LOVE TO SUCK COCK" scrawled on the walls of poorly lit, poorly maintained and sour-smelling coach restrooms.

When we made it to Cleveland I thought that the station looked a lot like Birmingham's: the same checkered floor, general shape and design, color scheme. A few things were switched around. Maybe all stations had that checkered floor and I only noticed it in Birmingham and Cleveland.

For a second I thought of working a few weeks to get another Ameripass and then heading off to find the tomb of America's first home-grown Sufi saint, Samuel L. Lewis, who studied directly under Hazrat Inayat Khan. Born in San Francisco in 1896, his father Jacob was V.P. of Levi-Strauss and his great-grandfather invented the copper rivets used on Asma Gull Hasan's blue jeans... or I could try to find the Melungeons, a strange race of Appalachian hillbillies in Tennessee with allegedly Turkish or Berber Muslim ancestors and then I'd go up to Elkader, a small town in Iowa named for an Algerian freedom-fighter who achieved international celebrity in the nineteenth century; half-Melungeon Abraham Lincoln sent him a pair of ornately decorated dueling pistols.

Perhaps I'd just ride up to Alaska and learn how they figure out prayer-times when the sun stays up or down for six months. Allah being Lord of East and West, I can land anywhere and build—I could stay on the road until the time for Muslim Mardi Gras, heading down to New Orleans to toss zikr beads at drunk hijabi girls but then the tale will just go on unraveling forever. We could be within ten years of seeing a Muslim American sitcom on ABC's Friday lineup, which I'll watch if it revolves around the sassy teenage daughter (and I imagine it will). Of course, there was a whole Muslim network on the way: Bridges TV with its headquarters in the terrible suburb of Amherst,

New York, where I worked lame overnights—I think Warith Deen had something to do with it...

We could also be within ten years of seeing Senator Seeme Hasan (R, Colorado) while John Walker is within ten years of starting another ten years on the same cell bunk. The Vegan Kung-Fu Ayatollah, Isa Adam al-Naziri might be crazy enough to be within ten years of becoming the next household name.

I wonder how they'll all turn out but I can't go bumming around for the next decade trying to write while on a moving bus. In Boulder I had passed a motel with the sign reading, "FACE IT—YOU'RE TOO OLD TO SLEEP ON THE GROUND!"

Something like forty-five hours after leaving Houston, I was dropped back in Geneva. And then my summer was done. I still smelled like the algae of Mecom Fountain and my tailbone hurt really, really bad.

PART III: PURE PRODUCTS OF AMERICA

"I did not register on or about April 27, 1942, when the law of the U. S. said I should have, because of my religion, Islam. I have been advised by Allah, the Almighty Supreme Being, Mr. W. D. Fard, Mohammed, not to take any part in any wars - not even a holy war. To me, the act of registering is part of war, and this is why I will not register and then apply for consideration as a conscientious objector."

I went back to squatting in the Commuter Lounge at Buff State, where they had free Pop-Tarts and a computer to waste my time until I ducked out early in the morning.

While scrolling down a listserv discussion of Elijah Muhammad's mental health, I encountered the following post:

> As for W.D. Fard, he was perhaps from Iran. I do believe, as the development of the NOI has come about, that he was loyal to Ahlul-Bayt.

It never ends. But it's done for me.

Before tossing Fard's 816-page FBI file in the trash I flipped through it to see if I had missed anything, learning that the man had a small scar on the back of his left hand and a black mole on the right side of his stomach.

The file also included summaries of Elijah Muhammad's monitored phone conversations, such as:

> June 1, 1965
> [name censored] told ELIJAH MUHAMMAD that a man apparently CASSIUS CLAY was on his way back over there. MUHAMMAD stated he wanted CLAY by his side until he was straight on one course or another.

Two days later the feds noted a woman (name also censored) telling Elijah that since "God himself" had his tonsils removed, Elijah shouldn't be afraid to take his own medicine as instructed. For a second I wondered if Muhammad Abdullah's tonsils had been removed or if he had scars and moles but then got over it. Fard was and is my American Islam, and I still read his lessons more than the Qur'an, but I don't need a reliable origin story.

At the end of the summer came another ISNA convention. The year before I had stink-palmed Cat Stevens and Siraj Wahhaj, handed out Kinko's-made copies of my novel and aspired to chokeslam Muzammil Siddiqi through the roof of McCormick Place. This year I'd speak on a panel—the ISNA people even gave me complimentary registration and an invitation letter from Secretary General Sayyid M. Syeed. Hot damn, right? And my books now had an ISBN number, smooth covers, perfect binding, bar codes and review blurbs on the back. So I guess punk is dead.

I showed up Friday morning with twenty copies of *The Taqwacores* shoved into a Budweiser box. It had a convenient handle and the books fit perfectly, but walking around the bazaar got me some double takes. It almost hurt, which I enjoyed in a sad kind of way. I hadn't tasted beer since I was five years old and so their dirty looks came undeserved, but I still brought them on deliberately—like I could cart away all of their pettiness in a red-and-white cardboard box.

Then I saw some stretched-out deerskins with Ya Sin branded on them. The smaller one went for $200 and the big one was $400. The vendor saw me inspecting them, looked at my special speaker nametag and asked about the beer.

"It's not beer," I said and showed him. "It's books."

"But it doesn't look right!"

"Doesn't look right? Who's got the fucking Qur'an on a carcass?"

To stay mindful of my true place in the pecking order of American Muslim writers, I accepted Asma Gull Hasan's invitation to work at her booth for a few hours. The kicker was that she shared it with her brother Ali Hasan of Muslims for Bush. The combined booth was an impressive endeavor with six tables, leather furniture and a back display featuring Seeme and Ali with George W. Bush on one side, Asma's blown-up book cover on the other. I stayed on Asma's side and watched everyone take their respective dumps on her. Someone drew a moustache on her poster, people signed her mailing list as John Kerry or "BUSH IN HELL," and a middle-aged desi man pointed at her to announce, "that's the crap of the world sitting right there."

Asra Nomani was at ISNA to give a presentation on her Muslim Women's Bill of Rights but I couldn't find the right lecture hall until it was already over. I walked in and spotted a boom mic hanging over a huddle of people, Asra at the center with a cameraman's bright light in her face. Between her piece in *Time* hitting newsstands Monday and the AP wire on Muslims for Bush, I don't think an ISNA convention had ever been so tied to mainstream America.

Asra wanted to hit the main hall and hear Hamza Yusuf speak, his topic being "Only for the Love of Allah: Devotion Through Giving." The chairs in the main hall were all graced with envelopes and complimentary ISNA pens. I took a bunch of pens but they were designed to fall apart about twelve seconds after you wrote your check. I left before the Hamza Show but stopped by later, watched for a minute and decided that he's an excited little worm. I also decided that he takes sharp little shits that hurt him, even though they're not big. They're just sharp. If you look at him it makes sense.

Saturday night I rode away from the Donald E. Stephens Center in a chauffeured van with the Hasans, their cousin Omer, a hired bodyguard and Asma's two friends. The traffic slowed to a crawl and I looked out at a sidewalk flooded with Muslims of every background and category, knowing that if ISNA 2004 was a wrestling federation (which was naturally how I viewed it) I had found myself sitting with Triple H, the main-event villain that a sold-out arena cheers to see torn apart. Ali told me about his meeting with the American Muslim Task Force, an umbrella group covering ISNA, CAIR and the rest of them—the way I heard the story, he had single-handedly prevented the AMTF from backing Ralph Nader (who had actually been spotted at the convention that day). Of course, Hooper's call at the meeting for an endorsement of Nader was only his gift to the Bush-loving Saudis that left bloody riyals hanging out of his anus. Behind closed doors the Muslim Illuminati asked Ali Hasan for another meeting with Bush. Ali said he'd talk to his dad and see what he could do. The mind-blowing part was that his dad really could produce the president.*

---

* Dr. Malik Hasan began with a modest Colorado HMO called Qual-Med. As he acquired other HMOs, Malik made sure to appoint directors who'd cut down the medical-loss ratio:

> If an obstetrician wanted to keep a new mother in the hospital for a second or third day after delivery, Qual-Med directors would say no on the grounds that it wasn't medically necessary. If an orthopedist wanted to order a second MRI, he was told no as well, on the same grounds.
> —George Anders, *Health Against Wealth: HMOs and the Breakdown of Medical Trust*

After a series of acquisitions and mergers, Malik emerged as CEO of the fourth-largest HMO in the country. He became interested in politics, funding and chairing the Council for American Muslim Understanding (CAMU), whose existence was "encouraged" by the State Department for the flooding of the Muslim world with pro-American ideas. Malik's congressman arranged him a meeting with George W. Bush in 1999 at the governor's mansion. Malik received a tour of the place and they talked health care, and the good doctor liked what he heard.

I made my way back to ISNA and slept under an MSA table. The next night I hung out with an Afghan-Uzbek girl named Inur. She told me how she had met Hamza Yusuf and said that he seemed really cool and soft-spoken but then went to his speech where he screamed like it was a pep rally. And ISNA wouldn't even let him speak until they had collected a certain amount of money, she said. The convention was only a racket and Hamza brought in the marks.

If ISNA '04 was a wrestling federation, of course he'd be the Rock. Perhaps the time was ripe for Hamza to make his own foray into feature films.

Eventually Inur's aunt called and asked where she was. We walked back through the lobby past some guys complaining that Yusuf had just repeated his earlier speech verbatim.

Before she left I asked Inur what brought her to ISNA.

"I really like Cat Stevens," she replied. "My sister said he'd be here."

Maybe a month after ISNA I found myself riding around Los Angeles in Ali Hasan's Lexus 470.

"You know who's the most talked-about Muslim leader in America right now?" he asked. "And the most written-about?" I thought it over until Ali thumb-pointed at himself.

I was there to see him get some more juice, this time out of Dennis Miller. And then I'd be another guy writing about him. So I didn't have to sleep in a dumpster the night before the show, Ali put me up in the Atrium Hotel. Cihan Kaan called me while I sat in a king-sized bed watching TV.

"Oh, you're *in* with them," said Cihan.

"Maybe I am."

"They *love* you."

"Maybe they do. But Ali loves everyone."

"You're their maggot mascot."

"Their what?"

"Their maggot mascot—you know, when rich people put themselves over by slumming around with poor writers who write about them." Maria back in Denver had preferred the term "slut-puppy." The topic passed and we talked about doing a Muslim-Punk movie. Cihan suggested that we call it *Amazing Ayyub and Umar Go to Burger King.*

The next day Ali picked me up in a chauffeured car sent by NBC and we went to the studio.

"Should I say that I think Muslims are voting for Bush?" he asked me from the makeup chair. "Is that being dishonest?"

"Not if you believe it."

"Think I should go with my point about Pakistan?"

"Sure." Then they had him switch seats so the hair-lady could work with him. Ali wanted a high pompadour ("Techno-Reagan," he called it) but she knew better.

I watched the taping from Ali's dressing room while picking from his complimentary tray of candy. Miller introduced the audience to his Varsity Panel: Ali (who pumped his fist and went "Woo!" like Ric Flair), columnist Cathy Seip and Al Torres, chairman of the California Democratic Party and member of MPAC. Ali started with his Pakistan angle and won audience applause for "We need Pakistan a lot more than we need France." He added that America was the best country for Muslims and he wanted Osama bin Laden dead.

"Ali," gushed Miller, "you're the most beautiful Muslim I've ever met." Cathy Seip tried making some kind of point and then Miller asked her, "are you terrified of Ali?" Ali put his arm around her and started moving in. "How can you be terrified," beamed Miller, "of the only Muslim on the make?"

Coming back from the break, we were treated to Dennis Miller and Ali Hasan arm-in-arm singing "Ebony and Ivory." Miller called Ali his man and his brother. Ali said something in Spanish to Al Torres. All I could say was holy shit, what a long way I was from building with Azreal Kennedy at Harlem's St. Nicholas projects, or Lawrence Nixon on Philadelphia's Broad Street. I felt like the rug from *The Big Lebowski* because in terms of American Islam, somehow I tied the room together—or at least I saw it that way, building inside my head on all the characters I had found.

After the taping, Cathy Seip's daughter, completely star-struck by Mr. Muslims for Bush, told Ali about her school and synagogue and progressive rabbi. Ali said he'd be thrilled to come speak at her school.

"I love Jews," he said.

"So you weren't raised to be very religious?" asked Cathy from across the room. What the hell did that mean?

"The Qur'an says that Jews are our brothers," Ali answered.

"That's not how they're reading it now."

"Some don't, but I'm confident that most read it that way."

"Really." She did not say it as a question, but Ali had won; the daughter was enamored and he had killed us all with kindness.

I knew a girl in Irvine, an eighteen-year-old desi freshman at UIC who wanted to be a writer. Shaytan lives in the testicles, so I had Ali drop me off at the campus. I tried calling but she wasn't around so I just circulated myself among the college kids before finding a table to write at. Called my friend Tom up in Santa Cruz. We were both completely broke and powerless to feed or transport ourselves. I had already used my last $1.09 and the last of my Sub Club cards, which had been given to me by an Albanian Muslim kid from Brooklyn who wrote his name and address on the back. If Allah still accepts du'as from me, He'll be hearing a few on behalf of Afrim Djonbalic.

Before my trip to California, I had mopped some floors so I could at least look forward to a direct deposit whenever it decided to kick in. Tom didn't have a job and faced the added stresses of a) a ticket for not wearing his seat belt, and b) eating a fourteen-year-old mezcal worm. We talked about digging up nickels and dimes like we were in seventh grade again.

"There's a certain romanticism to it, at times," I told him.

"Only for you, because writing about it gets you laid. Suck my dick and tell me how romantic it is."

Wasn't getting me anywhere that night. I just wanted a place to crash, but the UIC girl wouldn't pick up her phone and my prospects of sleeping anywhere besides behind the Book Exchange tent looked pretty slim. Could have called Ali to get me another room at the Atrium but that seemed the lazy way out; there's no fun to rolling the dice unless you're actually prepared to lose. I walked around the dark campus for a while and considered hopping buses back to Los Angeles. I had the idea in my head to head for 8152 Sunset Boulevard, where once stood a famed hotel named the Garden of Allah. Established by film star Alla Nazimova at the twilight of her career, the Garden of Allah included a bar, restaurant, swimming pool and bungalows and had been home to Humphrey Bogart, the Marx brothers and Ernest Hemingway. F. Scott Fitzgerald was there too, showing up in 1937 with a six-month MGM screenwriter's contract and three years left to live. The hotel is gone now, the space occupied by a pink plaza with a McDonald's. A replica Garden of Allah survives at Universal Studios in Orlando, Florida.

I forgot about the Garden of Allah and went to sleep on the grass in UIC's Aldrich Park, which was great by me, compared to Buffalo State's concrete lawns. Aldrich was also a better place to sleep than anywhere in D.C., where I could have been for the CAIR convention that weekend.

CAIR pretty quickly reveals its defining struggles: how do you maintain as a grass roots, civil-rights outfit while getting support from a kingdom with no concept of civil or human rights within its own borders?

How do you serve your pro-Bush benefactors while saving face with the American Muslim community?

How do you appeal to left-minded Americans while entertaining the Saudi-styled intolerance of Siraj Wahhaj?

Enter Wahhaj's co-keynote speaker, Ralph Nader.

By the next night I had gotten my check and could rent space for a while in the Anthill Pub, the campus bar. Over a Coke and grilled cheese sandwich I examined the Progressive scene. *Muslim WakeUp* editor-in-chief Ahmed Nassef was getting the wheels in motion to start his own organization, the Progressive Muslim Union. After a phone conversation with Sarah Eltantawi, I agreed to sit on the board of directors. There was a chance that it could end up just a liberal version of ISNA or CAIR, but it could be cool. So one more time—what's Progressive Islam?

In December 2002 I asked Farid Esack and he said that it was the use of Islam as "liberation theology" the way that Christianity had been applied in his native South Africa. At ISNA '04 I asked Asma Gull Hasan and she defined it as "being Muslim and being American without a contradiction between the two," while allowing that the term was largely a media creation.

Ali Hasan had referred to George W. Bush as the "Muslim World's Savior." I contemplated the depth of self-awareness in the Muslims for Bush kids—whether they know who they are and what they are and what they do and why they're doing it. It's hard to say; they could be essentially good people that have just spent their whole lives in Candy Land and don't know any better. They're both charming but with a TV shine, and they were nice enough to me but knew that I was writing about them. I haven't yet seen a side of Asma that you wouldn't catch in a three-minute *O'Reilly* segment. Ali's all hugs and kisses but lays it on a little thick.

My source warned me that Asma was hypersensitive when it came to what people wrote about her, citing the foaming conniptions she had when Omid Safi called her an "apologist." She had even demanded that he write a formal retraction and publish it in a journal.

"So I'm worried about the political ramifications for you," said my source, "if you offend the Hasans."

"What are they going to do," I replied. "Come to my job and take the mop out of my hand?"*

---

* See Appendix

Then my source asked what I thought about Imam Feisal Abdul Rauf, chauffeured head of the American Sufi Muslim Association and author of *What's Right with Islam*, which would later come out in paperback with its title changed to *What's Right with Islam is What's Right with America*. I replied that I had no use for him.

"Well, have you checked out his book?"

"Yeah, I have."

"What do you think about that cover photo? What does it say to you?"

"I think he's posing his hands like there's a brilliant truth floating in the air in front of him and he's about to choke it to death."

According to my source, Abdul Rauf still eats off rich Muslims in the Gulf states. If you broke down Progressive Islam using W.D. Fard's model of percentages, he would be a straight Ten Percenter pimping the mystery god. Eighty-Five Percenters—the deaf, dumb and blind, slaves to mental death and power—would be those poor marks paying $24.95 for *What's Right with Islam* in hardcover. I'm still waiting to find the Progressive Muslim Five Percenters, the ones that see through it all. They're probably hard to find because they don't have anything to do with this intellectual-scenester foolishness, they just live their lives and none of these names come up in their conversations.

Meanwhile, Barnes & Noble need more shelves for those getting in on the Battle for the Soul of Islam, another round of the mush of books with names like *What's Right with Islam, The Trouble with Islam, The Crisis of Islam, Taking Back Islam, Why I am a Muslim, Why I am Not a Muslim*, books promising to *unveil* Islam or go *beyond* the veil or *under* the veil or whatever, and some more smirking little hustlers who say "ijtihad" and then look at you blankly, knowing they've got nothing. I'd like to see which ones end up getting waved around in lecture halls of the future as seminal texts of the great post-9/11 something-something...

My interest in mushrooms led me to correspondence with an eccentric ethnobotanist named Ali Bey, who has over six hundred pages of material on the matter. In long-winded, tryptamine-fueled emails he'd tell me things like "you probably had *psilocybe cubensis*, when the Soma was thought to be *amanita muscaria*," and hint at the mind-blowing hadiths he had found. His book should come out soon, only to get squeezed off the shelves to make room for Asma Gull Hasan's *Halal Dating* and Irshad Manji's *Islam for Zionists*. But that's the business we're in.

Then there was me, growing dangerously aware that I could have a place—

At a lecture in Arizona, Mohja Kahf called me the *"enfant terrible of American Muslim writers."* Asra Nomani told me "this is how you can

206

finance your life," and said that *The Taqwacores* had led her to consider that women could lead men in prayer. Referring to the scene in which Rabeya, my niqabi riot grrl, gives a khutbah and serves as imam, Asra promised, "we're going to make that a reality."

As it seems that every corner of Western media has a throbbing boner for Muslims, and Muslims are stepping over each other to present themselves as redeemers of the Good Islam or champions of the New Islam, someone ought to become a millionaire while the getting is good. The thought arrived as I stared across a table at Irshad Manji.

Here was Irshad's dilemma: the story that she sold to non-Muslim readers had required her to stand alone. To properly cash in on Islam's internal crisis, she had to prove that she *was* the crisis, the single challenge that mullahs had been dreading all these fourteen centuries. She promoted her steel-cage match with the marketing savvy of a Vince McMahon: Irshad Manji, Lone Gay Muslim Woman vs. a Billion Angry, Bearded, Clitoris-Cutting Mohammedans. For Irshad to have any allies or backup within the Muslim community would take away from her melodrama; so while writing about Islam's treatment of women, she made no mention of scholars like Amina Wadud that have been promoting feminist readings of the Qur'an for years. Describing her alienation as a lesbian Muslim, she completely ignored the presence of an LGBT community like Al-Fatiha.

However, in doing so (and presenting Israel as a model of tolerance and liberal democracy for Muslims to follow), she found herself isolated from the actual movement for Islamic reform. While funding for her nascent Ijtihad Foundation supposedly ran in the millions, Irshad's name remained poison even to the *cool* Muslims. To maintain her relevance, she desperately needed to be filmed as a leader in the rising Progressive Muslim scene. Back around the time of the Morgantown protest, she had courted the Daughters of Hajar with offers to supply a camera crew. Asra Nomani was open to including her, but others in the group shot it down. Dispute over Irshad became so vehement that the Daughters of Hajar ultimately disbanded.

Now Irshad was trying to buddy up to Ahmed Nassef. Hoping for a spot with PMU, she made an appearance at the Progressive Muslim Meetup at Skylight Diner on West 34th in New York. As Irshad tried to plead her case and defend her statements on Palestine, I studied the facial expressions of her audience. Everyone looked like they had brooms up their asses. Sarah Eltantawi appeared ready to explode; Irshad's presence went against everything that she wanted PMU to be. She couldn't believe that Ahmed would have such poor political judgment as to consider selling out the group's legitimacy for Irshad's supposed starpower.

Ahmed talked about the upcoming PMU conference and passed around a sign-up sheet for anyone interested in helping out. By her own signature Irshad wrote, "Media Committee." I heard her explain to Ahmed that in promoting her book, she had gotten to know a small army of editors and producers that could give PMU some publicity. "Not for myself," she assured him; "I've had enough of my own." I noted her use of "we" when referring to PMU. When asked if she identified with the group, Irshad spoke of the chance it offered her to learn and grow, "not only as a Muslim but also a public figure and author." After Irshad left, Sarah let Ahmed have it, and before long they were screaming at each other in the middle of a crowded restaurant.

Ahmed, journalist Mona Eltahawy, her boyfriend and I later met up with Irshad at an Afghan restaurant. Irshad ran our dinner like a televised roundtable discussion, making sure everyone got his or her air time. If I withdrew from the conversation she'd reel me back in with a question.

"I hate to write," she said. "I find it so *agonizing*. Do you like to write, Mike?"

"Yeah, it's kind of my thing."

"Oh, that's great!" She put a hand on my forearm. "You're prolific." Irshad said that her next project would be a documentary on the past year of her life with the book tours and controversy, most likely filming in March 2005—another subtle nod to her publicity machine, as PMU had tentatively planned its conference for March.

I wondered what action PMU would take. If included, Irshad would wear PMU like an accessory and put herself over as running the whole show. In public perception, Irshad's opinions would become PMU's opinions, destroying the group's image with both the Muslim community and anyone sincerely committed to change. If excluded, it'd give her another chance at self-promotion as the true revolutionary of her time, so brave and outspoken that even PMU couldn't handle her. She could then discredit PMU and keep strutting her Salman Rushdie fetish.

Looking back now, I know that none of it mattered, because PMU would fall apart and die on its own. I was never sure of the group's priorities. We had religious scholars that worked on issues within the community, but also secular activists that hoped to advocate for Arab/Muslim issues in Washington. Some on the board of directors were very serious about their religion; others related to Islam only as a cultural identity. "Progressive Muslim" was now defined as anyone that did not object to the term. There were serious fuck-ups early on: PMU's board of advisors included Malik and Seeme Hasan, as well as Nawaad al-Sadawi, who had supported the hijab ban in

France, and Farid Zakariya, who wrote in *Newsweek* that an invasion of Iraq could be the "single best path to reform the Arab world." An outraged Farid Esack leaked the news of PMU's formation to the media before PMU was ready to capitalize on any press, and circulated a formal statement cosigned by members of his own Progressive Muslim faction. The movement already had its first schism.

PMU and Asra Nomani would get together to organize a Friday jum'aa prayer with a woman giving khutbah and leading the salat. PMU had no money for a venue, so Asra's publicist paid for the rental of a chapel in Manhattan. The PMU side grew increasingly wary of the affair becoming just a publicity stunt for Asra's new book, *Standing Alone in Mecca*, and made her promise that her publicist wouldn't come to the prayer. When I showed up that Friday, however, the first person I met was her publicist, who directed media traffic. I was assigned to work security, like a Fruit of Islam for our new American heresy.

The event did seem distinctly American, which apparently rendered it a less valid expression of Islam. "People in America think they are going to be the vanguards of change," Georgetown's Yvonne Haddad told the Associated Press, "but for Arab Muslims in the Middle East, American Muslims continue to be viewed on the margins of the faith." My source informed me that Feisal Abdul Rauf had agreed privately with the concept of female imams leading men, but refused to go on record with it for fear of losing his "political capital."

Inside the chapel there might have been as many reporters and camera crews as there were praying Muslims. The imam of the day, Amina Wadud, was so distracted by the long rows of popping flash-bulbs that in the middle of the prayer she forgot her ayats. At PMU's first board meeting, Ahmed Nassef would read to us an email from Dr. Wadud that completely washed her hands of the event. Though she still believed in woman-led prayer, she wanted nothing to do with PMU or Asra Nomani. As Ahmed read the email, none of us could say a word or even look up at each other. Wadud had drawn a clear line between the Truth and the media whores, and we knew that PMU was on the wrong side. To avoid public criticism, PMU's website made no mention of Asra's role in organizing the prayer. Asra complained of PMU shutting her out.

PMU's conference never happened, and everyone with real intellectual muscle left the group. Ahmed moved to Dubai; his name stayed on PMU's website, but leadership of the group was passed to a Malaysian-American pop singer named Ani Zonneveld. PMU would amount to little more than an online listserv, occasionally offering public statements ("PMU calls for an end to the killing in Darfur") that nobody gave a shit about. Asra would go her own way. She received a booking from Dennis Miller, but Miller's show got cancelled just prior to her scheduled appearance. Last I saw of her, she was logrolling in *Time* for an anti-Islamic, neocon-praised bigot named Wafa Sultan. Asra praised Sultan as a "daring voice" who "calls for a new Islam" and "crystallizes the mission for the rest of us."

The Internet was filled with all varieties of Muslims spewing diatribes against Asra and PMU. Even though they hated me too (one site ranked me #5 on a list of "Top 10 Pro-Regressive Idiots"), I was starting to agree with them. Progressive Islam's self-appointed heroes had placed more value on non-Muslim audiences than the community they hoped to reform. There was no credibility.

Back to that Afghan restaurant in Manhattan:

As we made our way out, Irshad noticed the Allah (Clarence 13X) button on my Alternative Tentacles jacket. "Who's that?" she asked.

"He started the Five Percenters."

"What are they? I've never heard of them."

"They're a band. They're on tour right now with Green Day."

Irshad and Asra were giving a joint talk that evening about women in Islam. On top of that, Asma Gull Hasan was in town to speak at the United Nations alongside John Esposito and Feisal Abdul Rauf. A star-studded weekend to be sure, but I drove straight out of Mecca. On the road I remembered Asra once wearing a hooded sweatshirt and calling it her "ghetto hijab."

> The pure products of America go crazy.
>
> —William Carlos Williams

Malcolm X was a pure product of America, and his legacy had gone shit-house-rat nuts—they put his angry face on U.S. postage stamps, his last name became a baseball cap, the $34 million Warner Bros. biopic spawned thousands of John Walkers and Michael Knights, the imam of his Harlem mosque prayed with George W. Bush, and his grandson burned down Betty's house with her in it.

In 1997, Malcolm Shabazz was twelve years old and a diagnosed schizophrenic who entertained himself with an imaginary character named Sinister Torch. His mother Qubilah had been arrested for trying to put a hit on Louis Farrakhan (her boyfriend turned out to be an undercover FBI agent) and avoided prison by agreeing to undergo psychiatric and alcoholism counseling. The child went to live with his grandmother but figured she'd send him back home if he caused enough trouble. So he set a fire. Betty Shabazz received third-degree burns on eighty percent of her body and died after three weeks in critical condition.

As a teen Malcolm was jumped into the Bloods and renamed himself M.E.C.C.A., which stood for Murder Every Crip Child Alive. In October 2004, he turned twenty while serving a three-year sentence for attempted armed robbery.

In his letter, he told me that two weeks earlier the guy next to him committed suicide and he watched them drag his body down the corridor. Before that, he heard that a close comrade had been murdered in Florida.

Malcolm Shabazz's mother was four years old when she sat in the front row at her father's assassination. Malcolm Little was six years old when white supremacists crushed his father's skull, and his mother would spend twenty-six years in the State Mental Hospital at Kalamazoo. Brother Reginald saw snakes in Malcolm's beard and found his way to an institution after claiming to be Allah, and then greater than Allah. I tried to see it in an Ahlul-Bayt way—Malcolm X really was America's Imam Husain, so holy that his family tree could only be doomed to never-ending distress and torture, tragedy and atrocity one after the other until the Son of the Brilliant Fulfillers comes to set it right.

Upstate Correctional Facility was a maxi-max or super-max with twenty-three-and-a-half hours of lockdown and one half-hour of solitary exercise in a pen. No educational programs, no vocational programs, no social contact with other prisoners. It's for the bad-news guys; they call it the box. He had been transferred there for six months after failing a drug test. The place was set in the farthest reaches of New York's "North Country" region, an economically depressed wilderness near the Canadian border sprinkled with lousy little towns like Antwerp and DeKalb. I made it to Canton a little after midnight and stopped at Sergi's for a pizza-roll. Malone was just an hour from there so I slept in the Jubilee parking lot. When I woke up the sun was out. I turned the key and drove to Malone.

You look at mesh fences covered in coils of razor wire and realize that they were put there to tear men apart, and then you think about what's inside.

The Torment of the Grave has nothing on Upstate. Say your Fatihas here.

Three flags waved in front, on three separate poles: United States, New York State, and POW/MIA. The black POW/MIA flag had a silhouette of a man with his head down, barbed wire and a watchtower in the background.

At the front desk I signed the form and ledger.

Inmate's name: Malcolm Shabazz.

DIN: 02R4617.

Took my shoes off for the metal detector. They gave me a key and I emptied my pockets into a locker. Then they put a stamp on my hand.

At the first door I waved my hand under the infrared sensor and a guard opened the electrified bars. I walked down a hall to the second door where a guard took my form and sent me through another door to the visitors' room. He said to sit at D3.

So I went down the rows of visiting wives and families, found the D aisle and sat on the bench marked 3 in front of white bars. About ten feet to my left sat a girl reaching under the bars to hold hands with her boyfriend.

I waited. People came and went. Visitors that arrived well after me got to see their inmates. I went to the bathroom a few times. I checked out the vending machines. At one point I put my head down on the table and could have fallen asleep. Every time the door opened to produce a new inmate I'd look up and he'd go somewhere else. I wasn't sure how long I had been there. There were no guards to ask for help on the visitors' side of the cages.

Malcolm Shabazz finally showed up in a green jumpsuit and the round state-issued glasses that are now widely known as "Malcolm X's." He had grown his hair out to stovepipe off his head like a crown. He said *as-salamu alaikum* and reached under the bars to shake my hand.

When they told him he had a visitor, Malcolm said "give me three minutes" so they left him for two hours. They fucked with him like that all the time; most inmates were only their DIN numbers but Malcolm's name stood out. Guards liked to give him racial slurs and curse his grandparents.

Back at his old prison, they messed with his head by giving contradictory instructions—one would tell him to get his coat and go to the yard while the other told him to go to the gym. Then he'd get shoved around and thrown back in his cell. Once when Malcolm had his head wrapped in a towel, a C.O. demanded that he remove it. Malcolm asked for a reason and the guard got mad so he went ahead and took it off.

"I just wanted to see if you had red hair," said the guard.

Malcolm told me that at the time of his failed drug test, he had been in solitary confinement; where would he have gotten weed?

He had been all over the state. They had him in Comstock, they had him in Auburn. At one point he was in a special unit for high-profile cases alongside rappers Ol' Dirty Bastard and Shyne. Upstate's C.O.s were all white North Country racists but Malcolm said that black C.O.s were even worse, since they had something to prove to their white comrades. He told me how he called one a traitor and a sell-out.

I noticed the tattoo on his right forearm—a crown with the letter B and a five-pointed star—indicating his rank in the Bloods. Malcolm told me that a Blood had to see himself as the natural enemy of all Crips, and he had a hard time getting into that. He saw through it too easily, he said. He understood too much of why they really killed each other.

He knew the rage of the street and how it manifested. Everyone in Upstate was there for being poor, and Upstate did nothing for them. He told me to look at the thirteenth amendment to the Constitution, which abolishes slavery "except as a punishment for crime whereof the party shall have been duly convicted."

"We make their uniforms," said Malcolm with a nod in the guards' direction. "We make police uniforms." Then he tugged at his green shirt. "We make *these*." And for removing asbestos, an inmate is paid fifteen dollars every two weeks.

It was at that point in our conversation that some little kids ran past me and one crawled under my bench. Malcolm beamed a big smile. He smiles like his grandfather.

Malcolm Shabazz identifies as a Sunni Muslim today, though as a kid he spent more time in church. We talked about the NOI. He doesn't believe that Elijah was involved in his grandfather's death. Not sure about Farrakhan. We talked about the Five Percenters. Malcolm said there were Gods in every jail.

He mentioned the teaching of W.D. Fard that the devil must study for thirty-five to fifty years before he could wear the flag of Islam, and then he'd have to add a sword to it. He asked if I knew what that meant and explained,

"When you reach the highest degree of the Masons, they give you a Qur'an." The Shriners were Masons; what'd they have for an emblem on their buses and fezzes and letterheads? A star and crescent with sword attached. Shriners were the Muslim Sons; they knew who God really was, but guarded their secret under penalty of decapitation. I told Malcolm that the Shriner mosque in Chicago was now a Bloomingdale's, though they still have Allah's Name all around their door.

The ten-minute warning came. Malcolm said he'd send me a list of books to read. We shared salams and got up from our respective benches.

As I went back down the hall one of the windows provided a close-up look at the razor wire, close enough to touch if it weren't for the glass. Surprised me how big the coils really were, almost four feet in diameter.

The sky was gray. There's something to northern New York that you'll never get in southern California, a bite in the air that keeps you alert even when you can't hold your eyes open. In Los Angeles the lazy weather makes for lazy brains.

Malcolm Shabazz had quoted Ho Chi Minh as saying that when prison gates are opened, the real dragon flies out. And he told me that the race goes not to the swift but to those that can endure until the end. I think he's living his grandfather's life all over again. Every day is Ashura, every land is Karbala. Some cry tears and some cry blood.

GLOSSARY

abaya: a black cloak worn by women

adhan: the call to prayer

ahlul-bayt: literally "people of the house," refers to Muhammad's daughter Fatima, her husband Ali, and their sons Hasan and Husain

akh: brother

al-Fatiha: the opening sura of the Qur'an; also name of a GLBT Muslim organization

al-hamdulilah: "all praises due to Allah"

al-Kauthar: a pond or lake in paradise

alim: a religious scholar

Allahu Akbar: "God is the Greatest"

Allahu Alim: "God knows best," or "God is the knower"

as-salamu alaikum: "Peace be unto you"

Asr: the third prayer of the day

ayat: a verse in the Qur'an

ayat-Allah: a sign of God

bismallah: "In the name of God"

Bukhari: collection of hadith named for the scholar Imam Bukhari

dashna: a dagger

daw'ah: the propagation of Islam

deen: religion

du'a: a supplication to God

Fajr: the first prayer of the day

fatwa: a religious ruling by a qualified scholar

fiqh: jurisprudence

fuhsh: indecency, obscenity, atrocity, and abomination

Gatta: special mark of prostration on the forehead

Ghaliya: a heretical Shi'a group

ghusl: a ritual bathing after intercourse, to achieve a state of purity before prayer

hadith: a saying of the Prophet

hafiz: someone who has memorized the entire Qur'an

hajj: the pilgrimage to Mecca

haram: forbidden

Hazrat: title of respect for a prophet or saint

hijab: head-covering for a woman

hijra: the Prophet's migration from Mecca to Medina

houri: a virgin of Paradise

imam: a leader of prayer

iman: faith

insha'Allah: "if God wills"

Isha: the final prayer of the night

istimna: masturbation

jahennam: Hell

jalab: a robe

jamaat: a group in prayer

jihad: a struggle

jinns: spirits made from smokeless fire

jum'aa: a congregational prayer

Juz Amma: suras comprising the final 30th segment of the Qur'an

Kaaba: the house of God built by Abraham in Mecca; object of Muslim pilgrimage

Karbala: site of Husain's martyrdom

Khattabiyya: a heretical Islamic group

khutbah: sermon

kifaya: Arab scarf

Kufic: Arabic script

kufi: a skullcap

kufr: a disbeliever

lun: "penis" in Urdu

madhab: Islamic school of jurisprudence

Maghrib: the fourth prayer of the day

Mahdi: the Messianic figure of Islamic eschatology

mahram: the group of people who are unlawful for a woman to marry due to marital or blood relationships *marabout*: a saint

mash'Allah: "as God willed it"

masjid: a mosque

maulana: a scholar

mazar: a tomb

muezzin: person who gives the call to prayer

mihrab: niche in the wall indicating the direction of Mecca

minbar: pulpit

Mu'ammariyya: an Islamic heretical group

Mughiriyya: an Islamic heretical group

Muharram: month in the Islamic calendar in which Husain was martyred

mujahideen: holy fighters

mullah: scholar

mumin: believer

munkar: ignorant, detestable behavior

murtad: apostate

nafl: a nonrequired and non-sunna prayer

niqab: a woman's face covering

desi: person of South Asian descent

Qalandari: a member of heretical Qalandar group

qiblah: the direction of Mecca

khuda hafiz: "God protect you"

rakat: a unit of prayer

riyal: unit of Saudi currency

Sahih Bukhari: a collection of hadiths

Salafi: a modern conservative movement

salam: peace

salat: prayer

sayyeda: a female descendent of the Prophet

shahadah: bearing witness that there is no god but God, and Muhammad is the Prophet

shaheed: martyr for Islam

shaikh, shaykh: a religious scholar

shalwar kameez: long shirt and pants worn in South Asia

shaytan: a devil

shirk: associating others with Allah; a major sin

shukran: "Thank you"

silsila: religious lineage

siwak: a twig or stick used to clean teeth

Staghfir' Allah: "God forgive me"

sujdah: prostration

sunna: practice of the Prophet

Sura Ya Sin: chapter in the Qur'an read for the dead or dying

sura: a chapter of the Qur'an

Suratul-Kauthar: a sura of the Qur'an

Tabligh: Islamic missionary group

Takbir: a cue to say "Allahu Akbar"

takfir: a declaration of disbelief made on another person

taqwa: consciousness of God

Tashahud: a passage recited in Islamic prayer

tawaf: circumambulation of pilgrims around the Kaaba

tawhid: the oneness of God

tayammum: wudhu made in the absence of water

Tayyariyya: a heretical Islamic group

thobe: a robe or long shirt

topi: a kind of hat

turba: a piece of clay from a holy site used by Shi'as in prayer

Wali-Allah: "Friend of God"

wudhu: ritual washing before prayer

yakub: the scientist who created the white race, in NOI tradition

zikr: remembrance of Allah, reciting of Allah's Names

zuhr: the second prayer of the day

APPENDIX

<table>
<tr>
<td>
DISTRICT COURT, CITY & COUNTY OF DENVER
STATE OF COLORADO

Court Address:
City & County Building
1437 Bannock Street, Room 256
Denver, Colorado 80202
</td>
<td>

Δ COURT USE ONLYΔ
</td>
</tr>
<tr>
<td>
ASMA GULL HASAN,

Plaintiff,

v.

MICHAEL MUHAMMAD KNIGHT; BASIM USMANI;
SHAHJEHAN MALIK KHAN; ARJUN RAY; KARNA
RAY; DANIEL JOYNER; and *THE KOMINAS*, a general
partnership performing as a musical group,

Defendants.
</td>
<td>
Case No.: 07-CV-_____

Div. ____ Ctrm:____
</td>
</tr>
<tr>
<td>
Attorneys for Plaintiff:

Name: Glenn W. Merrick, No.10042
Address: G.W. MERRICK & ASSOCIATES, LLC
           Suite 912, 5445 DTC Parkway
           Greenwood Village, Colorado 80111
Telephone No.: (303) 831-9400
Fax No.:   (303) 771-5803
E-mail: gwm@gwmerrick.com
</td>
<td></td>
</tr>
<tr>
<td colspan="2" align="center">

COMPLAINT AND JURY DEMAND

</td>
</tr>
</table>

Plaintiff, Asma Gull Hasan ("Hasan"), through her undersigned counsel, G.W. MERRICK & ASSOCIATES, LLC, hereby brings this Complaint against Defendants, Michael Muhammad Knight ("Knight"), Basim Usmani ("Usmani"), Shahjehan Khan ("Khan"), Arjun Ray ("A. Ray"), Karna Ray ("K. Ray"), Daniel Joyner ("Joyner") and *The Kominas*, a general partnership performing as a musical group, as follows:

APPENDIX

I.   Parties, Jurisdiction and Venue

1.   Hasan is an individual over the age of 21 years who is a resident of the City and County of Denver, State of Colorado. Hasan is a descendent of Pakistani immigrants, an observant follower of Islam, a graduate of Wellesley College and New York University School of Law, and member in good standing of the New York, California and Colorado bars. She is also a respected authoress whose books include *American Muslims: The New Generation* (published by HarperCollins Publishers in 2004) and *Why I am a Muslim: An American Odyssey* (published by Continuum Publishers in 2000). Hasan has been a columnist for *The Pueblo Chieftain, The Denver Post* and *The Pakistan Link* newspapers. Her op-eds have been published in *The New York Times, The San Francisco Chronicle, Beliefnet.com*, and *The Dallas Morning News*. She is a frequent guest on the Fox News Channel, *From the Heartland with John Kasich* and *The O'Reilly Factor*. Hasan has also appeared on *Faith Under Fire* and *The Dennis Miller Show*. She has also been featured on: *Fresh Air with Terry Gross, Morning Edition* and *Weekend Edition* on National Public Radio, CNN, CNN International, C-SPAN and *Politically Incorrect with Bill Maher* on ABC. She has been profiled in *USA Today* and interviewed in *The New York Times*. In September 2002, Hasan appeared in the History Channel documentary *Inside Islam*.

2.   Knight is an individual over the age of 21 years who, upon information and belief, is a resident of the State of New York. Knight is a Caucasian convert to Islam who has written accounts about the Muslim experience in the United States. His published works include *The Taqwacores* (a fictional novel about a group of Islamic punk rockers who smoke marijuana, read scriptures, pray and engage in sex) and *Blue Eyed Devil: A Road Odyssey Through Islamic America.*

3.   Usmani is an individual over the age of 21 years who, upon information and belief, is a resident of the State of Massachusetts. Usmani is bass player and the lead vocalist for *The Kominas.*

4.   Khan is an individual over the age of 21 years who upon information and belief is a resident of the State of Massachusetts. Khan plays lead guitar for *The Kominas.*

5.   A. Ray is an individual over the age of 21 years who, upon information and belief, is a resident of the State of Massachusetts. A. Ray plays guitar for *The Kominas.*

6.   K. Ray is an individual over the age of 21 years who, upon information and belief, is a resident of the State of Massachusetts. K. Ray plays drums for *The Kominas.*

7.   Joyner is an individual over the age of 21 years who, upon information and belief, is a resident of the State of Massachusetts. Joyner plays dhol (an Indian percussion instrument) for *The Kominas.*

8.   *The Kominas* is a Boston-based, punk rock band formed in 2004. The band's name is a Punjabi swear word meaning persons born out of wedlock.

9.   This Court possesses subject matter jurisdiction to adjudicate the claims for relief alleged herein pursuant to Art. VI, Sec. 9(1) of the Colorado Constitution.

10.   All of the defendants are subject to the *in personam* jurisdiction of this Court under the provisions of C.R.S. §13-1-124(1)(b) as they have committed tortuous acts within this State.

11.   Venue is proper in this Court under the provisions of C.R.C.P. 98(c)(1).

II.   General Allegations

12.   Hasan incorporates each of the allegations contained in Paragraphs 1-11 of this Complaint as if set forth in full here.

13.   Sometime during 2004, Knight was introduced to Hasan, a colleague Muslim writer whose views about the Muslim experience in the United States differs dramatically from his. Knight's book *Blue-Eyed Devil* later characterized Hasan in a highly unflattering fashion. It is fair to say that the book portrays Hasan as wealthy, self-absorbed, insensitive and acutely uniformed.

14.   By late 2004, Usmani and Khan -- who had read and were impressed with Knight's earlier fictional novel, *The Taqwacores* -- had formed *The Kominas*. Shortly thereafter, and following his introduction to Hasan, Knight met and befriended Usmani and Khan. From and after that initial meeting, Knight -- and his perspectives -- remained strongly influential on Usmani, Khan and *The Kominas*.

15.   *The Kominas* first musical release was a song entitled "Rumi was a Homo (but Siraj is a Fag)," featuring lyrics written by Usmani. In part, the song refers to Mowlana Jalaluddin Rumi ("Rumi"), a revered Thirteenth Century Sufi poet. In describing Rumi, the first verse of this musical piece announces, in pertinent part:

> I want to be stoned on your love,
> you give better hand jobs than Asma Hasan …

16.   The purpose, intent and effect of these highly offensive, denigrating and defamatory lyrics (written and performed by *The Kominas* with Knight's knowledge, encouragement and support) was to mock, deride and ridicule Hasan, and to hold her up for public scorn and contempt. Of course, the verse was written and has been performed with actual malice toward Hasan -- it was written and performed as knowingly false within the meaning of the applicable law of defamation.

17.   Prior to being introduced to Knight, none of Usmani, Khan or any other member of *The Kominas* had met, or had any knowledge or information about, Hasan. Moreover,

APPENDIX

Hasan has never had any sexual contact of any kind with any of the individual Defendants named in this Complaint.

18. Knight used his strong influence with Usmani and Khan to communicate an inflammatory, demeaning and insulting view of Hasan. Usmani accepted, adopted and perpetuated Knight's offensive and denigrating perspective when he penned the grotesquely defamatory language about Hasan described in Paragraph 15 of this Complaint.

19. The disgusting lyrics referred to herein were subsequently published on the official webpage of *The Kominas, http://sinsanctuary.com/kominas,* and they remain there. In addition, the defamatory lyrics were uploaded to the Internet (and could be downloaded to MP3 players) in a December 10, 2004 article authored by Knight -- introducing *The Kominas* to a broader base of readers -- in *Muslim Wakeup!,* an online magazine and website.

20. *The Kominas* has played "Rumi was a Homo (but Siraj is a Fag)" in engagements all across the United States, and the defamatory lyrics relating to Hasan have impacted numerous persons of diverse backgrounds, cultures and perspectives. In addition, the band has gained popularity with the Muslim population in Great Britain. Finally, the band and its handiwork have become significant on Myspace, a popular social networking website offering interactive user-submitted data respecting persons, profiles music and blogs on an international basis.

21. The defamatory lyrics referred to in Paragraph 15 of this Complaint were published in (and proximately caused Hasan damage, injury and loss in) Colorado by virtue of the official website of *The Kominas* and by virtue of the ability of Colorado-based Internet users to access, read and download the lyrics. In addition, when Hasan first learned of the defamatory lyrics (which discovery by Hasan occurred within the last six months), they caused her substantial economic and non-economic loss within the State of Colorado more particularly described in Paragraph 22 of this Complaint.

22. As a direct and proximate result of the outrageous, defamatory, tortious and continuing misconduct of the Defendants, Hasan has sustained substantial and incalculable damage, injury and loss. Such damage, injury and loss includes (but is not limited to) harm to Hasan's personal and professional reputation; loss of royalty and other earnings; disappointment and disillusionment; severe emotional anguish, distress, trauma and suffering; acute embarrassment and humiliation; loss of self-worth and self-esteem; and disruption and impairment to the quality of Hasan's life.

23. Unless the Defendants are enjoined – both on a preliminary and permanent basis – requiring them to: (a) remove from "Rumi was a Homo (but Siraj is a Fag)" those portions of the current lyrics that are defamatory in respect of Hasan, (b) remove from all publications and performances over which they have control or influence the defamatory lyrics relating to Hasan, and (c) forbear from publishing or performing these defamatory lyrics in the future -- there is a real, immediate, palpable and substantial risk and danger that Hasan will suffer further damage, injury and loss for which there is no plain, speedy and adequate remedy at law.

III.   First Claim for Relief
(Libel and Slander)

24.   Hasan incorporates each of the allegations contained in Paragraphs 1-23 of this Complaint as if set forth in full here.

25.   Usamani, Khan, A. Ray, K. Ray, Joyner and *The Kominas* repeatedly published to third persons, in written and oral form, the highly defamatory statement described in Paragraph 15 of this Complaint (the "Statement").

26.   The substance or gist of the Statement was false at the time that it was published.

27.   At the time of each publication of the Statement, each of Usamani, Khan, A. Ray, K. Ray, Joyner and *The Kominas* each knew that the Statement was false.

28.   Publication of the Statement has directly and proximately caused (and will continue to cause) Hasan substantial actual damage, injury and loss in an amount to be proved at trial.

29.   The tortious and outrageous misconduct of Usamini, Khan, A. Ray, K. Ray, Joiner and *The Kominas* described herein were attended by circumstances of malice and willful and wanton misconduct within the meaning of C.R.S. §13-21-102(1)(a).

30.   All conditions precedent and subsequent to Hasan's right to initiate and maintain this claim have been performed, waived or have otherwise occurred.

IV.   Second Claim for Relief
(Civil Conspiracy)

31.   Hasan incorporates each of the allegations contained in Paragraphs 1-30 of this Complaint as if set forth in full here.

32.   Each of the Defendants agreed, expressly or tacitly, by words and/or conduct, to engage in defamatory communications about Hasan to third persons.

33.   On or more overt acts were performed in furtherance of this unlawful and tortious goal.

34.   As a direct and proximate consequence and result of this unlawful civil conspiracy among the Defendants, Hasan has sustained substantial damage, injury and loss in an amount to be proved at trial.

APPENDIX

35.   The unlawful civil conspiracy in which the Defendants each engaged was attended by circumstances of malice and willful and wanton misconduct within the meaning of C.R.S. §13-21-102(1)(a).

36.   All conditions precedent and subsequent to Hasan's right to initiate and maintain this claim have been performed, waived or have otherwise occurred.

V.   Third Claim for Relief
(Outrageous Conduct)

37.   Hasan incorporates each of the allegations contained in Paragraphs 1-36 of this Complaint as if set forth in full here.

38.   Each of the Defendants engaged in extreme and outrageous conduct more fully described herein.

39.   Each of the Defendants engaged in the extreme and outrageous conduct recklessly or with the intent of causing Hasan severe emotional distress.

40.   As a direct and proximate cause of Defendants' extreme and outrageous conduct, Hasan did, in fact, suffer severe emotional distress and trauma. The amount of Hasan's damages shall be proved at trial.

41.   Defendants' extreme and outrageous conduct was attended by circumstances of malice and willful and wanton misconduct within the meaning of C.R.S. §13-21-102(1)(a).

42.   All conditions precedent and subsequent to Hasan's right to initiate and maintain this claim have been performed, waived or have otherwise occurred.

WHEREFORE, Hasan respectfully prays that this Court enter judgment in her favor and against each of the Defendants, jointly and severally, as follows:

A.   Entry of preliminary and permanent injunctive relief – both on a preliminary and permanent basis – requiring Defendants, and each of them, to: (a) remove from "Rumi was a Homo (but Siraj is a Fag)" those portions of the current lyrics that are defamatory in respect of Hasan, (b) remove from all publications and performances over which they have control or influence the defamatory lyrics relating to Hasan, and (c) forbear from publishing or performing these defamatory lyrics in the future.

B.   Judgment for money damages sufficient to fully compensate Hasan in respect of all of her actual, compensatory, special, consequential and incidental damages.

C.   Awarding Hasan reasonable attorney fees, expert witness fees, pre-judgment interest, moratory interest, post-judgment interest, costs of suit and such other and further relief to which she may be entitled.

JURY DEMAND

Hasan respectfully demands a trial by jury on all issues so triable.

Dated: October 19, 2007.

G.W. MERRICK & ASSOCIATES, LLC

By: _/s/_ Glenn W. Merrick
      Glenn W. Merrick

ATTORNEYS FOR PLAINTIFF, ASMA GULL HASAN

Plaintiff's Address:

P.O. Box 101178
Denver, Colorado 80250

Printed in the United States
by Baker & Taylor Publisher Services